Economists have devoted considerable effort to explaini.., ..v., ... economy functions, but they have given a good deal less attention to explaining how a market economy is formed. In this book, Jean Ensminger analyzes the process by which the market was introduced into the economy of a group of Kenyan pastoralists.

Ensminger employs new institutional economic analysis to assess the impact of new market institutions on production and distribution, with particular emphasis on the effect of institutions on decreasing transaction costs over time. Having compiled an extraordinary longitudinal data set that tracks a group of households over an extensive period, she traces the effects of increasing commercialization on the economic well-being of individual households, rich and poor alike. In addition, employing anthropological methods, she analyzes the process by which institutions themselves are transformed as a market economy develops. Changes in labor relationships, property rights, and the transfer of political authority from the council of elders to the state are considered in particular detail.

This case study points to the importance of understanding the roles of ideology and bargaining power – in addition to pure economic forces, such as changing relative prices – in shaping market institutions. The combination of new institutional economic analysis and richly detailed anthropological case study produces a work full of insights that may serve as the basis for a more adequate theory of economic development and social change.

MAKING A MARKET

MAKING A MARKET

*The institutional transformation
of an African society*

JEAN ENSMINGER
Washington University in St. Louis

Published by the Press Syndicate of the University of Cambridge
The Pitt Building, Trumpington Street, Cambridge CB2 IRP
40 West 20th Street, New York, NY 10011-4211, USA
10 Stamford Road, Oakleigh, Melbourne 3166, Australia

First published 1992
Reprinted 1996
First paperback edition 1996

Printed in the United States of America

Library of Congress Cataloging-in-Publication Data is available.

A catalog record for this book is available from the British Library.

ISBN 0-521-42060-1 hardback
ISBN 0-521-57426-9 paperback

For demonstrating the value
of asking the right questions,
I dedicate this book to
Ronald Cohen and Douglass North

Contents

vii

Tables, figures, and maps

TABLES

ix

Tables, figures, and maps

FIGURES

MAPS

Series editors' preface

This Cambridge series, The Political Economy of Institutions and Decisions, is built around attempts to answer two central questions: How do institutions evolve in response to individual incentives, strategies, and choices; and how do institutions affect the performance of political and economic systems? The scope of the series is comparative and historical rather than international or specifically American, and the focus is positive rather than normative.

This book breaks new ground in applying the tools of the new institutional economics to anthropology. The result is rich fare for both anthropologists and other social scientists. It is rich for anthropologists because the author convincingly demonstrates the power of the new institutional economics to shed light on the way a group of Kenyan pastoralists known as the Orma evolved in the context of the spread of a market economy and the way Orma society was transformed as a result. Jean Ensminger makes a convincing case that anthropologists will find this approach congenial because the new institutional economic perspective combines the individual-actor approach of economics, a strong appreciation of institutional constraints, incentives, and ideology from anthropology, and the attention to power that we associate with Marxist analyses. As the author says, "The goal is a more complete and realistic model of social change than that afforded by any of the approaches on their own."

The study is equally rich for other social scientists because of the body of empirical data the author developed in the course of years of close contact with the Orma. These data provide solid support for the author's analytical insights, as well as important new insights into the process of institutional change.

A melding of the analytical insights of the new institutional economics with the voluminous body of empirical data that anthropologists have developed is long overdue. This study should provide solid incentives for other anthropologists to combine these two perspectives.

Preface

In the 1970s and 1980s, neo-Marxist perspectives predominated in economic anthropology and political economy. Many studies documented the tendency for market relations to increase economic differentiation in the developing societies typically studied by anthropologists. The rich always seemed to get richer, sometimes the poor got poorer, sometimes the poor got richer, but rarely did the poor do as well as the rich; the gap widened. This story was documented over and over again (including in my own work), to the point that anthropology was becoming a "dismal science." Frustrated both by the pessimism of these conclusions and by the seeming dead end of the story, I began searching for a new theoretical direction. This I found in the form of the new institutional economics.

Institutional economics combines an individual-actor-oriented perspective with rich attention to institutional constraints, and it specifically addresses the relationship between market forces, indigenous institutions, and economic performance. The underlying assumption is that institutions directly affect economic outcomes (distribution and growth), that individuals realize this, and that they attempt to change institutions to serve their ends more effectively, whether these ends be ideological or materialistic. The relative success of different actors in getting the institutions they want derives in part from their bargaining power in the preexisting institutional structure. The outcomes of this process often have unintended consequences, and by no means need result in institutional arrangements that better serve the interests of society as a whole. This book uses an institutional economic framework to tell the story of how the market came to a group of Kenyan pastoralists known as the Orma and what effect it had on local institutions, economic performance, and welfare.

I owe my discovery of new institutional economics to being in the right place at the right time. I was hired by the anthropology department at Washington University in 1985. Thanks to the encouragement of Robert

Canfield and Andrew Rutten, I began attending seminars at the Center in Political Economy (then under the direction of Douglass North) and became a fellow in 1988. Douglass North's work on transaction costs, property rights, and institutional change had a tremendous influence on the direction of my own research agenda. It appeared to me (and still does) that economic historians had more than a chronological edge over economic anthropologists when it came to the theoretical questions of interest to us both. Anthropologists, for their part, have invaluable data and deep intuitions about issues of mutual theoretical concern. I owe a great deal of my intellectual development and stimulation to the weekly seminars at the Center in Political Economy and to all of the participants, especially Lee Benham, Arthur Denzau, John Drobak, Thráinn Eggertsson, Jack Knight, Gary Miller, Douglass North, John Nye, Andrew Rutten, and Norman Schofield.

Just as my discovery of new institutional economics was an accident, so too was my introduction to African studies. I originally went to Africa at the invitation of Louis Leakey, who needed someone to edit his ethnography of the southern Kikuyu. Though he died several months after my arrival, I continued working on the manuscript for several years at Mary Leakey's request and in collaboration with Louis's sister, Gladys Beecher. Louis told me when I arrived in Kenya, "No one ever visits Africa only once." Indeed, five trips later, I have now lived in Kenya for six years, four of them with the Orma, who are the subjects of this work.

I had the great fortune upon arrival among the Orma to settle with the Shambaro family in the village of Wayu. I doubt that any anthropologist has been more graciously and thoughtfully cared for by a host family. Shambaro Elema died at the age of eighty-seven during the last month of my fieldwork in 1987; he was a remarkable man and I am grateful to have been there for his passing. Hagufu Shambaro, his surviving senior wife, is one of the most noble and socially perceptive people I have ever know; she also helped provide me with the most treasured commodity an anthropologist can find in the field – occasional privacy. Shambaro's son Hussein was my research assistant for nearly three years between 1978 and 1981. By the time I returned for my restudy in 1987 Hussein had become chief, but nevertheless kindly welcomed me to reside again with his family, by then including his two wives, Galgalo and Esha, and a new, younger generation.

The richness of the quantitative data reported in this study is the result of the slogging efforts of Hussein Shambaro and my other Orma research assistants, particularly Omar Bonea and Hassan Galgalo (1978–81) and Kolde Abalaga, Dendole Balesa, Osman Elema, Mohamed Hanti, Omar Kampicha, Mahad Komoro, and Zeituni Shambaro (1987). Hundreds of

Orma families tolerated the inconveniences of panel survey demands. It is my hope that their investment in this project will be repaid.

The Kenyan government has twice granted me research clearance to study among the Orma. On the first occasion (1978–81) I was affiliated with the National Museums of Kenya and benefited greatly from the open academic atmosphere prevalent in Kenya at that time. Shem Migot-Adolla kindly facilitated my affiliation with the Institute for Development Studies at the University of Nairobi during my restudy in 1987. Some of the most highly regarded research in Africa has been done in connection with IDS at the University of Nairobi, and it was an honor to be associated with this institute. I am also grateful to numerous agencies that generously funded these two periods of fieldwork and data analysis: Fulbright-Hays, the Ford Foundation, the National Science Foundation (BSN-7904273), the Rockefeller Foundation, the National Institutes of Health (SSP 5 RO1 HD213427 DBS), and faculty research grants from Washington University.

Portions of Chapter 5 appeared as "The Political Economy of Changing Property Rights: Dismantling a Pastoral Commons," coauthored with Andrew Rutten and published in the *American Ethnologist* 18(4), November 1991. Portions of Chapter 6 appeared as "Co-opting the Elders: The Political Economy of State Incorporation in Africa" in the *American Anthropologist* 92(3), September 1990. Passages are reproduced in this volume with the permission of the publishers.

Several people read various versions of the manuscript. No one gave more willingly of his time than Andrew Rutten, who read several drafts of the entire book and with whom I discussed many of the ideas. Eliot Fratkin took the time to make page-by-page comments on the entire manuscript, which were all the more helpful because he admitted to being unsympathetic to my theoretical direction. An anonymous reviewer perceptively targeted key weaknesses in an early draft and provided much appreciated encouragement. Jack Knight's insightful comments on the several chapters he read significantly improved the book. Lois Beck, John Bowen, Karen Brison, Robert Canfield, Ronald Cohen, Arthur Denzau, Thomas Håkansson, Gary Miller, and Douglass North read parts or all of the manuscript and contributed their special and diverse expertise. Two foot soldiers were intellectually underemployed for several years doing much of the drone work involved in data analysis and manuscript preparation; James Hauf coded most of the 1987 quantitative data, and Danielle Glossip worked on the manuscript preparation. Their superior intellectual skills are reflected in the final product in many undetectable ways.

Finally, for providing emotional support, and for teaching me to believe in what I know, I thank John Chaves and Eugene Trunnell.

I

A proper marriage: new institutional economic anthropology

The market has become the dominant mode of economic organization the world over. Economists welcome this as a triumph and stress the virtue of increasing economic efficiency. They assume that the spread of the market is inevitable, the natural outcome of superior performance. Anthropologists, however, are generally less enamored of the market. They point out the social costs of transition that accompany growing market relations, as well as the economic and political inequalities that typically result. Marxists are inclined to focus on the detrimental consequences of *imperfect* markets – for example, the power that monopolists are granted by the political system. Despite the claims of proponents, these approaches are not necessarily mutually exclusive. Some traditional concerns of anthropologists – distribution and ideological legitimacy – may well be central to the efficiency of markets. In a system held to be illegitimate, where people are inclined to cheat every time they can get away with it, there may be little profit. Similarly, more than neoclassical economic theory is needed to help us understand the conditions under which markets become corrupted by the political process and facilitate the formation of politically induced inequality; these issues are often the subject matter of Marxists. The narrowness of the neoclassical approach, however, does not diminish the desirability of better economic performance to support a higher quality of life, especially among the peoples of the developing world with rapidly growing populations. On the subject of economic performance and growth, economists have much to offer. To address these issues, this book develops a new institutional economic (NIE) perspective that combines the individual-actor approach of economics, anthropology's appreciation of institutional constraints, incentives, and ideology, and the attention to power that we associate with Marxist analyses. The goal is a more complete and realistic model of social change than that afforded by any of the approaches alone. To illustrate the approach, this book tells the story of how the market spread among the pastoral Galole Orma of northeastern Kenya and transformed Orma society in the process.

For anthropologists, the Orma offer much evidence of the corrosive effects of the market on social institutions.[1] Indeed, one could make a case that their society is disintegrating in the wake of increasing market relations. Pasture that used to be held in common is gradually being privatized. Political power that used to reside with the council of elders is flowing to the central government and is being increasingly vested in the office of the government-appointed Orma chief. Young men openly show disrespect for their fathers and elders, to the point of selling off their elders' livestock without permission. Family herding cooperatives are giving way to pure wage contract herding. Clan exogamy is breaking down as more young people marry for love even within their clan. Widows are refusing to be inherited by their brothers-in-law in levirate marriage and are increasingly living on their own. Even domestic disputes formerly heard by the council of elders are increasingly being taken to the government for adjudication.

One could also make the case that the "moral economy" of the Orma is collapsing. A moral economy (Scott 1976) is one in which a subsistence ethos guarantees at least minimal provisioning to all households. Among the Orma, rich nomadic stock owners used to share their surplus milk freely with poor neighbors. With the increased sedentarization that accompanies market production, most livestock are sent far from the village to cattle camps offering more favorable grazing conditions. Consequently, households purchase their foodstuffs rather than depend on subsistence production. The "value" of milk has risen enormously, and consequently milking stock are almost never loaned, resulting in the disappearance of this once readily available aid.[2]

---

1 This study is based on research conducted from 1978 to 1981 and a restudy in 1987 among the Galole population of Orma. The Orma are divided into three groups, from north to south: the Hirman, Galole, and Chaffa. As of the 1979 Kenyan census, the Orma numbered 32,127. Although this study applies technically only to the Galole population, the specifics closely parallel those among the other two subgroups of Orma, the main difference being that market relations are more advanced among the more sedentary Chaffa and less so among the more nomadic Hirman. For simplicity, hereafter I refer to the population merely as "Orma." Where it is used, the ethnographic present refers to the time of the restudy, 1987.

2 I do not wish to imply here that I subscribe to Scott's interpretation of the "moral economy." One could also explain the milk transfers of the past as payment in kind for labor, since poor dependent households often did much herding for their patrons. In any case, the point holds that there has been a change in relative prices between the value of labor and the cost of subsistence support. Whether there has been a change in ethos is debatable. For example, because the value of milk was so low, we do not know the strength of the past commitment to provide subsistence support to the poor. In other words, it is possible that the ethos has not changed,

As Marxists would predict, there is also considerable evidence that commercialization has meant monopolization (at least until recently) and led to proletarianization. The means of production have fallen into relatively few hands, and at least some of the poor are left with no choice but to labor for those few. The percentage of livestock controlled by the poorest sector of the population has been consistently shrinking, at least in the period for which I have data – 1974 to 1987. Smallholders are increasingly turning to wage labor and trade as they lose control over stock (the primary means of production). What is more, these trends show no sign of reversing themselves.

Anthropologists' and Marxists' observations notwithstanding, however, the Orma case offers data that confirm economists' hunches about the benefits of the transition to the market. Many of the recent changes have had some positive economic consequences. My impression is that the poor Orma I had known in the late 1970s, although still poor in relative terms, were somewhat better off in absolute terms in the late 1980s when I carried out my restudy. In particular, they appeared to be better clothed and better fed. This was puzzling, because the Orma had suffered tremendous livestock losses during the 1985 drought, a mere two years before my return. In the end, a quantitative resurvey of the identical area and many of the same households confirmed my impression of economic improvement; income among the poorest third of the population had risen 37 percent in real terms. These income patterns ran contrary to developments in livestock production, where there was a clearly discernible movement toward larger economies of scale. As a result, small- and medium-sized producers were losing ground to larger producers.

The proliferation of alternative income sources prevented the trend toward larger economies of scale in stock production from leading to economic disaster for smallholders (especially given the reduced availability of subsistence support). Flood plain agriculture increased substantially, as did trade and wage labor.[3] The opening of six tea kiosks (small restaurants) in the largest village in my survey, where no such cafés had previously existed anywhere in Galole Orma territory, dram-

---

but rather that people were never prepared to pay a very high price to support those in need. If this were the case, one could argue that the change in relative prices has resulted in a greater cost than people were ever prepared to pay for this value. See Popkin (1979) for a detailed critique of the moral economy approach.

3 One should not overemphasize the significance of agriculture in the economy; harvests are successful on average only one season in four, or roughly once every two years, owing to erratic river flooding. Agriculture continues to be a supplemental windfall rather than a reliable subsistence strategy, and it will remain so in the absence of irrigation.

atizes the extent of change between 1980 and 1987. That one village could support such an expansion of the service sector pointed to the likelihood of substantial diversification and specialization within the economy.

Can these contradictory accounts of the same facts be reconciled? Yes, but in order to do so we need to understand how the economic, political, and social institutions changed into the forms seen in 1987. To comprehend these changes we must look both at individual motivation (institutional patterns result from individual choices) and at the socially determined constraints and incentives that influence what individuals strive for and how they go about realizing their goals. Ideologies determine what people value, while institutions and organizations determine what power people will have and what price they must pay to pursue their goals. Thus the approach I employ explores the interaction of ideology, institutions, organizations, and bargaining power, on the one hand, and individual choice and calculation in the context of changing relative prices, on the other.[4] This approach shows how individuals, acting in the shadow of society, forge the institutions that ultimately determine economic performance and distribution.

IDEOLOGY, INSTITUTIONS, ORGANIZATIONS, AND BARGAINING POWER

Any complete account of the growth of the market must focus on the role of ideology, institutions, organizations, and bargaining power. Together, these directly affect economic performance by determining the extent to which people cooperate and realize the gains from trade. Most economists tend to ignore these issues unless they impinge directly on markets. But even informal institutions and values such as notions of social justice and what constitutes "fair play" have a significant impact on economic performance. One of the costs of widening the scope of economic analysis is less "precise" theory, for cognitive and social phenomena are generally "messy" subjects. Works by anthropologists and Marxists have suffered from imprecise theory in part because they have not eschewed the study of such murky phenomena as ideology, institutions, organizations, and bargaining power. Given the many extant usages of these terms in the social science literature, some definitions are in

---

4 I use the term "relative prices" rather than "real prices" to focus the reader's attention on the fact that prices are relative phenomena. Choice depends on the value of something in relation to what one must give up for it. Examples of changes in relative prices include changes in terms of trade – for example, the exchange rate between maize and beef or, on a more abstract level, the increasing value of land due to increasing population pressure.

order. It is helpful to discuss these terms together, because the boundaries between them are not entirely clear.

"Ideology" refers to the values and beliefs that determine people's goals and shape their choices. In the jargon of economists, ideology defines what individuals consider to be in their self-interest. This definition is consistent with *any* values that people hold. For example, self-interest could (and often does) include concern for the well-being of others. Of course, values may also be inconsistent (Barth 1981: 49), thus greatly confounding scientific analysis. In addition to defining the ideal world, ideology includes people's mental models or theories of the way the world actually works (North 1990: 23). Asad (1979: 621), for example, notes that, to many anthropologists, ideology is the "culturally inherited lens of a given society by which external reality is filtered and internalized for its members." Together, these aspects of ideology have considerable implications for the actions we take: ideology provides the model we invoke to determine both what we "ought" to do and "how" we might best do it. In this sense, mental models are vulnerable to flaws stemming from both cognitive limitations and informational constraints. As Geertz (1973: 198) notes:

First, where social science, shaped as is all thought by the overall values of the society within which it is contained, is selective in the sort of questions it asks, the particular problems it chooses to tackle, and so forth, ideologies are subject to a further, cognitively more pernicious "secondary" selectivity, in that they emphasize some aspects of social reality – that reality, for example, as revealed by current social scientific knowledge – and neglect or even suppress other aspects. ... Second, ideological thought, not content with mere overselectivity, positively distorts even those aspects of social reality it recognizes, distortion that becomes apparent only when the assertions involved are placed against the background of the authoritative findings of social science.

Even more than ideology, institutions add predictability to human social behavior and facilitate cooperation. For these reasons the study of institutions is critical for understanding economic behavior. Following North (1990: 3–4):

Institutions are the rules of the game in a society or, more formally, are the humanly devised constraints that shape human interaction. In consequence they structure incentives in human exchange, whether political, social, or economic....

Institutions reduce uncertainty by providing a structure to everyday life. They are a guide to human interaction, so that when we wish to greet friends on the street, drive an automobile, buy oranges, borrow money, form a business, bury our dead, or whatever, we know (or can learn easily) how to perform these tasks.

In the sense in which North uses the term, and that adopted here, an institution consists of a combination of *formal rules* (such as those regulating the structure of the polity, property rights, and contracting), *informal constraints* (by which North means norms of behavior or the customary rules of the game), and *enforcement* (including that occurring by self-imposed standards of behavior).

This definition is quite similar to some usages in anthropology.[5] Thus Bailey (1969: ch. 1, 1988: 62) defines institutions as the "rules of the game," and Barth (1967: 663) describes an institution as a "pattern of the allocation of time and resources." Similarly, Douglas (1986: 46) notes, "Minimally, an institution is only a convention. David Lewis' definition [Lewis 1968] is helpful: a convention arises when all parties have a common interest in there being a rule to insure coordination."

Although most definitions of institutions emphasize their permanence and universality (see in particular Hechter, Opp, and Wippler 1990: 1–2), it is important not to exaggerate these features. Indeed, while institutions are significant in reducing uncertainty precisely because they are widely shared and have some degree of permanence, nevertheless there are significant differences in the interpretations of institutional rules (e.g., across gender and class lines) and institutions are continually changing.

Organizations are the easiest to characterize. Again, following North (1990: 5):

> Organizations include political bodies (political parties, the Senate, a city council, a regulatory agency), economic bodies (firms, trade unions, family farms, co-operatives), social bodies (churches, clubs, athletic associations), and education bodies (schools, universities, vocational training centers). They are groups of individuals bound by some common purpose to achieve objectives.

Unlike ideology and institutions, organizations are not merely ideas. Organizations are the groups people form to achieve their goals. In this sense they are central to collective action and may be organized with the express purpose of campaigning for changes in the institutional structure or even the underlying ideology of society. The confusion between organizations and the other two concepts arises in part because of the role organizations often play in furthering ideological ends – churches and schools, for example – and in providing a forum through which institutions are played out – Congress, for example.

Like ideology, bargaining power is often overlooked by economists focusing exclusively on exchange within competitive markets (see Knight 1992). In the study of exchange in less competitive markets, however, it is important to analyze the role of bargaining power. Bargaining power

---

5 Malinowski's (1945: 49–50) definition of institutions differs substantially from that laid out here. Malinowski effectively lumps together under the term "institution" what have been defined here as the separate concepts of ideology, institution, and organization.

is one's ability to get what one wants from others. It may come from greater wealth or social position or the ability to manipulate the ideology of others.[6] Bargaining power is consistent with "voluntary" exchange, as when one uses wealth to get compliance, or "involuntary" exchange, as when one uses force to compel others to act in one's interest. In Taylor's (1982: 11–12) terms, this is achieved by altering the incentives of others through rewards and/or threat of penalties. Bargaining power is determined by the preexisting institutional, organizational, and ideological configuration. But the causal relations are more complicated than this; bargaining power can also be used to effect changes in each of these domains. As Bates (1989: 35) points out, power plays a crucial role in institutional change. Changing institutions may be a costly undertaking; those who have the resource endowments to do so may be more effective in influencing the course of subsequent institutional change. Some are also better favored by the current institutional structure to effect further changes. For example, the chief among the Orma is in a powerful position as a consequence of the institutional structure set up by the national government. As chief, he is frequently given a forum for public speaking and often uses it to influence the ideology of the population. For example, he has exercised this option in order to promote the value of education. Other institutions and organizations at his disposal, such as laws mandating compulsory primary schooling, and administrative police, can be used to reinforce this and other objectives. His authority, however, is limited by the ideological legitimacy accorded to the chief by the populace.

OUTLINING THE THEORETICAL FRAMEWORK, PART I: MODELING CHANGE — THE ANTHROPOLOGICAL TRADITION

Since the pioneering work of Karl Polanyi (1944), economic anthropologists have recognized the study of institutions as a natural field for exercising their disciplinary comparative advantage.[7] Yet we remain a long way from bridging the gap between economics and anthropology.

Within economic anthropology, from the 1950s onward, there were significant contributions by Firth (especially 1967), who not only emphasized the role of individuals, but also attempted to model processes

6 This definition subsumes both the common usage of Weber (1947), i.e., the ability to coerce others into doing what they would otherwise not perceive to be in their best interest, and the popular contemporary usage of Foucault (1980), i.e., the ability to control the consciousness of others.

7 See Hechter (1983), North (1977), and Rutten (1990) for new institutional critiques of Polanyi.

of change without neglecting the strong constraints of social institutions. In the 1960s those associated with the formalist school carried on the tradition of centering analysis on rational choice makers, but tended to give less attention to the domain of institutional analysis, much as neo-classical economists used to do.[8] This, of course, was the complaint of the substantivists (notably Dalton 1968; Polanyi 1968; Sahlins 1972), who, in contrast, focused on the socially embedded nature of the economy but lost individuals in the process. In the 1970s some of the formalists and their descendants went on to more focused studies in economic decision making[9] and development anthropology, while others (Cook 1977, 1982), as well as some substantivists (Halperin 1984), turned to neo-Marxist orientations.

Within anthropology, those best known and most obviously compatible with the actor-oriented emphasis on processual change taken here include Bailey (1968, 1969, 1977, 1983, 1988), Barth (1963, 1965, 1966, 1967, 1981), Boissevain (1968), and others associated with the transaction approaches of the 1960s and 1970s (see Heath 1976; Kapferer 1976; for reviews of the literature see Hedican 1986; Vincent 1978).[10] These approaches provide a good starting point. After examining them, we can see more clearly the benefits of adapting the rational choice perspective to the study of institutional change, thereby adding more formality and precision to the discussion.

Among anthropologists, Fredrik Barth is quite possibly the best known for his processual approach to social change.[11] It is worth citing his

---

8 For examples of early formalist writings see Belshaw (1965, 1970), Burling (1968), Cancian (1968), Cook (1968), LeCiair (1968), Nash (1958, 1968), Salisbury (1962, 1969), and Schneider (1974).

9 Studies of economic decision making in anthropology are far too numerous to list, but some of the best early ones include the following: Barlett (1980, 1982), Cancian (1979), Fjellman (1976), Gladwin (1979), Howard and Ortiz (1971), Ortiz (1967), Plattner (1975), Prattis (1970, 1973, 1976), and Quinn (1975).

10 Several other traditions within anthropology are broadly compatible with the position argued here, among which one might note in particular cultural materialism (Harris 1979) and cultural ecology (Johnson 1972; Netting 1968, 1977; Service 1962; Vayda 1969; Vayda and McCay 1975; White 1959). For a fine recent example of work in these traditions see Johnson and Earle (1987).

11 Barth's perspective is also similar to Nash's (1958: 149) earlier writing on social change:

A theory of social and cultural change capable of dealing with the consequences of social decisions in situations of uncertain outcome is yet to be fashioned. I believe change is best understood as the result of the ways in which individuals choose to combine time, effort, and resources in the face of new opportunity. These factors, in their purposeful combination, underlie the emergence of new social relations and cultural understandings.

As these and similar ideas are elaborated by further research, a theory of change will emerge in which the role of choice will be analytically coordinate with the characteristics perspective at length, because it provides a familiar foundation on which to build (Barth 1981: 51–2).

> I have envisaged an hypothetical, initial situation of an unordered set of arbitrary, disparate values.... The logical effects of processes of social transactions on such a minimally integrated set of values would seem to be clear. Values become progressively systematized as they are used to mediate the comparisons of prestations in transactions: over-arching canons or principles of evaluation are necessary for persons engaged in such transactions. Secondly, values become progressively shared by being made known through transactions: the principles of evaluation, and their uses, become public and serve as guides in the choices of others. The process of transaction thus simultaneously generates trends towards integration and institutionalization. Finally, in an on-going system, where patterns of behavior are generated from a set of shared values, the resolution of individual dilemmas of choice by the construction of over-arching principles of evaluation will have a feedback effect in the direction of greater consistency and integration, and other patterns of choice and behaviour will in turn be generated.
>
> ... Clearly, every instance of transaction takes place in a matrix of values and statuses, the latter being a basic social arrangement....
>
> ... there is one further feedback effect which should be emphasized. Through transactions, evaluations are not only "corrected" with reference to consistency and sharing; they will also be modified in the direction of consistency in terms of natural and external criteria, i.e. they become less arbitrary. This will result because through being offered in transactions, prestations are also made subject to the cost–demand–price mechanisms of the market. Regardless of our initial evaluations – if something becomes dirt cheap, we may start treating it as dirt; in other words, we tend to revise our evaluation. I am not suggesting an identity of value and market price, but merely an effect of market price on value.

Barth's description of the processual relationship between relative prices (market price), ideology (values), institutions, and bargaining power (status) includes many of the elements considered here. Barth's model has been extensively criticized, most notably for insufficient consideration of power.[12] While he may have given insufficient *emphasis* to the role of power, it does not follow that it is impossible to rectify the existence of differences in power with the presence of choice, as argued by Paine (1974). Following Barth, the position argued here is that choice is fundamental to any model of institutional change; furthermore, giving appropriate attention to power is compatible with Barth's perspective.

Figure 1.1 presents these relationships graphically. Inside the "black box" are the characteristics that generally receive the most attention from

---

of the social and cultural systems. In fact, I envision an approach which deals with social systems as conditioning choice in two ways: (1) by generating sets of alternatives, and (2) by defining the means by which alternatives may be implemented.

12 For critiques of Barth's work see Asad (1972), Evens (1977), Hedican (1986), Kapferer (1976), Paine (1974), and Skvoretz and Conviser (1974). For Barth's reply see Barth (1981: ch. 5).

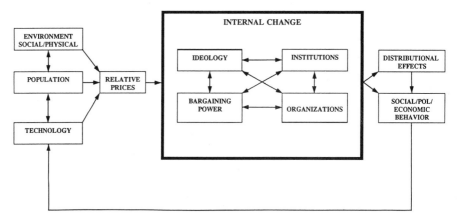

Figure 1.1. Modeling change.

anthropologists. Outside the black box are those causal elements most often crucial to economists' models, particularly population, technology, and relative prices. While economists have been successful in explaining a great deal of economic behavior in terms of these factors alone under some circumstances, they have not fared as well under other conditions, especially those likely to be of interest to anthropologists and development experts. The reason is that the factors inside the black box are not fixed – they can change. The endogeneity of these factors renders complete prediction, and even understanding, impossible without attention to these components.

Following economists' lead, changes in relative prices exert pressure on the black box, including ideology and institutions. Some anthropologists might have difficulty with this assumption, viewing ideology, for instance, as resistant to such pressures. To a degree, they are correct; ideological beliefs are resistant to change. Nevertheless, ideology does change over time, and so we must try to pinpoint the threshold at which ideology is altered to conform with changes in bargaining power, institutions, and organizations, which in turn may be brought about by changes in relative prices.[13] As Eggertsson (1990: 78) notes, each tem-

13 As I see it, one of the best measures of ideology is the extent to which such commitments withstand change in the face of increasing relative costs. In other words, how else can we be confident with any degree of scientific certainty that an ideological commitment exists except in terms of what people are prepared to forgo in its service? However, the relationship between changing costs and ideological commitment is subject to the same intentionality limitations of the cognitive models noted earlier. In other words, a precise correlation between cause and effect is unlikely to occur even when people intend to so respond.

porary change in relative prices may not warrant changes in the rules or institutions. The same is certainly true of ideology. Thus it is perfectly possible that the threshold at which one will forgo an ideological commitment, say to support one's relatives, is not breached, despite considerable pressure from rising costs. This is the phenomenon known as cultural conservation or cultural lag.

Ideologies are also less vulnerable to change than we might predict, even in the face of considerable change in relative prices, because they are "lumpy"; that is, they are indivisible and operate across numerous frontiers (cf. North 1990: 16, who similarly characterizes institutions as lumpy). Ideologies are not terribly precise guidelines, and they often allow for a wide variety of behavior. As Bailey (1969) notes, ideas are general, but situations are specific. For example, the Orma believe that it is right for people to support their fellow clan members in times of need. Such support may take the form of material contributions, but also includes such things as help with herding and political and legal disputes. While changes in food prices might rapidly lead to a decline in material support, they would not necessarily affect support in the other domains; thus the ideology might remain virtually intact.

A key difference between economic and anthropological analyses of economic behavior lies in what they typically assume to be endogenous. Even when explaining the same phenomena, the anthropologist and the economist adopt very different approaches. While the economist takes tastes (preferences) and institutions as constant and analyzes the effects of changing relative prices on economic behavior, the anthropologist is more inclined to take relative prices as constant and look to changes in the ideological or institutional structure to explain changes in economic behavior, and specifically economic distribution. The perspective here is that these approaches are not mutually exclusive, nor are they independently complete. But the answer is not to try to make all factors endogenous simultaneously.

Barth (1981: 80) has referred to the problem of where to locate endogenous sources of change as the "impasse" that troubles much contemporary anthropology. I suggest that we must shift back and forth, sometimes trying to understand the effect of demography and environment on relative prices, sometimes focusing on the effect of relative prices on ideology and institutions or the effect of ideology on institutions and vice versa. Moreover, we must constantly look at how an individual's current standing in the existing structure affects his or her motivations and relative bargaining power. Barth (1981: 77) proposes exactly this sort of "step-wise presentation of a model" in which forms are not generated from "scratch," but "with reference to a set of values . . . [and] a pre-established matrix of statuses." To create such an empirically rich, valid model demands the joint efforts and tools of anthropologists and economists.

While anthropologists have more expertise in describing relationships among ideology, institutions, organizations, and power, economists have one of the most powerful theories to explain what drives such relationships. I refer to rational choice theory, which as we shall see means very different things to different people.

OUTLINING THE THEORETICAL FRAMEWORK, PART II: RATIONAL CHOICE THEORY

Rational choice theory is controversial, especially among anthropologists and sociologists (see, e.g., Friedland and Robertson 1990: 6, 9; Peters 1987, 1989; Sahlins 1972, 1976; and for a review of critiques Johnson 1991; Mansbridge 1990a: 16–19).[14] Because of this controversy, it is worth discussing at length what rational choice theory is, and is not. Some of the greatest confusion has revolved around the definition of "rationality." Rationality is assumed by many of the critics to be equivalent to the assumption that people act only in their narrow economic self-interest. Perhaps some of the strongest aversion stems from the fear that failure to acknowledge the existence of altruism and cooperation in the world may actually contribute to the creation of a world based on more self-interested motives.[15]

All too often, rational choice theorists have indeed come close to endorsing the caricature of completely rational, perfectly informed, narrowly self-interested *homo economicus*, maximizing his (*sic*) way through life by mechanically calculating the narrow costs and benefits of every decision. One of the extreme proponents of the significance of self-interest, Tullock (1976), asserts that 95 percent of human behavior is narrowly self-interested, so we can safely make this assumption and merely forgo the other 5 percent of behavior as trivial.[16]

Recently, the crudest versions of rational choice theory have been replaced by a more realistic approach to human behavior. Rational choice

---

14 Much of the work in the substantivist tradition in anthropology (cited earlier) can also be considered an implicit attack on rational choice theory.

15 Some research suggests that this view is correct. Experimental economics has demonstrated, for example, that economics majors show the lowest level of cooperation (Marwell and Ames 1981). It remains to be seen whether this reflects the fact that more self-interested people are drawn to economics or that those who have internalized the ideology of *homo economicus* consider it legitimate to practice what they preach and avoid at all costs the "sucker" designation.

16 Tullock has since revised his position on the relative significance of behavior that is deemed to be non-self-interested.

retains the tenet of methodological individualism, the claim that social institutions and change must be explained in terms of individual actions and interactions (Elster 1989a: 13).[17] But it avoids assuming that individuals always act in their narrow economic self-interest, make choices in a largely unconstrained environment, have complete information, and have accurate cognitive models.[18] One could summarize the insights of this recent work simply as follows: While rational choice concerns means –ends relationships, economists have used far too narrow a concept of ends, neglecting obvious evidence of considerable behavior motivated by ideological or altruistic ends, and far too broad a concept of means, neglecting the costliness of information and the considerable constraints placed on choice by social norms and institutions. Most germane to the central concept of rational choice, economists have neglected to take into account the cognitive limitations stemming from individuals' imperfect models of the world (see Simon 1957).

There are several ways in which rational choice moves away from narrow self-interest. The most surprising is by showing that even altruistic behavior may be self-interested in the long term. This finding emerges in several ways. Game theorists who study cooperation note that, in repeat dealing, partners are able to use the threat of future noncooperation to punish cheaters, thus ensuring a high degree of cooperation even when that might run against one's short-term interests (Axelrod 1984; Taylor 1987).[19] Others assume a genetic foundation for cooperation which results in cooperative behavior even when there is no repeat dealing (R. Frank 1988).[20]

These findings are interesting, but as North (1990: 21) notes, and I suspect most anthropologists would agree, they do not exhaust the sources of altruism. In particular, to understand altruism we must ultimately come to terms with the role of culturally determined values (ideology) in human motivation. Through detailed ethnographic descriptions of diverse societies, anthropologists have already made a substantial contribution in this arena. The development of a more rigorous, but realistic,

---

17 See also Wilson (1977: 21), who writes: "Most changes in a society begin as a divergence in the behaviourism of one person, who is then followed by others. As the number following the innovator increases, the new pattern becomes the norm for a sub-group in the society."

18 Examples of new approaches to rational choice include the six recent volumes by Elster (1985a, 1985b, 1986, 1989a, 1989b, 1990), Johnson (1991), Knight (1992), the contributions to Mansbridge's (1990b) volume *Beyond Self-Interest*, as well as Cook and Levi's (1990) *The Limits of Rationality*. See Kalt and Zupan (1984) for a particularly interesting empirical study of rationality and ideology.

19 See Hechter (1990) and Schofield (1986) for critiques of game-theoretical approaches.

20 See Hayek (1978) for a discussion of the limits of sociobiological explanations.

theoretical perspective with which to organize these rich data should also lead to yet more valuable insights.

Altruism may be especially important in determining behavior outside the market. It may be, as Tullock and other economists claim, that self-interest dominates in markets where competition punishes those who ignore narrow goals.[21] Much behavior (including that in developing societies) studied by anthropologists is not subject to such competition. In these settings, other motives cannot be assumed away. Even in our own society, experimental research indicates that one can generate 40 percent altruistic behavior among strangers (Hornstein, Fisch, and Holmes 1968; Hornstein, Masor, Sole, and Heilman 1971; for a political example see Kalt and Zupan 1984). Unfortunately, the domain of narrowly self-interested economic behavior carved out by Tullock and many other economists is the most easily modeled and predicted, and leaves the more difficult work for anthropologists and other social scientists. Thus it is not that narrow self-interest is unimportant, but that it leaves too much other human behavior unexplained.

In addition to restrictive assumptions about ends, crude rational choice makes insupportable assumptions about the accuracy with which individuals can predict the relationship between means and ends. Recent work in psychology indicates that cognitive limitations make the precision assumed by economists impossible (Tversky and Kahneman 1987; see also Quinn 1978; Simon 1957). In response to this criticism, economists increasingly recognize the erroneousness of the complete-information assumption employed in most traditional economic models. But incomplete information is only one part of the problem. Concerns about means–ends calculations relate also to the significance of ideology in determining behavior. Ideology includes the theory or model of the world on which people base their calculations of effective means–ends relations, so we must also recognize the limitations imposed by these other cognitive imperfections of individuals' models. Individuals' operational perspectives are potentially severely flawed. In economic jargon, the gap between expected and actual outcomes of a given behavior may be extreme, thus rendering explanation and prediction based on simple rational choice models quite weak (see North 1990: 15). This may account in large part for the confusion demonstrated in examples of intransitive preferences and imperfect maximization.

Barth (1981: 90) discusses this issue, which he refers to as intentionality:

---

21 There is a growing body of literature that suggests people take fairness into account even in markets (see, e.g., Kahneman, Knetsch, and Thaler 1986a, 1986b, 1986c).

I have emphasized the central role of values and intentionality in shaping human behaviour; but this does not assume perfectly aware and deliberate actors, only that awareness and intention are formative of what such behaviour does show of regular pattern. It is enough that we posit that people intermittently deliberate over their desires, acts, and achievements, and have the ability sometimes to recollect experience and devise plans. Otherwise we can acknowledge that behaviour is often automatic, habitual, impulsive, passionate or random.

Again (on p. 102):

Essentially, "Models" sees social life being generated by actors who go about their activity by pursuing their interests fitfully, often thoughtlessly, and generally conventionally.

In short, social science is destined to remain an imprecise science because considerable cultural lag and imprecision are built into individuals' actions.

Even as modified, rational choice theory is an impotent tool in the absence of knowledge about existing "ends" and "means." Rational choice theory concerns means–ends relations, not the specific configuration of preexisting constraints and incentives created by institutions, nor the specific makeup of antecedent ends and means.[22] In order to be realistic, rational choice theory must be stripped of the simplistic assumptions with which it is frequently coupled. So corrected, rational choice remains a necessary theory for understanding human behavior. It offers promise for understanding the processes by which new means and ends come to be the way they are. This large domain, the subject of much anthropological analysis, is now viewed by economists (Eggertsson 1990; North 1990), political scientists (Bates 1989; Johnson 1991; Mansbridge 1990b), and sociologists (Coleman 1986; Hechter et al. 1990) alike as one of the most exciting and yet unexplored areas in the social sciences.

These criticisms of rational choice, while significant, have not been devastating, but they have forced a severe modification of the theory. With what, then, are we left? Elster (1989a: 22) sums it up this way: "When faced with several courses of action, people usually do what they believe is likely to have the best overall outcome." Or as Barth (1981: 38) puts it, "... a clear concept of transaction, leads us to a recognition of a very fundamental social process: the process which results where parties in the course of their interactions systematically try to assume that the value gained for them is greater or equal to the value lost."[23]

---

22 Neo-Marxists and anthropologists generally (Donham 1981, 1990) are especially bothered by this failing, which they argue does not necessarily render neoclassical theory wrong, but means that it begs the most interesting questions.

23 Paine's (1974: 7) criticism of this perspective notwithstanding, I do find this

Making a market

The following story (Dawes and Thaler 1988: 145, cited in Mansbridge 1990a: xiii) illustrates the level at which this author finds rational choice theory useful:

In the rural areas around Ithaca it is common for farmers to put some fresh produce on a table by the road. There is a cash box on the table, and customers are expected to put money in the box in return for the vegetables they take. The box has just a small slit, so money can only be put in, not taken out. Also, the box is attached to the table, so no one can (easily) make off with the money. We think that the farmers who use this system have just about the right model of human nature. They feel that enough people will volunteer to pay for the fresh corn to make it worthwhile to put it out there. The farmers also know that if it were easy enough to take the money, someone would do so.

As Mansbridge (1990a) notes, this story illustrates two points: first, that human motives are complex and include significant quantities of duty and moral self-enforcement in addition to self-interest, but equally important, that human behavior based on such mixed motives can be modeled and predicted using rational choice theory.

How do we get from rational choice theory about means–ends relations to a processual theory that can help us model changing ends, means, their relationship to asymmetries of power, and the development of social, political, and economic institutions? Economists assume that ends (preferences) are fixed and known by inference from past "revealed preferences." This necessarily results in a static model that cannot account for changing ends as a consequence of changing ideology. What is needed is a rational choice model explicitly accommodating the possibility of changing ideology, institutions, and bargaining power. It is to such a model, developed by the new institutional economists, that we now turn.

The NIE provides a framework for examining the process of change. It helps us understand how and why social, political, and economic institutions change over time, and what role the intentions and bargaining power of individuals play in this process. In short, it demonstrates how rational choice theory can be modified to meet many of the objections that critics have raised to it, namely, that it cannot account for altruistic behavior, that it cannot deal with asymmetries of power or changing preferences, that it cannot explain suboptimal or economically inefficient behavior, and that it ignores the most interesting questions, particularly the development of the institutional constraints that may so restrict the options of individuals as to make the study of their actual behavior trivial.

statement consistent with an assumption of unequal distribution of power. At the point of choice, such constraints are given. Each choice, in turn, further alters the power dynamics of the future choice set.

A proper marriage

OUTLINING THE THEORETICAL FRAMEWORK, PART III: THE NEW INSTITUTIONAL ECONOMICS

It is one thing to say that institutions matter; it is another to explain how they matter. This is the task of the new institutional economists.[24] Most work in the NIE is concerned with explaining the effects of institutions on economic performance and distribution; more recently, attention has also turned to the determinants of institutions and their evolution over time. The relevance of such work to anthropologists should be obvious. Similarly, the relevance to institutional economists of anthropological insights gleaned from detailed examination of these issues across hundreds of diverse societies should also be obvious. Despite these complementarities, only a handful of anthropologists have "discovered" new institutionalism.[25]

Nevertheless, within anthropology one can trace developments that parallel what was occurring in institutional economics in the middle of this century. As R. C. O. Matthews (1986: 909) noted in his presidential address to the Royal Economic Society:

The idea of deliberate institutional innovations was interestingly developed in the 1950s and 1960s by Frederick [sic] Barth, who introduced the so-called transactional approach into social anthropology (apparently without being aware of the similar movement in economics). Barth (1966) saw the entrepreneur as someone who initiates transactions between values that were previously incommensurable, in other words someone who creates a new market.

---

24 The adjective "new" differentiates contemporary institutional economics from the "old" institutional economics of John Commons, Wesley Mitchell, and Thorstein Veblen (for a brief review see Gunnarsson 1991). Like the old institutional economists, the new also criticize neoclassical theory for failing to pay sufficient attention to institutions and for making unreasonable assumptions about human behavior. Beyond this, however, there is little resemblance between the rather atheoretical original approach and the identifiable body of literature that began to coalesce as the new institutional economics (NIE) in the 1960s. Langlois (1986: 5) summarizes it this way: "The problem with many of the early Institutionalists is that they wanted an economics with institutions but without theory; the problem with many neoclassicists is that they want economic theory without institutions; what NIE tries to do is to provide an economics with both theory *and* institutions."

25 Acheson (1982, 1985, 1988, 1989a, b), Behnke (1985), Cashdan (1990), Ensminger (1990, 1991), Plattner (1989), and Wade (1988) have employed the perspective most explicitly. Increasing interest in the perspective among anthropologists is evidenced by the fact that the Society for Economic Anthropology devoted its annual meeting to the subject in 1992. Innumerable anthropologists, like Barth and Bailey, have written from a clearly compatible perspective. Among the earliest and most famous, one might cite Linton (1936) and Morgan (1974 [1877]) and, in African studies, Colson (1974) and Wilson (1977).

Indeed, if Barth did not influence the new institutional economists, he at least deserves credit for independently inventing many of the same ideas.

The new institutionalists rely on two assumptions to extend the traditional economic approach to institutions. The most important is that transaction costs are not zero: it takes resources to gather information, negotiate, monitor, and enforce property rights and contracts.[26] Transaction costs are incurred whenever people try to measure the quality of the goods and services they want, to monitor the performance of agents (employees), to find trading partners, or to enforce contracts (see North 1985).[27] In short, exchange is not free, nor even cheap.[28] The second assumption is that the goods and services have more than the two dimensions (price and quantity) usually assumed by economists. In particular, quality is a crucial dimension and exists over so many planes that its complete measurement is impossible. For example, when the Orma hire a herder and entrust him with the family's entire assets in lion-infested territory, the extent to which he utilizes his common sense, intelligence, knowledge, and strength is at least as critical to the profitability of the employer as how many hours he works (see Bradburd 1990). Even more significant than all of these may be the yet more elusive quality of trustworthiness.

Although simple, these two assumptions have powerful implications for the impact of institutions and ideology on economic performance. While institutional economists accept the insight of Adam Smith (1976 [1776]) that economic growth stems from gains from trade and increasing specialization and division of labor, they do not accept that such gains are automatic or costless (North 1981: 176). Societies may *not* benefit from trade or specialization if the "transaction costs" incurred in the process of exchange outweigh the benefits of that exchange. It is exactly these costs that governments reduce by clearly specifying property rights, by regulating weights and measures, and by providing third-party enforcement of property rights and contracts. Institutional economists maintain that economic growth comes not merely from technological change, as has been the emphasis in most neoclassical analyses, but also from institutional change, particularly by a reduction in transaction costs.[29] In developing societies with weak institutions, in which anthro-

---

26 For an especially clear discussion of transaction costs, see Goldberg (1989: 21–3).

27 Geertz's (1979) study of the Moroccan market (*sug*) exemplifies the type of exchange one typically finds when information and other transaction costs are high.

28 See, e.g., Wallis and North (1986), who have measured the costs of transacting for the U.S. economy.

29 The importance given to institutional rather than technological innovation is a view familiar to anthropologists from Karl Polanyi's work (1944).

pologists typically work, such costs may be the primary impediment to development. This is not to suggest that institutional change always moves in the direction of increasing efficiency or economic growth.

These assumptions also imply that people cannot establish institutions to control all dimensions of exchange, having the consequence of either raising transaction costs or forgoing some gains from exchange. Indeed, it is impossible even to enforce all of the rules that they do make. As a result, people will always have opportunities to ignore at least the spirit of some rules. How any particular rule affects behavior depends on exactly how the rule is specified and enforced, the costs and benefits of noncompliance, and the role of ideology in making the rule self-enforcing. For example, we often do not cheat or shirk even when we know we could do so undetected. In many cases, this is because we *believe* the rule is just. Thus the same institution in different circumstances may elicit very different behavior. Even more significantly, many institutions that might facilitate economic growth cannot be feasibly implemented.

These assumptions obviously have important implications for people's choice of institutions. While some institutions exist primarily to channel behavior based on religious and ideological norms, others have more explicitly economic effects. In all cases, institutions impose costs (social, political, or economic) on certain forms of behavior, and therefore those who wish to engage in such proscribed behavior have an incentive to change the institutional structure. Furthermore, individuals try to structure institutions toward their own ends (see Bates 1981, 1989) by committing resources to bring about changes in the institutional environment.

The analysis of institutional choice is a three-step process. The first is to consider how the available institutions distribute costs and benefits across society. The next step is to model the desires of the people and groups who are choosing, to see how they rank the alternatives, including what they consider to be the legitimate distribution of costs and benefits. Ideology must be explicitly considered in these assessments, because people may consider more than narrow economic effects on themselves. The final step is to consider the politics of institutions, or the way in which the political system treats the desires of different groups. This determines how the various groups control the outcomes. This three-step approach is especially useful for analyzing the path of institutional change, including the timing and direction of change.

The two assumptions associated with institutional economics were originally used to analyze the organization of exchange within markets. The first application was Ronald Coase's 1937 study of the firm. In effect, he asked, if markets are so great, why is so much economic activity carried on outside the market, in firms? He argued that this question could be answered using simple economic reasoning. In particular, he claimed that firms allowed people to avoid the transaction costs of the market. Following his lead, the new institutionalists examined the economic logic underlying the organization of market transactions. Like Coase, they assumed that people will structure their relations to reduce the costs of exchange. Since organizations will be tailored to the problem to be solved and to the cost structure, those that serve one purpose in one setting may not serve another purpose in another setting. This approach has been used to explain a variety of otherwise puzzling forms of economic organization, ranging from franchise agreements to farm tenant contracts.

The aspect of the NIE most interesting to development specialists is its application to economic growth. While these specialists accept that growth depends on exchange, their assumptions do not imply that the process of growth is automatic or smooth. When it is costly to exchange, people may not be able to make the trades that offer them the greatest benefits. Much research in the NIE has focused on identifying precisely these institutional and organizational constraints on growth.

The new institutionalists have extended this logic beyond the market to include nonmarket institutions, such as politics. In doing so, they have continued to apply the basic approach. In nonmarket settings, however, competition does not act as effectively to reward efficiency. Exactly how competition works, and what it rewards, depends on the structure of specific institutions. In particular, the outcomes of many nonmarket institutions do not simply mimic market outcomes. Those who are choosing institutions will not always choose ones that benefit society at large. Many political institutions insulate people so effectively from competition that they are free to extract monopoly rents or otherwise pursue their ideology. It is this application of the NIE that goes a long way toward satisfying some of the criticisms of Marxists who have found little within neoclassical theory with which to address their concerns (see Bardhan 1989a: ch. 1 for a similar conclusion).

In analyzing institutions, the new institutionalists proceed at three different levels. These levels are distinguished by which features are taken as endogenous. Eggertsson (1990: xiii) characterizes the different research agendas as follows:

As I see it, there are several levels of analysis in Neoinstitutional Economics, depending on which variables are treated as endogenous. At the first level, the structure of property rights and forms of organization are explicitly modeled but are treated as exogenous, and the emphasis is on their impact on economic outcomes. At the second level, the organization of exchange is endogenized, but the fundamental structure of property rights remains exogenous. Exchange within firms, across formal markets, and in non-market situations is organized by means of contracts that constrain economic agents. For instance, the firm is defined as a network of contracts. At the third level, attempts are made to endogenize both social and political rules and the structure of political institutions by introducing the concept of transaction costs.

To this, anthropologists might want to add a fourth level, in which ideology is endogenous.

Most research in the NIE proceeds at the first and second levels. That is, the social and political institutions are considered exogenous (given), and at most the effects of different forms of organization (e.g., firms) or contracting (e.g., sharecropping vs. tenant arrangements) are tested against economic performance. While these are fascinating issues in the developed world, they are not necessarily as useful to social scientists interested in the developing world. Far more relevant may be applications at the third level, where considerable attention is given to the effect of different institutional arrangements on transaction costs, which may well be critical to economic development (see Bardhan 1989a, 1989b; Bates 1988; Behnke 1985; Nabli and Nugent 1989; Wade 1988).

Many anthropologists, however, are more concerned with how ideology and institutions come to be. Much other work in the NIE, although not as well known, is concerned with exactly these issues. The scholars involved are attempting to create models of behavior that treat institutions and even ideology as endogenous. For example, how do individuals attempt to alter institutions to serve their interests more effectively? Here I would note especially the works of Bates (1981, 1989), Hechter (1987), Higgs (1987), Levi (1988), and North (1981, 1990). This attempt to make institutions endogenous is similar to the research orientation advocated by Friedland and Robertson (1990: 13), who make a plea for models that make political power endogenous, and that of Johnson (1991), who does the same for ideology.

While the differences noted so far are a matter of research interest and context (market vs. nonmarket) rather than theoretical disagreement, one can also discern some disagreements within the ranks of the NIE.

After some thirty years of considerable work in the NIE, one can no longer easily generalize to the entire field. In particular, one might note a key difference between what could be labeled the "Williamsonian" (after Oliver Williamson) and the "Northian" (after Douglass C. North) approaches.[30] While the differences between these approaches should not be overdrawn, they also ought not be overlooked, because they have important implications for the application of the NIE to the developing world. Williamson (1975, 1985) and his students have made enormous contributions to the NIE, especially transaction cost economics as applied

---

30 These correspond closely to what Eggertsson identifies as the new institutional versus the neoinstitutional approach.

to Western, capitalist, competitive market environments. In this context, Williamson (1981) takes the position that institutions are expressly designed to reduce transaction costs and that, in a competitive market, those that fail to do so will not survive. He has posited both the cause (high transaction costs) and effect (increasing economic efficiency) of institutions. In some contexts, and perhaps most particularly the Western capitalist domains of his concern, such assumptions may hold. In the less competitive markets of the developing world, where anthropologists generally work, these are not particularly accurate assumptions, even as applied to economic behavior. Furthermore, the concepts of the NIE have vast applications for the analysis of institutional change other than that which is transacted in markets, where the concept of economic efficiency has even less relevance.

The works of Robert Higgs (1971, 1987), Douglass North (1981, 1990), and other economic historians are likely to be a far better starting point for those working in development or anthropology and interested in adapting this perspective to their needs. This is not surprising, for economic historians are asking many of the same questions about historical development that anthropologists ask in the contemporary context.

Along with others from this group, North (1981: ch. 3, 1990: 8, 52) vehemently eschews the notion that institutions are created only to reduce transaction costs and increase economic efficiency. As North puts it (personal communication), "If institutional change results in increasing efficiency, it is usually an accident." One of the best illustrations of the sort of motivation that may drive institutional change is Bates's (1981) study of African agricultural policy. He finds that politicians promote agricultural policies that satisfy their political aspirations to be reelected, but are far less successful in promoting general agricultural development. As Bates notes, far more effective institutional methods exist to increase agricultural production, but they are not implemented, because they could not be selectively employed to achieve the ends most desired by the politicians, namely, their personal gain. The logic here is familiar to anthropologists as the difference between individual and group rationality (Popkin 1979: 31; Rutz 1977). Firth (1953: 152) articulated this notion when he wrote, "One may adopt the assumption that in all social life there is necessarily and inescapably a clash between interest or values of individual and society." Given that some actors have more bargaining power than others, as well as diverging goals, it is not surprising that the institutions they promote rarely represent the most efficient outcome for society as a whole.

Some of the sources most accessible to anthropologists and development specialists who deal with the NIE have lumped the Williamsonian and Northian perspectives and ascribed the efficiency error to both (see particularly Bromley 1989; Friedland and Robertson 1990; Granovetter 1985; Langlois 1986).[31] The danger is that many social scientists, especially empirically oriented anthropologists, who recognize the obvious error of assuming that institutions are created to solve efficiency problems, may dismiss the entire contribution of the NIE. It is crucial, therefore, that they understand that this assumption is neither central to the theory of the NIE nor shared by all of its practitioners.

Many of the considerable differences among new institutionalists concern emphasis, not fundamental theoretical disagreements. Again, invoking the analysis introduced earlier in the quote from Eggertsson, some of these differences relate to what one assumes to be endogenous or exogenous in the model. Those in the Williamson camp are most concerned with explaining different forms of organization, and consequently they consider both ideology and institutions to be exogenous. They also often treat organizations as exogenous when analyzing their effects on economic performance. Furthermore, because the driving force behind institutional change is assumed to be greater efficiency, the role of individual bargaining power is neglected altogether.

Those in the Northian camp, however, are far more catholic in their orientation. While they also have an interest in explaining organizations and economic performance, they are as interested in explaining why different institutions arise and in examining the role of ideology in the process (Higgs 1987, 1989; Hinich and Munger 1990; North 1981, 1990; Siegenthaler 1989). Because of their orientation, these studies have a greater appreciation of both history and relative bargaining power.

Many of those in the Northian group are economic historians and as such have a special appreciation of the fact that existing institutional and ideological structures place constraints on future behavior (path dependency). Because institutions are "lumpy" and serve multiple purposes, institutional change is difficult to achieve and is rarely revolutionary.[32] In many cases this precludes alternative courses of action that those using a traditional economic model might expect to find.[33]

---

31 North's (1981) position (reflected in all subsequent publications) also represents a clarification of his former position (North and Thomas 1973) on this issue.
32 This is akin to Gluckman's (1956) observation that individuals have innumerable cross-cutting ties that serve to reduce conflict even in the absence of a state.
33 Scarlett Epstein (1962: 9) has captured the essence of the path dependency perspective (see David 1985; North 1990: ch. 11) in her study of social change in South India. She studied two villages of common cultural heritage, one of which (Wangala) had received irrigation twenty years before her study, while the other (Dalena) had not. Because irrigation was built on traditional patterns of labor allocation and social structure, particularly the caste system, it brought relatively minor incremental change to Wangala. In the absence of irrigation, Dalena was

To bring these diverse applications into better focus, I turn now to an introduction to the four research areas in which this analysis will be applied in the book: transaction costs (Chapters 2 and 3), contractual choice (including principal–agent theory – Chapter 4), property rights (Chapter 5), and collective action (Chapter 6). The increasing commercialization of the Orma economy, including the transition to larger economies of scale in livestock production, has led to continued pressure for change in many institutions. The theoretical framework laid out in this chapter is intended to help us understand this social transformation.

APPLYING THE NIE IN ANTHROPOLOGICAL AND DEVELOPMENT CONTEXTS

Economists for the most part agree that economic growth stems from increasing the gains from trade, specialization, and the division of labor.[34] Much less agreement exists, even among economists, about the best means to achieve this end.[35] Until relatively recently, economists have focused a great deal on the effect of technology and production on economic growth. The costs of transacting have long been ignored in neoclassical economics generally, as they have been specifically in the development field. Yet according to a growing number of economists, transaction costs are the key to the performance of economies (Nabli and Nugent 1989; North 1981, 1990; North and Thomas 1973; Williamson 1985; see Bardhan 1989b for a critical discussion). Transaction

forced to change far more radically by adopting altogether new economic strategies including labor migration and new labor contracts that undermined the caste system. In Epstein's (1962: 9–10) terminology, "unilineal change" is similar to the concept of "path dependency" as utilized by economists. The difference in application, however, is that the economists employing the concept of path dependency are more concerned with examining the economic losses of forgone opportunities as a consequence of historical antecedents, while Epstein looks more to its function in maintaining the status quo: "Irrigation of Wangala land brought what I may term unilinear changes in the sense that the new opportunities were in line with the former mode of economic organization. The interests of Wangala's population continued to be vested in agriculture.... because these economic changes were unilinear, they brought about only minor changes in the traditional social system. By contrast Dalena's social system has changed considerably in the same period. Irrigation in the [neighboring] region brought multifarious economic opportunities to Dalena villages: their economic activities and their interests diversified.... These multifarious opportunities were responsible for a radical change in Dalena's former farming economy."

34 By "economic growth" I mean change in the total output of society, regardless of the distribution.

35 Among other social scientists, the desirability of economic growth itself has been questioned. Nevertheless, whether one considers economic growth a good thing or not, it is still valid scientifically to ask what processes bring it about.

costs derive in turn directly from the formal and informal institutions within a society.

In many of the societies studied by anthropologists, the transaction costs faced in daily life are extremely low. Most exchange occurs between individuals who are known (if not related) to one another and with whom one can expect to engage in repeat dealings. Often such individuals also have complex ties that cross-cut social and political domains. A shared ideological orientation may ensure that both individuals have a great deal of information about the likely behavior of those with whom they are exchanging. This predictability may considerably reduce transaction costs. For example, it may greatly facilitate the negotiating, monitoring, and enforcement of contracts.

Even if individuals in small-scale societies were deceitfully inclined, there would be good reasons for them not to act on their inclinations, because their reputations might be destroyed and in small communities such information would be widely known. In a purely economic sense, then, those who deceived might well destroy their chances for future exchanges. Cross-cutting ties in the form of kin linkages, especially through affines, generate innumerable mechanisms by which such undesirable behavior can be negatively sanctioned. Similarly, corporate cooperation in the form of clan and lineage support may not be as forthcoming to those with bad reputations. These are examples of positive and negative incentives and sanctions that work through local institutions to discourage shirking, lying, and cheating in small-scale societies.

Given that many transaction costs are relatively low in small-scale societies, one might well ask why the NIE has much to offer. The explanation rests in the fundamental assumption of neoclassical economics, that there are gains to be realized from exchange. Societies may *not* benefit from trade or specialization if the transaction costs incurred in the process of exchange outweigh the benefits of that exchange.

As long as small-scale societies remain small and exchange takes place in a limited face-to-face sphere among known individuals with whom repeat deals are common, transaction costs are minimized. The problem is that limited networks also minimize the gains from trade. Those who are the most easily trusted trading partners may face the same ecological constraints as oneself and therefore have few desired trade goods. The natural limit of such exchange is also obvious. In order to capture the gains from broader trade and specialization it may be necessary to develop more complex institutions which ensure that people who have no previous knowledge of one another, no kin relations, and perhaps no prospect of future dealings will cooperate in good faith. If institutional economists are correct, this is the domain where much development economics ought to be focused, rather than where it has historically been concentrated, on technology and production. This does not mean exclusive attention to the formal legislative and judicial sectors, however. North (1990: 39), for example, notes that informal constraints that operate through social norms are often far more important (even in modern economies) in reducing transaction costs than are formal sanctions like police forces and courts. It is likely, therefore, that new institutional studies of the developing world will necessitate a thorough understanding of existing ideology and institutional structures that only a rich anthropological approach can give us.

The significance of transaction costs is demonstrated in part by the forms of organization to which they give rise. This is well illustrated in Abner Cohen's work (1971) on the Hausa trading diaspora of West Africa. As is the case in many developing societies today, state structures capable of ensuring free exchange across ethnic boundaries were weak. For example, institutions intended to facilitate the free flow of information about supply and demand and to adjudicate disputes relating to credit, contracting, property rights, or any number of other potential sources of friction were unreliable or nonexistent. As a consequence, in the Hausa case, as in many others (cf. Greif 1989), one found a high degree of vertical integration, with one organization (an ethnic group) involved in many different stages of production and distribution of a particular commodity. Because transaction costs were otherwise high, members ensured a greater degree of trust and cooperation by establishing an ethnic trading diaspora, thus reducing costs over what they would have been if members had been forced to interact in the marketplace for all production and marketing components.

A situation analogous to Cohen's trading diaspora existed among the Orma for most of this century, and it illustrates some of the economic consequences of a poorly developed institutional environment. One Arab family from the coast dominated much of the livestock trade in the Galole area from at least the 1920s to the early 1980s. It had an enormous organization spanning all aspects of production and marketing, from breeding herds in Orma territory and permanent agents who bought stock for them, to a fleet of lorries for transporting stock to market, ranches for fattening, and finally the butcheries where the stock was slaughtered. One could easily make the case that this degree of vertical integration was in part a response to extraordinarily high transaction costs stemming from the general lack of institutional structure in the area and consequently higher level of insecurity in livestock trading. For example, secure title to property in livestock was not easy to determine, information costs were high between point of production and point of consumption, capital and credit markets and banks were absent, and courts to enforce contracts were often nonexistent or bribable, and at least in later years bandit attacks on traders were common.

Given a weak institutional environment, the rewards of vertical integration, in the form of reduced transaction costs, are great. In fact, the rewards are so considerable that the small trader finds it very difficult to be competitive in any segment of the trade. In the developing world, therefore, a weak institutional structure commonly facilitates a monopsony situation (presence of only one buyer). Indeed, livestock trading in much of northern Kenya has followed exactly this pattern.

Institutions that decrease transaction costs include the simple notarizing of legitimate traders and property rights by third-party agencies, security forces that reduce banditry, banking facilities that extend credit and reduce the dangers of travel with cash, the regulation of weights and measures, courts that enforce contracts and property rights, and telecommunication and roads (which increase the flow of traffic and information). These institutions not only make trade more profitable, but may also increase competition in different sectors of the trade, thus affording the opportunity for those with less capital to break into one stage of the marketing process. Institutional changes like these were accelerated in Tana River District between 1981 and 1987, and one consequence was an increase in the level of Orma involvement in all aspects of livestock marketing, as well as increased competition and the opening of new stock markets.

North (1981) has argued that the state can realize economies of scale in the provision and regulation of institutions such as those just described, thus further reducing transaction costs. However, the state can also impose institutions that have the opposite effect on transaction costs.[36] Typical examples in Africa are agricultural marketing boards (see Bates 1981), excessive regulation and licensing, bribable courts, and police forces that operate as licensed bandits. While the history of state institutional development in Tana River District has by no means moved unilineally toward decreasing transaction costs for traders, I would hold that on balance the net effect has been in this direction, with the resultant increase in trade that one would predict from such a trend.[37] As more

36 De Soto's (1989) study of the informal economy in Peru is one example of the sort of consequences that can result when governments not only fail to provide the institutional support necessary to reduce transaction costs, but actually increase such costs by the creation of excessive regulation and licensing. By forcing a huge percentage of the economy to operate outside of governmental control, enormous inefficiencies result. Maliyamkono and Bagachwa (1990) document similar effects in Tanzania.

37 The impact of changing institutions on social justice and human rights is far more

economically efficient state institutions reach out into peripheral areas such as Tana River District, the costs of transaction in larger spheres decline, the relative profitability of trade increases, and more and more actors are pulled into exchange. This has been the pattern among the Orma in this century.

Thus far, nothing has been said about the distribution of the increased gains from trade, an area of great concern to anthropologists. It should go without saying that while substantial gains may be realized for the economy overall by the expansion of trade and increased specialization, these may certainly not be shared equally, and in fact some people can be, and often are, worse off.[38] This outcome is ultimately related to the preexisting division of power in the society, which may be marshaled to revise the institutional structure to further the gains of small interest groups even more.[39] The perspective taken here predicts neither the inevitability of increasing nor the inevitability of decreasing inequality as a result of economic growth; distribution may vary independently of growth.[40] As we shall see in Chapter 3, for the Orma the data are mixed, showing a *relative* decline in wealth for the poor, but an *absolute* improvement in income and a variety of other indicators.

The concept of transaction costs in commodity exchange can easily be adapted to an analysis of labor relations (see Goldberg 1981). Contracts between principals (owners) and agents (workers) are forms of organization. As forms of organization, much of their composition depends on the institutional structure. For example, in the absence of effective government and a legal system capable of enforcing contracts, people in small-scale societies might be far more inclined to restrict contractual relations to kin members whom they can trust rather than total strangers or members of other ethnic groups. This is a commonsense notion to an anthropologist, but becomes much more profound when considered in the context of the NIE, which asks what economic gains may be forgone

complicated to evaluate and measure, and deserves considerable attention. Human rights abuses in Kenya are well documented (Amnesty International 1987).

38 Numerous studies of the green revolution have taken this position (Frankel 1971), though many others have contested it (Leaf 1984).

39 The effect of bargaining power on choice of institutional change and its consequences for distributional effects is taken up more fully in Chapters 5 and 6. However, the actual distributional effects of change on the Orma between 1980 and 1987 are dealt with in Chapter 3.

40 This statement applies equally well to neoclassical and Marxist notions. While neoclassical theorists might be inclined to assume that all will benefit from the gains of trade, Marxist theorists equally might predict that the poor will be worse off. Numerous scholars studying East African pastoralists have found support for the latter position (see Fratkin 1991; Fratkin and Roth 1991; Little 1985a).

by such restricted networks of cooperation. In other words, what are the costs to such societies of forgoing the gains from increasing specialization and division of labor because alternative forms of contracting cannot be guaranteed?

In Chapter 4 I examine the many forms that contractual labor relations take among the Orma. The transformation of labor relations provides a perfect illustration of the fact that commoditization does not lead automatically and rapidly to what we might think of as "pure contractual" wage markets. While largeholders have clearly increased the size of their production units in order to realize economies of scale, they have employed a variety of means to achieve this end. Wealthy households stay together longer in extended families, they adopt more foster children, they maintain patron–client relations with young men who herd in the cattle camps, and they engage in more "pure" wage contract hiring. There are clear reasons for the persistence of informal means of expansion over the more market-oriented contract hiring. These have to do with the exceptionally high risk associated with livestock production and the enormous difficulties involved in monitoring labor in the distant cattle camps. Patron–client relationships provide better solutions to these problems by endowing the "hired herder" with many of the privileges and responsibilities of a son – most notably trustworthiness.

A major focus of research in the NIE deals with property rights. Property rights are rules governing the use of resources and, as such, are institutions. By their nature, they are also major determinants of the distribution of rewards within society. Like transaction costs, therefore, property rights provide incentives for some to seek changes in the rules of the game, while others have a vested interest in preserving the status quo. It is worth bearing in mind that "incentives" need not be material. For example, people with strong ideological convictions about environmental preservation might commit their own resources to support changes in property rights that they deem will best accomplish this end, in spite of the potential long-term economic costs of such a change to themselves or others.

In Chapter 5 I examine the changes in property rights in common grazing that have resulted from increasing economic growth among the Orma. As economic diversification and differentiation have intensified, it has been increasingly difficult for individuals to come to agreement over a solution to increased pressure on the common grazing. Which property rights eventually evolve is a function of their economic consequences, ideology regarding the proper distribution of benefits that accrue from property rights, and the bargaining power of the various interest groups that wish to pursue their desires over those of others. We shall see in Chapter 5 that the interests of those who now control the majority of the stock production are being served by a partial privatization of what was previously common grazing.

A final area of considerable research in the NIE concerns collective action. Collective action arises when individuals join together to work for the collective good. Problems typically arise over imbalances among contributions to the effort (especially in time, risk, and capital) and the distribution of benefits from the creation of collective goods, known as the "free rider" problem. It may be impossible to measure individual contributions to the effort, or even if differences in contribution are known, it may not be possible to divide the benefits in such a way that those who made insufficient contributions can be excluded. Realization of these information and measurement problems may be cause alone to discourage cooperation.

Those who study collective action have focused as much on the conditions that prevent successful collective action (Olson 1965) as they have on successful outcomes (Wade 1988). The key question for many theorists who study this problem is why we do not find more collective action than we do. Nevertheless, quite obviously, collective action problems are often overcome. It remains to be seen under what conditions collective action is most likely to be successful. Collective action is sometimes undertaken for more ideological reasons, for example, the anti-abortion movement's efforts to effect legislative and judicial change and the civil rights movement (see Chong 1991). At other times, collective action has specifically materialistic ends (e.g., changes in property rights, taxation, or price controls). In all cases, an incentive of some sort motivates people to organize themselves with the goal of changing the institutional structure.

The study of collective action highlights a major difference between the new institutional perspective and that of neo-Marxists. Neo-Marxists begin with groups (although not necessarily the classes of Marx and Engels) and analyze their interactions.[41] I begin with individuals (albeit individuals who are embedded in a specific social and economic context) and work up. Thus while I acknowledge the importance of groups, I believe that it is more fruitful not to take them as given. Instead, my approach is to consider explicitly the conditions under which individuals will come together as members of groups and when they will not do so (or when they will cease participating in groups they have formed).[42] For

41 There are, of course, exceptions, the most obvious being Elster (1985a), who, like other rational choice theorists, begins with individuals.
42 My position here is similar to that of Skocpol (1985: 25), who puts it as follows: "Marxists may be right to argue that classes and class tensions are always present in industrial societies, but the political expression of class interests and conflicts

example, in the Galole case, preferences for particular property rights are based not so much on simple class interests as on more specific economic interests and kin alliances.

Because of increasing economic differentiation and diversity, collective action among the Orma has become more difficult. This has occurred at a time when the Orma greatly need to cooperate over changes in their use of grazing land (both to prevent Somali encroachment and to prevent overgrazing). As a consequence, there have also been significant changes in Orma political institutions, which are described in Chapter 6. In general, this transition has been one from more consensual rule by the council of elders to more use of third-party enforcement by the state. In 1983 a young and educated chief replaced the illiterate elderly chief, who was more aligned with the council of elders than with the state. In the Kenyan system the chief is a member of the local ethnic group, but works for the national government as a civil servant. He is appointed by the government, although usually with the consent of the local populace, because an unpopular chief is of limited effectiveness. During the young chief's brief tenure up to 1987, he played a role in effecting significant changes in state–society relations. He was much more inclined to use force to implement policy than had been the previous chief. However, since he was careful to get the backing of a widespread segment of the population, his use of force was considered legitimate by most Orma. The chief also used soldiers to enforce more restrictive property rights, which were gradually leading to a de facto breakdown of the commons. This development was part of a gradual, but broad transition of authority from the council of elders to the central government. This could be interpreted as part of the decline in the elders' control, which had been eroding steadily since before the turn of the twentieth century. However, it also reflected the increasing ability of the elite, who now controlled most of the livestock production, to influence the direction of change in political institutions. In short, it was probably easier for them to control the chief than to control the population at large.

CONCLUSIONS

These topics do not exhaust the potential applications of the NIE even as it is currently formulated. There is much more to be learned by marrying the rigor of institutional economic theory with the rich understand-

is never automatic or economically determined. It depends on the capacities classes have for achieving consciousness, organization, and representation. Directly or indirectly, the structures and activities of states profoundly condition such class capacities. Thus, the classical wisdom of Marxian political sociology must be turned, if not on its head, then certainly on its side."

ing of institutions and ideology that anthropologists have to offer. Many anthropologists already employ some of these perspectives, perhaps quite unknowingly. But what we take for granted as "common sense" often turns out to be far less obvious than we thought once we try to state it in more formal terms: with assumptions, hypotheses, and predictions. Similarly, overly formal and untestable models are of little use, and new institutional economists can learn a great deal about the diversity of actual institutions and organizations from anthropologists. A common theoretical language will do much to further this end.

2

Transaction costs: the history of trade among the Orma

A fundamental difference between neoclassical, neo-Marxist, and new institutional analyses regards the relative merits of exchange. While neoclassical economists are inclined to believe that the benefits of exchange outweigh the costs, Marxists (especially dependency theorists) are more inclined to argue that exchange is "unequal" and therefore detrimental to all but the elite in what they call the peripheral nations (Amin 1976; Emmanuel 1972; A. Frank 1967; and for Kenya, Leys 1975).[1] New institutional economists, for their part, would agree with neoclassical economists that economic growth stems from the gains from exchange and that these can be realized for both sides, but they would not accept that such gains are automatic; to do so would be to ignore transaction costs.[2] New institutional economists accept that people may well resist trade as long as the costs of exchange are higher than the perceived benefits, and they would also accept the possibility (though not the inevitability) of the Marxist prediction that some may be made worse off as a result of unequal distribution of the new benefits.

In this chapter I examine the evidence on precolonial, colonial, and postindependence exchange among the Orma. Has "coercion" played a role historically, and if so, when and how? If so, does this mean that exchange is undesirable, at least for the poor? How have the costs of transacting changed, and what institutional changes have accounted for this? How have the increased costs and/or benefits of exchange owing

---

1 In keeping with this perspective, some neo-Marxists emphasize the coercion that was necessary to pull peasants into exchange in colonial Africa. Taxation, forced labor, and expropriation of the means of production were used to force peasants into market relations, since the terms offered to them were not favorable enough to attract them otherwise (for Kenya, see Berman and Lonsdale 1980; Heyer 1981; Kitching 1980).
2 See Hart (1982: 2, 16) for a critique of dependency theory as an explanation for the failure of development in Africa.

to changes in transaction costs been distributed between traders and producers? For all but the most recent period we cannot assess the actual impact of these changes on individual households. For the 1970s and 1980s, I have collected such household economic data on the population, and in the next chapter I shall address the effect that recent increases in commercialization have had on the economic well-being of the population, in both absolute and relative terms.

The early history of exchange among the Orma is intricately bound up with their pattern of migration, ethnic relations, and institutional structure before this century. Before turning to the subject of exchange *per se*, therefore, we must briefly address the broader historical and ethnographic context.

ORMA ORIGINS

The Orma are related to the large Oromo population of southern Ethiopia and northern Kenya.[3] Their closest ethnic and linguistic relatives are the better known Boran, from whom the Orma have been separated for centuries.[4] Although there has been much independent variation in the social structure of the Boran and Orma, the Orma do continue to share with the Boran some characteristics also common to most East African pastoral populations. They are, for example, patrilineal and largely patrilocal. Land is held in common and stock are owned individually.[5] While men own the stock, women own the milk and hides. Like the southern Boran in Kenya, the Orma are recent converts to Islam, having universally converted between 1920 and 1940. Even more so than the Boran, the Orma continue to be primarily cattle pastoralists, although they do keep a small number of sheep and goats; camels are totally absent. Only since the turn of the century have the Orma practiced any significant amount of agriculture, and in most cases it continues to be of an opportunistic variety dependent on highly unreliable river flooding.[6] Like most pastoral

---

3 The Orma are often referred to as Galla in both travelers' accounts and early colonial records of the day. "Galla" is a derogatory term (meaning pagan, infidel, or non-Muslim) used by many of the Oromo's Muslim neighbors to refer to them. Where it appears in quotations in this chapter it should be considered synonymous with the Oromo of Ethiopia or their descendants in Kenya, the Orma.

4 Some excellent ethnographies on the Boran exist. See, in particular, Baxter (1954), Dahl (1979), Dahl and Hjort (1976), Helland (1980), Hogg (1981), Legesse (1973), and, among the closely related Gabra, Torry (1973). Hilarie Kelly is completing an extensive ethnography of the Orma as a Ph.D. dissertation in anthropology at the University of California, Los Angeles.

5 See Chapter 5 for a discussion of changes in property rights.

6 The degree of dependence on agriculture among the Orma varies widely by location. This study was carried out with the population known as the Galole, who live

areas in Africa, Ormaland tends to be far less economically developed than agricultural areas; there is, for instance, no piped water – wells are hand-dug each season in dry riverbeds, and these are the only source of water during most of the year. The Orma currently populate most of Tana River District, Kenya, on the west bank of the Tana River, with heavy concentration also in the Tana River delta and some settlements in Lamu District to the east of the Tana.

There are two schools of thought on the migration of the Orma to their current position and, more particularly, their position between the Tana and Juba rivers in the seventeenth century (Map 2.1). It was previously believed (I. M. Lewis 1960) that the Orma migrated from Ethiopia to Somalia, where they were pushed by the Somali migration southward into present-day Kenya. More recently (H. Lewis 1966: 32; Turton 1975: 519), scholars have speculated that the greater Oromo expansion that began in 1537 in southwestern Ethiopia was responsible for the Oromo migration directly into northeastern Kenya, and that the Orma (representing the southern vanguard of this expansion) came via Moyale, the Lorian Swamp, and the Tana River, not via Somalia. This is supported by linguistic analysis and the absence of evidence of an Oromo presence in Somalia before the seventeenth century. The sudden appearance of the Oromo at Malindi and the Juba, where they were observed by Father Lobo in 1624, seems consistent with the fact that we know the Oromo were expanding in the 1500s and 1600s. H. Lewis argues that rather than being pushed westward and southward by the Somali, it is more likely that the Oromo were on the advance during this period. This is consistent with Turton's (1975: 529) speculation that the Somali inhabited the Tana–Juba area before the Oromo arrival and were displaced by the Oromo. These reconstructions also agree with statements made by Orma elders in 1980, who spoke of a migration from Ethiopia, through Moyale, down the Tana, and thence to places such as Wama in present-day Somalia.[7]

What all accounts agree on is that the Orma came from Ethiopia, and by 1624 were certainly in residence on the coast of Kenya as far south as Malindi and north to the Juba. Father Lobo observed several thousand Orma camped near an Arab town at the mouth of the Juba River in 1624 (cited in Turton 1975: 533). Lobo reported that their territory stretched

along the banks of the seasonal river of the same name. The Galole River floods sufficiently to produce a crop approximately one out of four rainy seasons, or once in two years.

7 It must be noted, however, that the Orma do not devote the degree of attention to oral history that we commonly associate with pastoral peoples such as the Somali; consequently, their account could be confounded by secondary reports they have heard from others about their history.

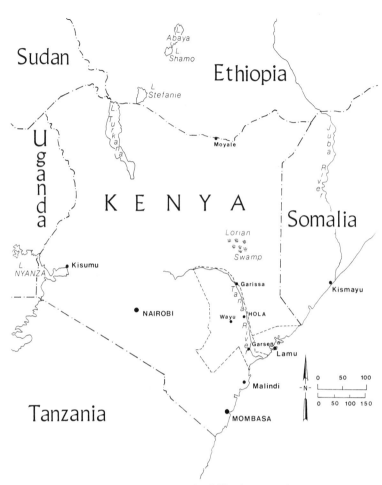

Map 2.1. Kenya and neighboring countries.

to the southwest from the Juba and that they had migrated from the interior. It is significant that he reported that the Somali were being attacked and enslaved by the Orma upstream on the Juba.

For the purposes of this study, the path of Orma migration itself is less important than what it implies about their institutional structures and their early experiences with trade.

INDIGENOUS ORMA POLITICAL INSTITUTIONS

Father Lobo (in 1624) was the first to have reported the presence of a "leader" among the Orma. Almost without exception, the explorers and

36

missionaries who traveled to Ormaland over the succeeding centuries also remarked that the Orma had a "chief," referred to as *hayu* (in 1823, Boteler 1835: 394; in 1844, Arc Angelo 1845: 280; in 1845, Krapf 1845; in 1867, Brenner 1868: 463 and New 1873: 209, 273). Some travelers also mentioned the existence of councillors (*luba*) subordinate to the chief. Given the looseness with which the term "chief" was used by Europeans of the day to describe the political authority of all sorts of individuals who were often nothing more than heads of councils of elders (see in particular Krapf 1860, passim), it is worth discussing in some detail exactly what is known of the actual political structure and roles associated with this institution among the Orma.

New (1873: 273) was the most detailed in his discussion of the political system among the Orma before their wars with the Maasai and Somali in the 1860s:

> The country is governed by a chief (heiyu), sub-chief, and their "lubu" (party) of toibs or councillors. Chiefs are elected from five distinct families, each chief retaining office eight years.

This early account of Orma political structure is consistent with living elders' recollections of Orma history, although the elders note that these institutions had disappeared before they were born (e.g., at least before the turn of the twentieth century). According to elders currently living in Tana River District, the Orma previously had elected chiefs (*hayu*) from each of three Orma districts: Chaffa (the Tana delta area and Witu), Wayama (the northern Hirman area up to Garrisa), and Galole (the middle region west of Hola and the Tana River). The chiefs of these areas were chosen from one clan, Galech (which is composed of three subclans: Meta, Karara, and Garjeda). The Galech clan was believed to contain the most "pure" and "clever" Orma.[8] Rulers were often wealthy, and there was a tendency for people from the same families to be elected.

Above these three chiefs was a senior chief (*haicha abadaga* – father of the people).[9] Some elders said the senior chief always lived at Golbanti, referred to as the "capital" of Ormaland (Map 2.2); others disagreed.

---

8 This is supported by Alice Werner's (1914: 140) discussions with Orma elders. She was told by Abarea, then the headman of Kurawa, that two central clans, Meta and Gardyed, were considered to be *galich,* and that members of these clans had to be present at weddings and other important transactions to act as witnesses. She inferred that their presence was necessary "to impart a legal sanction to the proceedings." Abarea also told her that they acted as "umpires" in time of war and were like "Sheikhs."

9 New (1873: 209) also makes reference to an "Aiyu" among the Orma, which he translates as "king-chief." This may be the senior chief described by the Orma elders, but New is not clear on this point, and it is possible that he was himself confused about the political structure among the territories.

Map 2.2. Tana River District.

Each chief and the senior chief himself had four elders to help and eight soldiers to enforce the law. The division chiefs handled disputes in their own areas without the senior chief's help. The four assistants were like judges, and they decided cases. Once they had come to a conclusion, they presented it to their district chief, who gave the final verdict. If the dispute was large or dangerous, it might be sent to the senior chief.

The chiefs also had important responsibilities for defense. They were responsible for deciding to wage war and raising an army for that purpose. In this event, the tribe gathered and the four councillors called the names of each clan one by one. Each clan was given fire and had to go off by themselves to sit by it. When they had all divided into their clans, one man from each clan was chosen as leader. They then went to war. All of the elders agreed that clans had been far more significant in the past, especially in war, than they are today.

The historical accounts of Orma political institutions, together with the reconstructions of living Orma elders, seem consistent with what one might expect of a people who were as militarily successful as the Orma in conquering large tracts of new territory very rapidly and a long way from their original homeland.

This organization, and indeed many Orma social institutions, were destroyed at the end of the nineteenth century. While the government of Kenya appoints chiefs among the Orma, the institution as just described no longer functions. The Orma claim that this indigenous system has not existed in their lifetimes, and that it was destroyed with the coming of Europeans.

THE RELATION OF ORMA POLITICAL INSTITUTIONS TO LONG-DISTANCE TRADE

Several early travelers specifically noted the role of the Orma chief in long-distance trade (Brenner 1868: 463, cited in Ylvisaker 1979: 105). Some noted that he was personally in control of all negotiations with outside traders. Many talked about the tribute exacted from the nearby hunter-gatherers in the form of one tusk for every elephant killed. Even the resident Swahili sultan paid tribute to the Orma chief. Further evidence of the degree of centralized control exerted by the Orma is found in the fact that they were able to prevent much penetration by outsiders into their territory right up to their conquest by the Maasai and the Somali in the 1860s.

Krapf (1845, quoted in Spear 1981: 140) provides the most detailed description of the way in which trade was carried out, at least for one area and one period of time. His description here is of Takaunga (see Map 2.2), the major southern trade center used by the Orma in the early nineteenth century:

When the Sultan of the Gallas [Orma] (as he is called by the Swahilis) makes his appearance at Takaongo every second or third year, he is accompanied by several hundreds of his savage followers, and he must be received in state and pomp by the governor of Takaongo, who meets him at the outskirts of the village under a salute of a large volume of firing from the Swahili musketry. When this has been accomplished, the Galla Majesty is placed on a new arm chair and carried by free-born Swahilis in procession through the streets, and at last deposited at an open and large place, where the Governor sits at his side and delivers the presents which consist of the chair (which the Sultan already occupies), of a slave, of a hundred clothes, or a quantity of Tobacco (which the Galla love more than silver and gold, and for which they will readily deliver up their cattle, their copal and their ivory) and some other petty articles. After the Sultan has received these presents, he returns them by giving the Governor a number of cattle and ele-phants'-teeth. After these transactions a cow is slaughtered by the Muhammedans, and a few bloody parts of the heart are eaten by the Swahilis and the Galla, who both swear in this manner and renew friendship and fidelity to each other. When all these ceremonies have been duly performed, the Galla soldiery is regaled with Tobacco, rice and other eatables. His sable Majesty remains then some ten or twenty days at Takaongo and its vicinity, during which time the Galla sell their goods and buy their commodities from the Swahilis.

The best description of the tributary relationship between the Orma and their neighbors (the agricultural Pokomo and hunter-gatherer Was-ania) is that of New (1873: 276, 278), who visited Ormaland in 1866 just after the Orma had suffered a devastating defeat at the hands of the Maasai:

They [the Pokomo] do a little trade, transporting grain, ivory, etc., to the coast, in exchange for cloth, wire, and beads. Some of them told us that they do not hunt so much as they would otherwise do, on account of the exactions of the Gallas, to whom they are tributary. They say that after their masters have taken what they deem to be their right, there is so little left that it does not pay for the trouble and cost of hunting and carriage. Naturally unwilling therefore that others should reap the rewards of their toil, they lay the spear aside, and seek profit in other ways [p. 276].

. . . The Wasania are the subjects of the Gallas, but they indignantly resent the application to them of the term slave. The Gallas take from them a heavy per-centage on all fruits of their toil, which I believe it does not enter into their minds to refuse. They are therefore, at least, a subordinated race. . . . On the flesh of the animals slain the hunters subsist; and with the proceeds of ivory, horn, etc., after they have paid the Gallas their tribute, they purchase clothing, ornaments, etc. [p. 278].

Further evidence of Orma centralization and strength sufficient to exact tribute comes from Boteler, who visited the area in 1823. Boteler (1835: 394) observed that the former Swahili sultan of Pate, recently forced to move his headquarters to Orma territory, also paid an annual tribute to the chief of the Orma for the privilege of trading in the area (see also Owen 1833: 297; Schmidt 1888: 133, cited in Fischer 1877: 350; Ylv-isaker 1979: 87).

Finally, almost all of the early travelers to Orma territory remarked on the reputation of the Orma as "fierce" and/or "aloof" (see also Ylv-isaker 1979: 24). Many noted that caravans and Arab traders never went to the Orma, out of fear of attack, but rather had to wait for the Orma to bring their goods to them. New (1873: 161), the last observer to visit the Orma before their wars with the Somali, described the incredulity with which the Arabs greeted the news that he intended to visit the territory.

... it is a remarkable fact that while the Arabs and Wasuahili had travelled over the whole of the country south of the Galla-land, and had established friendly relations with most of the tribes, not only along the coast but for hundreds of miles inland, yet up to the time of which we write [1866] none of their trading parties had ever ventured into the Galla-land, and they would have looked upon a proposition to do so as the act of a madman.

This "closure" of the territory by the Orma almost certainly would have retarded the development of trade, but it is also likely that it aided the chief in keeping a monopoly on trade and extracting tribute from the local hunters and gatherers. One would guess, therefore, that the chief assumed he and/or the Orma as a whole had more to gain by monopolizing a small trade than by opening the territory to more competitive trade. Had traders been allowed in, it would have been far easier for the hunters and gatherers to have circumvented their Orma overlords.

THE EXTENT OF PRECOLONIAL TRADE

Despite the relative dearth of interior trade, the Orma had considerable trade dealings with the Arabs and Muslim Swahilis at a number of locations along their borders. Relations between the Orma and the sultan of Witu, formerly of Kau and Pate, were especially close. Despite their long-standing hostile relations with the Somali, the Orma also engaged in trade with Somali along the Juba (Cassanelli 1982: 153; H. Lewis 1966: 37; I. M. Lewis 1960: 226).

Nevertheless, the overall level of long-distance trade in which the Orma engaged up to the twentieth century was not substantial. One gets the distinct feeling while reading the early accounts of Ormaland that the Orma were quite indifferent to trade – they could take it or leave it. They certainly did not go out of their way to facilitate it.[10] In addition to fear of losing control of tributary relations, this hostility to trade probably stemmed from the fact that the Orma were relatively self-sufficient and valued little what trade had to offer above what they already had and would have had to give up. Ivory, however, was an exception, all the

---

10 Descriptions of Orma interference with the caravan trade and refusal to permit traders of any sort into their territory abound in the literature. For example, it is reported that at the beginning of the nineteenth century the Nyika, who dominated the coastal–inland caravan trade until they were superseded by the Wakamba, tried to negotiate a treaty with the Orma in order to facilitate trade. The Orma refused to cooperate (Gray and Birmingham 1970: 78).

more so if they did not even need to devote time to its procurement, but could merely tax the hard work of their subordinate neighbors.

Evidence of Orma self-sufficiency and general indifference to trade goes back to their homeland in Ethiopia. Abir (1968) reports that the Oromo were not used to trade when they overran Ethiopia in the sixteenth and seventeenth centuries. Trade had been common in the Christian empires of Ethiopia before this time, but was dominated by Muslim traders from 1000. After the Oromo expansion, however, trade diminished on the Red Sea to a negligible level and stayed that way until the 1850s. Abir attributes this to the tendency of the Oromo to raid. In their new home, the Orma seem to have maintained the same tradition, although the ivory trade offered rewards too great to ignore.[11] The flavor of their attitude toward trade, as well as the mechanics, is captured in the following account recorded along the Juba River in 1844 (Arc Angelo 1845: 279):

> These [Somali] carry on a rather precarious trade with the Galli [Orma], who bring down from the interior ivory, bullocks, honey, and gee,[12] (the gee has a very aromatic taste different from all the other gee on the coast,) which articles they exchange with the Somaulles [Somali] of Juba, for a coarse kind of cotton cloth, (made at Juba, Brara, Marka, and Mokadosha, and is of different degrees of fineness); also tobacco and sometimes even *spears*. This trade is frequently broken off in consequence of an attack of one party on the other, in which event (as it was on my arrival there) all trade is stopped, sometimes for a considerable time, and *guerre à outrance* is proclaimed far and wide, for the Somaulle and Galli are implacable enemies, with whom no treaty is considered binding longer than *necessary* to each; amity is never known to exist long between them, their trading with each other is only a case of necessity, more especially on the side of the Somaulles, as without their trade with the Galli, they are completely destitute of even food.

While there has been an effort in the recent African historical literature to correct the past tendency to underreport the degree of precolonial trade in Africa, we must not err in the other direction either and obscure our ability to make relative assessments of the level of trade and its impact on the average person. One of the best indicators of the extent of trade among the Orma is the nature of what they were importing. Cloth almost always figures most prominently, with tobacco a close second, and some reference to spears, beads, copper, iron, and other items used for ornamentation. Given that at least until the 1860s it was uncommon for any

---

11 According to Ylvisaker (1979: 38), the Orma became involved in the ivory trade with Pate at least by the mid-seventeenth century, or almost immediately upon their arrival in the Tana–Juba area.

12 Ghee (spelled "gee" here) is clarified butter. It is much prized by both the local populations and the Asian and Arab communities, who use it extensively in cooking. It can be stored for a long period of time, and thus is far easier for the women to market than is perishable milk.

but men to wear cloth (New 1873: 271), and even by 1914 (Werner 1914: 126) women were still wearing animal skins as well as cloth, one has to question the level of long-distance trade in which the Orma were involved at this time.

Most scholars appear to agree that the Somali were far more engaged in trade than the Orma. Indeed, the Somali were known all across northern Kenya for their long-distance trading in the nineteenth century, over which they held a virtual monopoly (Dalleo 1975: 117). Yet Dalleo (1975) supports the general thesis that the Somali who lived in the area bordering the Orma were themselves also relatively little involved in trade:

The majority of Somali, however, especially those in the hinterland between the Daua and the Tana, remained nomads. Except for the occasional caravan they remained untouched by trade. Pastoralism remained the core of their economic system. Trade was a stronger factor in the areas near the Juba [p. 116].
...trade in northern Kenya was precarious. During the last half of the 19th century the Ogaden gained control of the area along the Juba down to Kismayu, and frequently raided along the Tana. Somali trade in this area, when compared to Lugh, was more recent, less in volume, and included more Arab involvement [p. 58].

Thus while the Orma and, even more so, their Muslim neighbors, the Somali, had some access to trade, and presumably could have had more had they so desired, it appears that they were little interested. Until trade could offer some considerable inducement, it had relatively little appeal. Such inducement, I would argue, came for Orma pastoralists when herd losses brought per capita holdings down to the point where they could no longer supply the necessary calories to the population without the added multiplication afforded by the conversion of meat to grain in the market. Consideration must also be given to the decline in the ivory trade brought about by European regulation, which began in 1896 (Ylvisaker 1979: 171). As the ivory trade declined, so too did the Orma incentive to keep traders out of their territory for fear of disrupting their tributary relations with the hunters and gatherers.

Trade also increased as the transaction costs of trade declined, thus affording better terms of trade, in part as a consequence of the spread of common institutional structures among both the Orma and their trade partners. Thus while the old institutions might have been adequate to handle the opportunistic trade in ivory, which was "pennies from heaven," as it were, they might not have been adequate to handle broader trade in subsistence goods on which people depended for reliable supply. I shall argue that these new institutions took the form of both conversion to Islam and state-imposed institutions such as courts, regulated weights and measures, and improved security. To the extent that such institutions were capable of reducing extremely high transaction costs due among other things to the insecurity of caravans, high cost of information, and absence of credit, they had the potential to reduce the relative prices of desired commodities to a more attractive level.

CRISIS IN THE LATE NINETEENTH CENTURY

The late nineteenth century brought changes to the Orma that completely altered their relations with the rest of the world, and ultimately left them in greater need of trade than before; consequently, they were more receptive to institutions that might facilitate trade. The immediate causes of this change were devastating wars with the Maasai and the Somali, which nearly resulted in the annihilation of the Orma. These events had their roots in a complex of ethnic and trading relationships on the coast of East Africa.

By the early eighteenth century, the Omani Arabs had replaced the Portuguese on the island city-states off the coast of East Africa. The Omani were not a unified body, however, and there were many rivalries among them. For our purposes the most significant was the rivalry between Pate (which, according to Ylvisaker 1979, traded more with the Orma) and Lamu (which traded more with the Somali). Lamu eventually gained ascendancy over Pate, and in 1812 the deposed Pate ruler took up residence on the mainland in Orma territory at the mouth of the Tana. Sultan Fumoluti (the deposed Pate ruler) supposedly had Oromo ancestry on his mother's side, employed Oromo (from Ethiopia) at his headquarters, and arranged for an annual gift to be paid to the Orma leader in return for a pact of nonaggression (Ylvisaker 1979: 74). This arrangement seems to have worked well until 1862, when the Lamu rivals again attacked and forced the Pate sultan and his followers to move further inland to a forest site known as Witu (see Map 2.2). Here he built a formidable walled town and, with his alliance with the Orma, was able to hold off the Lamu Arabs, despite serious attempts to dislodge him. The Orma, however, did not fare so well.

Beginning in the 1850s and intensifying in the 1860s, the Maasai made serious attacks on the Orma from the south. Charles New (1873) arrived in Orma territory right after one of the most devastating encounters with the Maasai in 1866, and his description of them already belied signs of a defeated people on the run. In all of his discussions with leaders and elders the main issue on their minds was whether the Europeans could aid them in some way to combat the threat of the Maasai. But the situation got much worse for the Orma shortly after New's departure.

Apparently taking advantage of the weakened state of the Orma, the Omani Arabs of Lamu, who for some time had been attempting to break the Orma–Witu alliance that challenged their control of trade on the mainland, took this moment to form an alliance with the Somali and encourage the latter to launch a massive attack on the Orma. The resulting Orma–Somali war of 1867–9 resulted in the near destruction of the Orma as a people. While the Maasai continued their attacks from the south, the Orma were now being hammered severely by the Somali from the northeast. A large number of Orma were captured by the Somali and sold into slavery. Others were taken as Somali clients, and their descendants are recognized today as the Wardei. Many Orma lost all of their stock. Although the war itself lasted only from 1867 to 1869, skirmishes erupted periodically until as late as the 1930s, with the Somali gradually pushing their boundary southward until they had taken exclusive control of most of the region between the Juba and the Tana.[13] In 1909 the Somali had reached as far as the Tana, and they were still on the move in 1912. Many of the captured Orma moved across the Tana for protection, but most remained behind as clients among the Somali. An agreement in 1919 to end the Orma–Somali hostility allowed former clients to rejoin their free kin on the west bank of the Tana, but few did, because a condition of their departure was that they leave their stock behind. Trouble flared up again in 1931, and in 1936 the colonial government accepted that those Orma still resident with the Somali were effectively absorbed (I. M. Lewis 1960: 227).

During the prolonged period of insecurity in the late 1800s, Orma social, economic, and political organization was severely stressed. Groups of Orma sought refuge in the Arab towns and Christian missionary compounds. Others migrated southward as far away as possible from the advancing Somali (Fischer 1877). The results were disorganization and destruction of the institutions of the chief and councillors. Other aspects of Orma social organization also fell into disuse. Just as the Boran practiced the well-known *gada* age-grade system (Legesse 1973), so too had the Orma. By 1978 the young among the Orma knew nothing about the institutions of the once powerful chief, nor did many of them even know what the term *gada* stood for. The kinship system among the Orma had also changed markedly. While the Orma once recognized two exogamous moieties (New 1873; Werner 1913a: 368), many young people in 1978 did not even know to which moiety they belonged, and in the 1980s even clan exogamy was being ignored.

---

13 In fact, the territorial competition between the Orma and Somali continues to the present. In the 1980s the Somali effectively occupied most of Hirman (northern Ormaland) and made many inroads in Galole territory (the middle zone). Since the 1930s both groups have been more inclined to seek political support for their claims through the central government in Nairobi rather than do battle in the field.

While it is unlikely that these social institutional changes occurred overnight, a strong case can be made that their demise was associated with the disruptions brought about by the warfare in the second half of the nineteenth century. Particularly destructive to social institutions was the scattering of the population due to the forced migration from their territory between the Juba and the Tana and the decimation of their numbers.

The first indication we have that Orma institutions were under attack comes from Charles New in 1866, even before the war with the Somali. On the basis only of their battles with the Maasai, he found their leadership to be in a state of disarray at the time of his visit. He complained first (1873: 161–3) of having difficulty in ascertaining who the chief really was. Later he learned that "a *bonna'a fide* chief for the time being was wanting." The previous chief had died heroically in a battle with the Maasai and "with him fell the good fortunes of the Gallas; they had never rallied since." Although New did eventually identify a standing chief, New characterized him as "effeminate" and ineffective.

The next indication we have of the status of Orma institutions comes from Alice Werner (1913a, 1913b, 1913c, 1913d, 1913e, 1914, 1915, 1919), who provided the most scholarly observations of the Orma and neighboring peoples for this period. While she went into detail about the Orma moiety, clan, age-grade, and chieftain systems, there were indications that these institutions were still remembered, but not practiced, because she got many conflicting and contradictory reports from different elders. Given the generally high level of her reporting, one is inclined to attribute the confusion to the Orma rather than to incomplete research on her part. For example, in describing the chiefship, Werner (1914: 134) noted that her account was accurate only "as far as I can make out," for the statements of her informants "were perplexing in the extreme and sometimes contradictory." With respect to the age-grade system Werner had similar difficulties, as the following discussion illustrates (1914: 142):

According to one informant the *luvus* [age sets] recur in cycles of seven; another said that there were eight, but without mention of their recurring, and repeated attempts to get the names enumerated landed us in hopeless confusion.

While it may be impossible to ascertain exactly how long it took for the Orma institutional structure of the mid-1800s to be transformed, we do know that elders as old as eighty in 1980 claimed that the *gada* age-grade system and the chiefship had not been practiced in their lifetimes. Given New's reports, it seems reasonable to assume that the attacks by the Maasai precipitated the transformation of Orma institutions, which were dealt further blows by the Somali purges and European entry into the territory in the late 1800s.

Ironically, during the period immediately following their military defeat, the Orma needed trade more than ever before, but due at least in part to the undermining of their institutional structures, trade was even more disrupted and limited than previously. After the wars with the Maasai and the Somali, the Orma experienced a protracted period of instability and shifting. For many years families lived in the Arab garrisons and Christian missions to escape further attack. Many Orma were destitute, having lost all or most of their stock in the wars. Families were split up by migration and slave raiding. Not surprisingly, the Orma practiced a wide range of new strategies, from begging to cultivation to banditry (Fischer 1877), to pull themselves through these difficult years.

The sultan still resided at Witu and continued to hinder Lamu Arab attempts to control trade on the mainland. Unable to control the trade himself, the sultan seems to have resorted to banditry, sometimes using the Orma to disrupt the trade. Among other things, Witu became a refuge for debtors from Lamu and other areas on the coast, thus disrupting to some extent the credit networks there (Ylvisaker 1979: 115, 123). In many other ways also, the sultan of Witu went out of his way to limit trade in the area. He taxed trade to the point of discouraging it (Ylvisaker 1979: 139), and when Carl Peters (1891: 69, cited in Ylvisaker 1979: 146) visited the area in 1889, he was amazed to discover that there was no credit system. "To buy even a coconut took cash – nor any idea of caravan commerce with the interior. Porters were not forthcoming."

The trade situation declined even further when the British took over administration of the colony in 1895. The government began by restricting the ivory trade and licensing traders in the area. The latter move was an effort to control what were considered exorbitant interest rates charged of the Pokomo (Ainsworth and Hollis 1909: 23, cited in Ylvisaker 1979: 171). Ylvisaker (1979: 172) discusses the situation of trade in the Tana area at the beginning of the twentieth century:

Between 1905 and 1909 the ivory trade declined considerably. . . . Oddly enough, the Tana River, which had twenty years before been considered a main artery of potential trade, became a neglected area. Beyond Kau, it could not be said "to be a factor in the existing trade of the country [Ainsworth and Hollis 1909: 55]." The Commission of 1909 could not understand why the administration had not long before brought the Tana into the scope of the trade resources of the province. Instead of being a highway to the interior, it was a closed district.

I attribute much of the depressed state of trade among the Orma from the late 1800s to about 1910 to the absence of functioning institutional structures capable of guaranteeing even minimal security to caravans and individuals. In the absence of a strong chief, the past trade in perimeter areas tightly controlled by the chief also slowed. With both the Orma and the sultan at Witu in virtual states of siege, trade was not possible. Many resorted to banditry, which required far less organization than the control of trade.

This period of arrested trade did not last long into the twentieth century. Through the persistence of Arab merchants at the coast, the growing demand for cattle, the colonial imposition of a cash tax, the increasing presence of colonial administrators, and demographic pressures, the situation gradually changed and trade increased substantially. As we approach the period within the memory of living informants, we see the development of the first significant trade in the interior of Orma territory. I turn now to the development of this trade, focusing specifically on the Galole Orma,[14] with whom the rest of the book deals.

THE DEVELOPMENT OF GALOLE TRADE IN THE TWENTIETH CENTURY

The history of the early trade in this century comes primarily from oral history accounts of Arab and Orma traders and the Tana River District (TRD) annual reports (beginning in 1917). The colonial presence in this area began, as in much of East Africa, with the appearance of British East Africa Company agents in Lamu between 1890 and 1905. The first local presence within Tana River District proper occurred between 1895 and 1905, when Mr. J. J. Anderssen was the district commissioner (D.C.) at Kipini, the initial district headquarters (see Map 2.2). The first official political involvement with the Galole Orma began at this time, when it was reported that the D.C. recognized Guyo Abajila (a Galole resident) as leader of the northern Orma. Abajila was gazetted as "headman" of the northern Orma at least as early as 1908 and remained so until his death in 1942 (see TRD Annual Report 1942).[15]

From the 1920s on, the colonial presence and involvement increased in fits and starts. It was estimated by J. S. S. Rowlands (1955: 108), who was D.C. in 1955, that from "1920 to 1948 for over twelve years there was no resident administrative officer in the district. With leaves, conferences illness etc. there must have been absentees for half this period."

In the TRD Annual Report for 1917–18, the earliest available, it is clear that hut and poll taxes (begun in Kenya in 1905) were already being

---

14 The Galole Orma live along the east–west Galole River, which runs through the center of Orma territory; Galole territory makes up roughly one-third of Orma territory and a similar portion of Tana River District.

15 Initially the office was "headman," but later became "chief." Although then, as now, this was a government civil service appointment, Guyo Abajila was also recognized as the traditional leader by the Orma themselves.

collected in Tana River District. Given that almost no knowledge of the Orma hinterland existed and such collections were based on exceedingly erroneous estimates of the population, as well as dependent on the collection capabilities of the government-appointed indigenous headmen, the extent to which such taxes affected the average Orma is not clear. One can assume that a vast number of Orma paid no tax at all for a long period of time.[16]

Even before the Europeans began taxation in the district, some venturesome Arab cattle traders were trading stock in the interior of the district. One of these men was the grandfather (Naji Thaja bin Ali) of Ahmed bin Said, whose family has dominated cattle trade with the Galole through most of this century. He met Ormas who came to trade with him in the south, and followed them back to their homes inside Orma territory to buy cattle for cash. Ahmed reports that his grandfather was trading cattle as far as Wayu probably even before the turn of the century. The Orma then had to travel themselves to use the cash to purchase cloth, bangles, and honey, for the cattle traders did not generally carry trade goods with them. Ahmed himself entered Orma territory in 1923 to trade commodities while his grandfather and father were trading cattle. By 1927 the family had opened several shops in Chaffa, the southern part of Orma territory (at Kone Derti, Odo Ergamso, Meti Characka, and Mkununi). In these early days the shops were supplied by boats and donkeys, since they were all relatively near the sea or river. Initially most trade was in cloth and bangles; sugar had not yet been introduced.

It is extremely difficult to estimate the extent of Orma dependence on trade for their daily subsistence during most of this century. We may assume, however, that before and during the early years of colonial government, the Galole Orma (a long way from the sea and these early shops) were not to any appreciable extent dependent on exchange for their daily subsistence. They did barter stock for grain with their agricultural neighbors in times of stress, most notably with the Kamba to the west and the Pokomo to the east.[17] The southern Orma (or Chaffa),

16 For example, in 1924 it was clear that the D.C. thought Orma territory extended westward from the Tana River only about one-third of its actual distance. This error appears not to have been definitively corrected until the D.C. in 1938 traveled as far as the western Orma settlement of Waldena. Similarly, even as late as 1952, the Orma population was estimated to be only 25% that of the Pokomo (4,228 vs. 16,940). In the far more reliable 1979 census, however, the Orma population is reported to be 80.8 percent of the Pokomo population (32,127 vs. 39,741). Since it is highly unlikely that the Orma rate of population growth in the interim has exceeded that of the Pokomo, we can assume that the population of the Orma was grossly underestimated through the entire colonial period. It was, of course, in the interest of the Orma to have it so.

17 Informants report that in the 1930s the standard rate of exchange between the

who live interspersed with the agricultural Pokomo, were probably more extensively involved in such exchanges than were the Galole. Until the 1940s, the Galole could be characterized as predominantly self-sufficient subsistence producers. During normal dry seasons (when yields of milk, the staple food, fell), most families survived by traditional pastoral adaptive strategies – bleeding their stock, hunting and gathering, and slaughtering when absolutely necessary. A typical household might, for instance, have slaughtered sheep and goats as necessary or even a steer, whose meat would be dried and consumed over the course of the entire dry season. Even as recently as 1987 during my last observations, nomads continued to subsist on a pure dairy diet whenever conditions so allowed. Due to the relative lushness of their environment, the Galole were in a better position to live off a pastoral diet than were most East African pastoralists.

Periods of extended hardship, however, forced the Orma to turn to the market and often led to greater involvement in trade even once conditions improved. One such period occurred in the early 1930s following a devastating outbreak of rinderpest (1933). This coincided with a large influx of population to Galole from the south; with this influx came the first Orma trader, Shambaro Elema.

Like many current Galole residents, Shambaro was raised in the south, in Chaffa. His father died while he was young, and he was left with few resources. He began trading as a young man in order to build up a herd. In the 1920s he began working for the Said family, which was already involved in the Galole area. In the 1930s Shambaro turned his trading interests to the north. He took such trade goods as salt, oil, and cloth (there was as yet little market for sugar) from his Arab shopkeeper, loaded them into a canoe in Garsen, and paddled up the Tana to Hola and Bura (see Map 2.2), where he at first sold them primarily to the agricultural Pokomo. Upon his return, he would clear his debt with the agent and take more goods on credit.

By the mid-1930s, Shambaro had shifted his trade from the agricultural

Orma and Pokomo was one medium goat for a very large *kikapu* (basket) or *mzigo* of maize (58 kilograms, or roughly one-half gunia bag). A goat then sold for 5/=, making the price of maize =/09 per kilogram. This agrees with the price reports derived from the TRD annual reports (see Table 2.1), in which the price of maize varied from =/06 to =/13 in the 1930s. The Orma reported that Pokomo maize was cheaper than Kamba maize, but the Orma went to the Pokomo, while the Kamba came to them. The Kamba were interested in exchanging maize for animals only, not for cash. It is also true that while the Kamba and the Orma did and still do have hostile relations, the Pokomo have a history of more subservient and peaceful relations with the Orma. In fact, something like patron–client relations often existed between families of Orma and Pokomo, and these included considerable exchange.

Pokomo to the Galole Orma. He still worked out of Garsen and sent his goods up the Tana in a canoe to Hola, but there he transferred them to donkeys for the 55-kilometer trek west to Wayu. At that time Wayu was not even a permanent settlement, although, as now, it had some of the best wells in the territory.

Shambaro was not at first involved in the cattle trade. He exchanged his goods either for cash, which people had earned from trading stock with the Arabs, or for ghee (clarified butter), which he purchased at that time for 1/= a bottle.[18] He reported that ghee (made from surplus milk) was then in relative abundance and people were happy to trade it for other commodities. It took twenty-five bottles to fill a "tin" (probably a 16.4-liter *frasila*), which Shambaro sold to Arabs in Garsen for 60/=, thus realizing a gross return of 140 percent. He reported that on a typical trip he took goods worth about 1,000/=, on which he made a profit of approximately 50 percent.

Not coincidentally, Shambaro had converted to Islam before his successful partnership with his Arab agent in the south.[19] Among other things, this afforded them the opportunity to share the institutions of Islam that are particularly conducive to long-distance trading, including codes of law. An example was the *commenda* arrangement, whereby the supplier provided the trader with goods up front and they split the profit. This is the same arrangement in practice today.

The next appreciable increase in trade between Galole and the coast took place in the early 1940s. In 1942 Shambaro opened a shop in Wayu.[20] This coincided with World War II and a severe drought in 1943.

18 The 1980 producer price for a 700-milliliter bottle of ghee was 13/=, while the 1987 price was 30/=.

19 Shambaro was an early convert to Islam, but by 1940 virtually the entire population of Orma had converted. For more details on the relationship between Islam and trade, see the section entitled "Evidence of Declining Transaction Costs."

20 An Arab by the name of Ali Mgedem also had a shop in Wayu. The circumstances surrounding the closing of Ali's shop, which occurred sometime in the 1940s, possibly before Shambaro's opened, are not entirely clear. Shambaro himself reported that the government made Ali give it up because it passed a law forbidding anyone to have shops in more than one location (the territorial unit into which districts are divided), and Ali also had one in Hola. This also kept much other Arab competition out of Wayu, because no one wished to give up his shop in Hola in order to do so, but many resented the substantial loss of business to Shambaro's Wayu shop. To what extent Shambaro's influence with colonial officials may have protected his trade monopoly in Galole is unclear. As the only literate individual in Wayu, he was acting as the chief's clerk, and consequently the government was much in his debt. However, Ahmed bin Said, Shambaro's supplier, denied that the Arab shop in Wayu closed because of the government regulation. He insisted that it was because the Arab could not compete with Shambaro, who brought his goods from Hola on donkeys himself, while the Arab hired others to do it and therefore had to charge higher prices.

The primary trade items were cloth, sugar, tea, coffee beans, and tobacco. People were just beginning to drink tea. During the drought in 1943 Shambaro began to sell maize, for the government provided little or no famine relief to the Galole area. Once the drought ended, most people abandoned the consumption of maize, but continued to drink tea with sugar. Thus trade stabilized at a higher level of market interaction than existed before the drought.[21]

By the mid-1940s Shambaro's trading business had escalated. Shambaro was still dealing with the Arab family of Ahmed Bin Said, based in Mambrui, just north of Malindi on the coast of Kenya. Ahmed's elder brother (Salim bin Said) agreed to supply Shambaro with trade goods on credit at his written request.[22] This alleviated the need for Shambaro to make trips south every time he needed to resupply.

It was also at this time (1945) that Shambaro began to buy and sell cattle, not just in exchange for goods from his shop, but as an agent for the Said family. Up to this point the Arabs had always come themselves to buy stock, but now Ahmed Bin Said's brother agreed to give Shambaro large sums of money to purchase stock on his behalf. Two- to three-year-old cattle were selling for 30/= to 40/=, mature cattle over four years from 50/= to 60/=, and the largest for 80/=. These prices represented a considerable increase over previous years (see Table 2.1). Shambaro would buy seventy to eighty head and pay someone to herd them down to the coast or sell them at government-sponsored auctions in Wayu, which were held beginning in 1944.[23] Ahmed Bin Said reported that while many other Arab traders were attempting to buy stock in the area during this period, the Said family had a significant advantage in that they could leave Shambaro with cash, so that he was always ready when the opportunity presented itself, whereas other Arabs, without local agents, merely visited the area occasionally. Shambaro found that there was much more profit to be made in trading livestock than in selling goods.

There were as yet few families living permanently in Wayu. Most of the Galole population continued to remain nomadic in order to provide the best grazing conditions for their stock. The desire to avoid taxation also undoubtedly provided an incentive to remain nomadic. Approxi-

21 Even after the end of World War II, sugar appears to have been in short supply in the district. Not until 1954 is there a comment in the TRD Annual Report indicating an improvement in the supply of sugar.
22 Unusual for his day, Shambaro had acquired minimal literacy from a Pokomo boy in the south; he had no formal education, however.
23 This is confirmed in the TRD Annual Report for 1952, which documents that Shambaro exported 100 head of cattle from the district, the largest number of any trader in the entire district.

mately ten households did settle in Wayu in the early 1950s, however. Many were headed by young to middle-aged men who are still resident there. Most were not wealthy then, although they are today. The grazing conditions around Wayu were at that time superb, due to the natural flooding and soil quality in the area. It was a place that could easily support a small permanent population.

While Shambaro gave up his cattle trading when he became the government-appointed chief in 1950, he did not give up his shop.[24] He continued to buy from the Said family, who by then brought his goods in a car. By 1955 Shambaro had purchased his own landrover, which he used both to supply his shop and to carry out government business.[25] Sugar was becoming an increasingly important commodity, and many people from the bush (nomads) now came to buy from him, sometimes even loading goods on donkeys to resell in more remote areas.

In 1955 Shambaro built a second shop in Chifiri (among the northern, Hirman Orma), and in 1958 he built a third in Moti (15 kilometers east of Wayu on the main road to Hola) and a fourth in Waldena (a western settlement among the Galole; see Map 2.3). These were as yet the only other shops in the territory. Wayu was still his most profitable shop, but Chifiri also did very well. Shambaro's senior wife, Hawalo, sometimes acted as shopkeeper in his Wayu store. For each of the satellite shops Shambaro hired shopkeepers. In 1959 he managed to buy a Bedford truck on credit, but Shambaro's good fortune did not last much longer. Owing in part to problems with collecting debts at his shops and the poor records kept by his illiterate shopkeepers, within four years he lost the truck and all but his Wayu shop.

For many years Shambaro was the only Orma with shops in Galole. When he opened his shops in Moti, Chifiri, and Waldena, however, he

24 Although the colonial government forbade chiefs to be involved in trade, they made an exception in Shambaro's case because it was the only way he would agree to become chief. The government was extremely anxious to have a literate chief in this area, which was difficult to visit and with which communications had therefore to be carried out through correspondence more often than was the norm. Evidence of just how unusual Shambaro's literacy was for the day is reflected in the fact that when he retired in the early 1960s he had to be replaced by another illiterate chief, because no literate candidates were available even then. Not until 1983 did Wayu location again acquire a literate chief, Hussein Shambaro, the son of Shambaro.

25 Shambaro also reported that he purchased a "secondhand car" in 1948, which he claimed was only the second privately owned vehicle in the district. The TRD Annual Report (1955: 8) mentions only his 1955 purchase of a landrover (the report includes a picture) and a comment that it was "believed that he is the first African individual to procure a vehicle for himself in the district." The new D.C. in 1955 may not have been aware of the earlier vehicle, for Shambaro reported that it was often broken down.

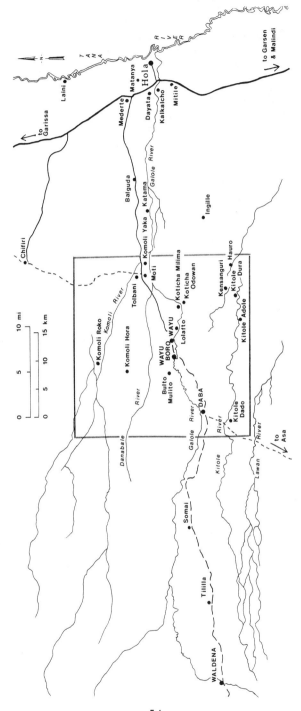

Map 2.3. Galole and survey area.

54

brought a number of people into his business as shopkeepers. Among these men were two relatively young brothers, one of whom worked in Waldena and the other in Chifiri. These men learned from Shambaro, and both went on to careers of their own in trading. In 1981 one ran a moderately successful shop in the district headquarters at Hola, while the other was the largest trader in Wayu.

At just about the time that Shambaro's empire began to collapse in the early 1960s, that of one of his former shopkeepers grew. Other shop owners attempted to make a go of it in the 1960s and early 1970s, but none were successful. Shambaro's successor particularly dominated trade through the early 1970s, which because of the drought was a period of considerable retail trade in foodstuffs. It was also a time when shopkeepers needed credit to be successful, since most households ran up large debts; small operators easily went under. Just after the drought, two young men, one the son of the chief who succeeded Shambaro and the other a former Qur'anic teacher (both educated to the sixth standard), opened shops in Wayu; the former shop survives to this day.

The number of people settling in Galole increased gradually through the 1960s, especially at the more popular settlements such as Wayu and its sister village 3 kilometers away (Wayu Boro). But it was when the drought of the early 1970s hit that the growth of these and other villages escalated. There were few places where the wells had not dried up, and this was one of the things that brought people to such permanent settlements. Wayu was particularly attractive, though, because there was a shop there, and with no milk, most people had to purchase food. Those who could afford to slaughter did so, but everyone became dependent on purchased food. Most bought on credit, and many had to turn over some of their few remaining stock at the end of the drought to shopkeepers who had extended them credit.

A large number of people were impoverished by the drought. Many chose not to return to a nomadic life-style when it was over. Instead, they remained in Wayu and other permanent settlements. By the late 1970s, the population of Wayu and Wayu Boro had grown to seventy-four households, and approximately 39 percent of the entire Galole population had settled in such market towns. The area did not have sufficient grazing to sustain the herds of so many households, especially as herds began to grow after the drought ended.

Even before this influx, people in the permanent villages had sent a large number of their dry stock to remote cattle camps to ensure their health and fertility. Now this strategy became crucial and an even greater proportion had to be sent, including as many lactating animals as could be spared. The result was that less milk was available for subsistence consumption. Furthermore, the milk yields of those cows that remained behind fell to about half of what they would have been under the more favorable conditions in the nomadic villages. Among the Galole, sedentarization necessitated a heavy commitment to the market economy. People had to depend on selling beef in order to purchase the usual staples of grain, cooking oil, and sugar.

The mid-1980s witnessed something of a repeat of the mid-1970s. Another devastating drought hit in 1984 with cattle losses again reaching 70 percent, just as had occurred in the mid-1970s. Again there was a major response in the form of increased sedentarization and dependence on the market for daily subsistence. By 1987 the two Wayus had a population of 119 households, and 63 percent of the Galole population was living in market towns. By 1987 six shops served this population of 214 households (2,414 individuals). In 1979 three shops served the population of 230 households (2,232 individuals).

This account brings the history of the Wayu retail trade up to the late 1980s. One thing is indisputable, and that is that market exchange increased steadily over the entire period, especially spurred on by droughts and stock losses in 1933, 1943, 1975, and 1985. However, unlike earlier historical periods when equally severe environmental disasters occurred, each of these periods left the Orma committed to market production at a significantly higher plateau from which they never fully retreated.

EXPLAINING THE INCREASE IN TRADE FROM 1920 TO 1980

It is well substantiated that commercial activity has steadily increased for the Orma over the course of the twentieth century. It remains to be seen, however, whether this has brought increasing prosperity, as neoclassical economists would expect, or has resulted in unequal exchange (as dependency theorists might predict), leading to a worsening of economic conditions for the poor. Alternatively, new institutional economists would not assume either, but would look first to the direction of change in transaction costs and the distribution of those increased costs or benefits between producers and traders.

The colonial records give us relatively little information specifically about the Orma. Tana River District, then as now, is composed primarily of two populations: the Orma, who inhabit the vast majority of the territory, and the Pokomo, who live almost exclusively along the roughly three-mile-wide Tana River flood plain and Tana delta, which are fertile agricultural lands. Because the district headquarters has always been along the river (at Kipini until 1960, and then at Hola; see Map 2.2), government officials, especially in the early days, when transportation was almost nonexistent, had far more contact with the Pokomo than with the Orma.[26] Indeed, it was not until the 1940s that the colonial officials had much knowledge of what was going on within Galole territory. Nevertheless, many details relating to the trading environment in the district have been recorded, especially regarding taxation, the regulation of weights and measures, the development of transportation and communications, number of traders, and changes in relative prices.

There is clearly some evidence to support the proposition that in the early period of colonial rule the Orma may not have engaged in trade altogether voluntarily. Most significantly, the colonial authorities imposed a hut tax. In 1921, when the tax was 8/=, we know that a head of cattle sold for about 10/=. For a man with two or three wives and one or more married sons, each of whom would have had a hut, this was obviously a considerable sum.[27] By 1937, however, the tax was 10/= (reduced from 12/= the previous year), and cattle sold for approximately 35/=, a considerable relative decline in the tax rate from the early 1920s. The Orma did not pay all of their tax by selling cattle. In the 1920s they still had considerable revenues from the ivory trade, though most likely far less than before the arrival of Europeans, who had created a government monopsony over it and paid far below the world market price. Ghee, which was produced and owned by women, also involved a significant amount of money. In fact, the D.C. wrote (not necessarily accurately) in the TRD Handing Over Report (1923: 5), "The Gallas [Orma] could easily pay all their taxes in Ghee." We may never know what percentage of the Orma cattle trade was induced by their tax obligations and what percentage by demand for other commodities. In my interviews with him, however, Shambaro did remark that in the 1920s people were not terribly eager to trade a head of cattle for a twenty-shilling note, and it was primarily in order to pay their taxes that they did so.

We do know from the historical accounts cited earlier that a substantial cattle trade predated the arrival of European administration and taxation. Also, there is evidence in the annual reports of a desire among the Orma to market livestock. The D.C. wrote in the TRD Annual Report (1923:

26 This was still the case in 1987. However, then even more than recently, this suited the Orma quite well, for the government's main interest in the Orma was the collection of hut and poll taxes, which no longer exist. Earlier colonial records such as that in the TRD Handing Over Report (1928: 16), for example, make reference to the fact that should the new D.C. contemplate a trip to the Orma interior, "you will, however, find the Galla [Orma], whose one aim in life seems to be to keep the district officer on the River, will put every obstacle in your way." See Chapter 6 for a detailed discussion of the transition in state–society relations between the Orma and the government of Kenya.

27 As noted earlier, however, only a small percentage of the Orma population was counted, thereby reducing such bills considerably.

6): "It has been a good cattle year and a great many more head were exported from Lamu than in 1922. The galla [Orma] had still a great many more to sell but could not find buyers." The 1925 TRD Annual Report recorded that many Arabs in the district were seeking trade with the Orma and many trade licenses were issued. In 1926 (TRD Annual Report 1926: 6, 14) the D.C. noted that cattle sales were up 33 percent, and he attributed this directly to a decline in the ivory trade, which he reported to be decreasing each year. In the TRD Handing Over Report (1945: 4) we find, "Sales are held at Wayu and Garsen and no difficulty has been experienced in obtaining cattle from the Oromo of this district." The 1950 TRD Annual Report (p. 12) stated:

Further sales would have been possible and desirable but, due to the glut of stock awaiting the butchers knife in Mombasa since the introduction of the Kenya Meat Commission none were organized. The Oromo appeared willing and even eager to sell their stock and this can be taken as a sign that they are becoming cash conscious, even in a world where cash values are practically negligible.

As noted, however, the Orma's increasing desire to trade livestock in the colonial era might have been motivated primarily by the need to meet their tax obligations. Some data from the Pokomo support this thesis. The 1933 TRD Annual Report (p. 11)[28] noted:

Labour [presumably Pokomo] was not offering at all until the date for collection of Hut Tax was very definitely published and there is little doubt that it would not have been obtainble [*sic*] at all locally had it not been for the Tax demands by Government. The rate of pay was Shs. 8/– a month, that is higher than at Malindi [a far larger and more developed area closer to the city of Mombasa]. When asked the reasons for their reluctance two reasons were given, firstly insufficient food, secondly too hard work.

We do have some evidence, however, that the Orma were doing much more than paying their tax with the money they earned from cattle sales in the 1920s and 1930s, at least during hard times. In fact, in the same year as the report just cited, 1933, it was reported that the Orma had trouble selling enough cattle to buy the grain they needed to supplement unusually low milk yields caused by extremely heavy stock losses from rinderpest. Thus, we read in the TRD Annual Report of 1933 (p. 17), "Petty traders, mostly Arabs, are established on the river at 10 villages and deal mainly with internal trade especially the supply of grain to the Galla [Orma]."

In short, there is clearly some evidence that, up to about the mid-1930s, trade was being spurred by the need to pay the government tax in cash, rather than by the advantages exchange might offer in its own

28 A similar comment appears in the TRD Annual Report of 1934.

right, but it is not possible to determine what percentage of the trade was driven by this imperative. By the late 1930s, however, it becomes increasingly difficult to explain trade primarily in terms of political coercion, though ecological and demographic necessity clearly played a role. In addition, there is substantial evidence that a number of changes, including declining transaction costs for local traders and cheaper transportation, made trade increasingly profitable for producers and traders alike.

EVIDENCE OF DECLINING TRANSACTION COSTS

Considerable data bearing on transaction costs exist in the colonial records for Tana River District. The history records the first regulation of weights and measures, and improved transportation and telecommunications, which among other things lower the cost of information. Before turning to these issues, I wish to take up the significance of conversion to Islam, which predated these later changes and brought the Orma under the same institutional structure as their primary trading partners, the Arabs.

The role of conversion to Islam

The Orma underwent an almost total conversion to Islam between 1920 and 1940. While one could attempt to argue that trade actually gave them an incentive to convert through opportunities for better terms of trade and access to credit, here I wish to make only the case that, whatever the reasons for conversion, it led to some considerable benefits in trade for the Orma, primarily in the form of decreased transaction costs. As Abner Cohen (1971: 278) puts it: "[Islam is a] blue-print of a politico-economic organization which has overcome the many basic technical problems of the trade." I shall argue that conversion to Islam made trade more profitable and contributed to its expansion.[29]

There is a well-researched connection between long-distance trade the world over and conversion to Islam (A. Cohen 1971; Geertz 1968: 26). For example, in Africa it was the long-distance traders themselves who did much of the converting, and Islam tended to follow the trade routes (Trimingham 1962). As we have already seen, this was also the pattern among the Orma. Shambaro was the first Orma trader to set up a per-

---

29 Orma elders report that it was young men who converted first among the Galole. It is quite possible that they did so in part as a challenge to the authority of their elders, much as Bunger (1979) argues for the neighboring Pokomo. This thesis would be entirely consistent with the perspective on institutional change adopted here.

manent trade station among the Galole, and he was responsible for converting many others. Other Orma from the south had also been converted by traders in Lamu, and as they moved north they were successful in converting others.

It is easy to understand the commercial advantages that Islam affords to trade, primarily as an institutional structure that reduces transaction costs. For example, conversion provides a ready-made way to turn outsiders, with whom one shares no binding institutional structures that might ensure the honoring of contracts, to insiders, who are subject to commonly shared sanctions for default on contracts, such as credit. The fact that Islam is also a religion and not merely a set of secular institutions further reduces the costs of exchange. Islam is a powerful ideology with built-in sanctions, which result in considerable self-enforcement of contracts. True believers have a nonmaterial interest in holding to the terms of contracts even if an opportunity to shirk or cheat presents itself. For the Orma, who witnessed the demise of their political institutions in the late 1800s, Islam may well have filled an institutional vacuum.

Considerable evidence on the relationship between Islam and trade exists for West Africa, and much of it is directly analogous to the Orma situation. Perhaps one of the most important institutions that spread through the trading diasporas was the Muslim *commenda*, or trading partnership. The widespread use of the *commenda* for long-distance trade in West Africa greatly facilitated the intensification of trade by relaxing the binding constraints of engaging in barter, or direct exchange of equivalently valued goods. Perinbam (1980: 465–6) describes the manner in which *commenda* was practiced in West African Islamic communities:

It enabled an investor or group of investors to entrust capital or merchandise to an agent-manager, who traded with it and returned the principal and previously agreed-upon share of profits to the investor. The agent received the remaining share of the profits as a reward for his time and labor. . . . The *commenda*, which combined the advantages of a loan with those of partnership, was a contract which regulated the use of capital, trading skills, and labor for mutual profit.

The *commenda* and other Islamic credit systems were widely used and had a profound effect on the level of trade in Africa. It was the institution Shambaro used in his partnership with his Arab supplier, and it is still the norm in Tana River today. Citing two early sources, Perinbam (1980: 464–5) describes the ease with which credit was managed among fellow Muslims in West Africa:

If Valentim Fernandes is correct, credit was sometimes given for a year, without collateral, witnesses, or any written statement (Fernandes 1938: 87). Dubois (1897: 301–2) reports that the period could sometimes be extended to two or three years, and if the jula never return "it [was] . . . less by dishonesty than by wars and insecurity of routes." If he died before meeting his debts, his relatives would honor them.

As credit contracts and partnerships such as the *commenda* facilitated the expansion of trade into new areas, long-distance agents could no longer cope on their own and had to leave behind agents who would deal on their behalf. This is similar to the way in which the Said family ran their cattle-buying operation through agents among the Orma, beginning with Shambaro in 1945. Murray Last (1979: 239–40) reports that in West Africa this process developed a chain of middlemen, with the pressure always building on those at the bottom of the chain to convert in order to move up the chain. Last provides a clear illustration of how this process functioned:

I suggest that if one draws a graph to show the growth of a trader's turnover for a number of years, there is a point on the graph where the size of the turnover is such that the trader must convert to Islam in order to maintain or increase the initial rate of growth.... Hausa trade is essentially dependent on networks. Growth depends on the number of trading friends, not on the cheapness, necessarily, of one's wares and the number of new customers one can thus attract. "Friends" are those to whom one gives goods on credit – in effect those to whom you can give capital. The more creditors one has, the greater the turnover – and the greater the profit to one's own creditors.

In the Orma case, the amount of credit extended by some of these agents (including Ahmed bin Said) was considerable and lends support to the argument that Islam provided a strong institutional framework that served to back up these contracts. For such a system to work, however, it is essential that people build "reputations" for trustworthiness and demonstrate that they are indeed true adherents of the faith on which these institutions rest. Demonstrating one's commitment to the institution, therefore, is beneficial in establishing a reputation. In addition to praying, giving up alcohol and fasting during Ramadan are two clear ways one can do this on a regular basis. As the credit stakes grow, however, more might be demanded, as Last (1979: 241) illustrates:

To mark his entry or, as often, to make his claim to entry into a bigger network, the trader is likely to go on the pilgrimage, an investment of at least $200. Some of it may be recouped by profits from merchandise brought back from Mecca, but the $200 can, I think, be seen as an investment with a good return; it is not so much conspicuous consumption but rather a kind of membership fee to an ostensibly religious club – but a club that controls a trader's credit rating. Now that more and more traders can claim the title of *Alhaji* (pilgrim), further acts of piety like building mosques or funding others' pilgrimages are required. Religious status, then is important in trade at other levels than merely that of the new convert who is starting to trade; it is seen not merely as the socially sanctioned goal that justified the accumulation of wealth, but also as the *cause* of the successful accumulation, and continued accumulation, of that wealth.

The first Orma pilgrimages to Mecca took place in 1950, a mere thirty years after the first conversions. Both Shambaro and his senior wife, who for a time was the shopkeeper of his Wayu store, made the hajj, as did other prominent traders in the district.

Probably the most substantial change afforded by the widespread conversion of the Orma to Islam was the extension of credit. Cattle are extremely "lumpy" goods; in other words, each unit is of relatively high value and it is indivisible. While people want to purchase goods throughout the year, they typically wish to sell cattle only twice a year, at the beginning of the rainy seasons.[30] Credit between shopkeeper and producer/consumer greatly facilitates this problem. Given the long distances involved in trade and the poor communication networks, credit also simplifies trade for wholesalers who can extend credit to agents such as Shambaro. Agents on site with cash ready to purchase stock when the opportunity presents itself are a great advantage.

Islam is also associated with basic education in literacy and arithmetic. Even in remote Muslim areas where secular schools have yet to develop, one often finds Qur'anic schools. For some time now, all but the smallest nomadic camps among the Orma have had a Qur'anic teacher offering rudimentary education in the form of literacy in Arabic and simple arithmetic. Basic arithmetic is invaluable for potential shopkeepers, who must keep accounts. But simple accounting may also give confidence to credit takers, who feel more comfortable if they themselves can "check the figures" kept by the shopkeeper. As we saw in Shambaro's case, a lack of literate shopkeepers who could keep accurate accounts contributed to his undoing in at least one shop.

In short, I would argue that Islam greatly reduced the transaction costs associated with trade among the Galole beginning in the 1920s and accounts for some substantial portion of the more favorable terms of trade and increasing volume of exchange over this period (see Figures 2.1–2.4).

The standardization of weights and measures

Another significant change to affect transaction costs was the standardization of weights and measures. It was the Pokomo agricultural producers themselves who in the mid-1930s put pressure on the British colonials to impose standardization. Accordingly to the TRD Annual Report (1936: 18):

---

30 Prices are typically highest at the beginning of the rains, because the risk of drought and the accompanying weight loss and possibility of death are reduced.

Yet another cause of discountent [*sic*] is that all produce, again excepting cotton, is sold by volume, and the measure used is varied to suit the shopkeeper's pocket. If a standard Government "pishi" [8 pounds] were introduced, it would be enthusiastically received by the cultivators and better class traders, who are constantly petitioning for the standardisation of the measure.

In the following year, the government actually implemented such a policy, and the degree of attention with which it was noted by the D.C. in the TRD Annual Report (1937: 5–6) is worth recording:

The most important piece of legislation immediately affecting the natives was the application of the Weights and Measures Ordinance to the Coast Province and the establishment of the half-bushel measure and subdivisions thereof as compulsory dry measures. This was very popular with the natives and with the better class of traders, as the situation had become chaotic with each person using his own measure, with no two measures holding the same quantity.

Later the report (p. 20) states:

Great satisfaction was caused in the district by the introduction of standard dry measures, the use of which is compulsory, instead of the many and various measures previously used by traders. Although there may still be occasional cases where illegal measures are used, there are sufficient semi-educated natives in all locations [this refers to Pokomo areas near the river, not the Orma hinterland], who can recognise the Government stamps, to make the use of such measures not worth the risk. Actually the traders themselves were very glad when standard measures were introduced, as they in their turn were being swindled by the Lamu traders who bought their produce and measured it with even larger measures than had been used by the buyers.

Finally, in the following year, the TRD Annual Report (1938: 14–15) records:

The introduction last year of the Standard Dry measures, the use of which is compulsory, has proved of considerable benefit to the natives, and also to the less intelligent traders, in preventing frauds.
The traders have willingly brought their measures to be stamped, and although some illegal measures may still be in use, their use is becoming increasingly risky.

While it is entirely possible that the colonial officials exaggerated the degree of compliance with standardized measures in these first years of implementation, the trend had clearly begun. It should also be borne in mind that while the policing of such ordinances would in those days have been all but impossible in the Orma interior, those who sold there had to purchase from the areas like the coast and the Tana River, which were far easier to police.

Transportation and communications

Another major handicap to trade, noted in numerous district reports, was the poor road network and absence of motorized transportation. Poor transportation adds not just to the cost of delivering goods, but also to the costs of information. Here the record is quite precise. The first lorry did not arrive in the district until 1929, and then it went only to Kipini (then the district headquarters in the far south of the district). The transportation situation remained very poor through the early 1940s, as noted in the TRD Annual Report (1941: 5):

Transport remains the great problem. There were good crops of choroko and rice on the upper river which could not be marketed advantageously. If the Garsen–Hola road is open earlier in future years [following the rains] it may help, but river transport cannot cope with a good crop. By the time traders were able to market[,] prices had fallen and the traders lost a lot of money. Some shops will probably close in 1942.

As instances of the kind of risks traders face, apart from fluctuations of price, 2 dhows [small sailing vessels] were stranded at Kipini [in the south of the district] in April and had to jettison cargoes of rice etc. worth £150, while a shop at Mjimkuu was gutted by fire in November and another at Laza [the business district in Hola] in December.

Shortly after this report was issued, the situation began to improve. The first privately owned vehicle was a military lorry purchased in 1943 by an Arab trader named Byusuf. By 1955, when Shambaro purchased his landrover, eleven lorries were owned by Arab traders in the district. Much of the trade volume in the district that necessitated this amount of commercial transport would have been with the agricultural Pokomo. This broad expansion in transportation, however, also coincides with evidence of increased trade among the Orma in the 1940s.

The presence of vehicles undoubtedly increased the flow of both trade goods and information. However, it also provided a capital barrier to competition in wholesale trade for most African traders, who (with the exception of Shambaro) could not afford vehicles.[31] For example, the TRD Annual Report (1954: 33) makes note of the fact that the Arab monopoly on transport renders the position of the African traders very difficult. For example:

... those [Pokomo traders who have ambition] know they would instantly incite the combined opposition of the Arabs. As the latter own all the transport, their

---

31 The dominance of Arabs in wholesale trade in the district continues to this day, although it was beginning to lessen in the 1980s. Significantly, since Shambaro lost his last vehicle in the early 1960s, no trader in Wayu has owned a vehicle; all depend on Arab wholesalers or free-lance drivers for transport.

position would be very difficult; indeed, there have been complaints of cases where Arab lorry-owners have refused to carry Pokomo crops to market, but found the truck was available immediately the crops had been sold to an Arab dealer.

The TRD Annual Report (1955) makes note of vast improvements in roads and telecommunications, which undoubtedly further facilitated trade in that decade and further reduced the costs of both transportation and information. One example of the transaction costs resulting from inadequate communications graphically illustrates the consequences engendered by poor communications. In the TRD Annual Report (1954: 19) an incident is described that probably typified the administrative headaches of the day. It resulted from the "garbling" of a telegram to Garissa, a Somali town just north of Orma territory:

The wire as sent reported an epidemic among Somalis at Walu, but as received read as the report of an epidemic among cattle at Wayu. This led to a considerable dislocation of the stock movement and a special trip by air to be made by the Provincial Veterinary Officer to contact the writer on safari and straighten out the tangle.

An error like this would certainly have had serious implications for the Orma, since cattle would have been moved rapidly to less desirable locations to avoid contagion and strict quarantines against movement and sales of stock would have been imposed in due course. Each improvement in the telecommunications system, therefore, had the potential to improve the efficiency of production and exchange, thereby decreasing costs.

The role of both transportation and telecommunications in increasing the flow of information regarding supply and demand and current prices also ought not to be overlooked. Especially in cattle trading, information about prices is critical before the moving of stock to market. Even nomads do not relish walking their stock a hundred miles or more to a central market only to find prices well below what they had anticipated. Under such circumstances they might easily be persuaded to sell at a very low price, rather than return with their (then weakened) stock and no purchases. As transportation and information costs fall to the Orma, fewer such mistakes are likely to arise, with the consequence that the Orma should (all other things being equal) be able to realize higher prices for their stock.

The Arab monopoly on transportation, however, possibly gave the traders an edge in reaping many of the increased profits associated with these declining transaction costs. Thus while it seems obvious that the stock trade would have become increasingly profitable in the face of declining transportation and information costs, we do not yet know how the increased profit was divided between producer and trader.

Government services

In addition to the changes already noted in the form of conversion to Islam (1920–40), standardized weights and measures (1937), and improved transportation and communication (especially in the early to middle 1950s), Tana River District was receiving more administrative support in the mid-1950s, which could also be related to the increasing profitability of trade through declining transaction costs. For example, we read in the TRD Annual Report (1953: 2):

... the year has also seen a marked change of attitude to the district on the part of Government. From being a place of which the less heard the better, Tana River has become a centre of interest, not all of which it is hoped, is entirely due to the Emergency.[32] This has shown itself in various ways. A District Officer was posted in July, so that the District has now regained its 1919 establishment of European Officers; a really determined effort to improve the Garsen–Witu road is being made; and many parties of technical officers have been in the district to set on foot schemes of development. The Asst. Agricultural Officer was provided with a habitable house, a boat, an effective vehicle, and even a typewriter, none of which he had last year.
... [the visit of His Excellency the Governor, himself to the district this year] has gone far to allay the belief, among the Tana River tribes, that they are a forgotten minority in whose welbeing [sic] nobody of importance takes any interest. The danger to them now is perhaps not that of being left behind, but that of being rushed too rapidly ahead; but if the proposed developments prosper without to [sic] sudden a disruption of the existing life of the people, the district may be approaching an era of prosperity the like of which it has not known before.

Again in 1955 (p. 1):

Some substantial development took place in 1955 and Tana River seems more on the map, metaphorically and literally. Several departments have shown a gratifying interest and thanks to better roads the District received a large number of visitors.

It is impossible to know how much the posting of new administrators and technical support staff added to or detracted from the profitability of production and trade. Some changes almost certainly provided benefits, such as the massive inoculation efforts against rinderpest and other stock diseases from 1935 onward, as well as the considerable efforts at locust

32 The "Emergency" refers to the Mau Mau war for independence, which was declared in 1952 and which ultimately resulted in independence in 1963. Most of the fighting took place in Kikuyu territory. Tana River District, however, is infamous because in 1959 eleven prisoners were brutally massacred at a prison camp in Hola.

eradication from the 1940s, including a major campaign in Wayu.[33] The government also attempted to centralize cattle marketing by holding preannounced public auctions. The first of these to take place in Wayu occurred in 1944. While the Orma associate a major rise in cattle prices with the first government efforts to organize the trade in the form of "Supply Board" purchases, it is not clear that the increased prices reflected this change in the organization of the exchange as much as they did increased demand for the product.

DIVIDING THE SPOILS FROM DECLINING TRANSACTION COSTS: TRADERS VERSUS PRODUCERS

While the evidence of declining transaction costs in the form of standardized weights and measures (imposed in 1937) and lower transportation and information costs is compelling, given the apparent monopolistic trade environment of this period, it is difficult to know how great an impact these increased profits had on the Orma producers.

We do know, however, that the more favorable conditions that developed for traders over the years brought many people into the retail business. Thus while the colonial officials complained about a shortage of traders in the district in 1923 and 1929, as well as their formation into something like a cartel, the situation reported in 1949 was quite different. The 1923 TRD Annual Report (pp. 5–6) noted:

Trade in the district is very depressed.... The chief factor militating against the River rice trade is the absence of trade competition. The Traders up the River are agents of others at Kau, Kipini and Lamu who are able to dictate the price. Another factor is the shortage of working capital among these traders and another in [*sic*] the shortage of canoes already referred to.

In 1929 the TRD Annual Report (p. 5) stated:

The trade of the Tana River is in the hands of a comparatively few traders, who are only in a small way of business, or agents of slightly larger concerns in Lamu. These work in together and to some extent form a ring, added to which the majority of the Pokomo are in their debt, and appear to have little desire (or at any rate make no effort) to get out of it. With these conditions prevailing complaints are sometimes made that market prices are not always given for local

---

33 In 1931 the Orma adamantly refused to have their cattle inoculated. However, once they saw the efficacy of inoculation against rinderpest, they were won over; some agreed to inoculations in 1935 (TRD Annual Report 1935: 17), and these served as an example, such that by 1944 inoculations were widely accepted. Today, the government still inoculates stock, but not as much as desired. Consequently, the Orma spend considerable sums on cattle medicines and inoculate their stock themselves against a broad variety of diseases.

produce, but it is difficult to see how it can be remedied until production increases sufficiently to entice larger and independent traders to come into the District.

In contrast, the TRD Annual Report for 1949 (p. 13) noted, "In all trading centres there are too many traders and the Native Markets have more than enough also."

The strongest evidence we have that the Orma producers were also sharing in the increasing profitability of trade comes from the data on changing relative prices, or terms of trade. Table 2.1 gives the price data for the most commonly consumed commodities for the period from 1923 to 1987; it also lists the prices received by the Orma for their cattle and ghee, as well as wages for labor.[34]

Until the 1980s, the vast majority of Orma income came from cattle sales. Consequently, to compare relative prices, we examine the quantity of each of the consumption commodities that the Orma could have purchased with a five-year-old steer over time (Figures 2.1, 2.2, and 2.3). In this way we are able to determine whether their relative prices are rising or falling. In Figure 2.1, cattle are compared with the three staple food-stuffs: maize, rice, and sugar. In all cases, the trajectory shows significant gains over time for the Orma from 1923 to 1987. The spike in the terms of trade for maize relates to the rescheduling of government-controlled prices for maize in 1955. The government had been attempting to subsidize Pokomo maize prices in the early 1950s, the result being higher costs to the Orma, but they reduced this effort in 1955, thus giving the Orma a windfall. Except for the period up to 1933, the most notable increases for the Orma came after the early 1950s.

Turning to cloth (Figure 2.2), we see that the Orma also benefited from a favorable turn in terms of trade. While a steer purchased 2.5 *leso* (two pieces of local cotton cloth more commonly known as *kanga*) in 1923, this had risen to 5 in 1926, 10 in 1944, 13 in 1980, and 14 in 1987. Then as now, cloth represented a major consumption item for the Orma. Unfortunately, the data points are few, but it appears that the real gains for the Orma in cloth preceded 1944.

Finally, in Figure 2.3 we see the terms of trade for paraffin and cooking oil. The Orma probably consumed almost no paraffin in the early days, and today use small quantities only for light, not for cooking. Cooking oil was also purchased in only small quantities in the past, because the much preferred home-produced ghee was in plentiful supply. But by 1980

---

34 The wage data for the colonial period reflect prevailing Pokomo and Orma wages for the period in Tana River District, but it is unlikely that any significant number of Galole Orma were involved in wage labor at this time. Most of those employed would have been Pokomo. Not until the drought of 1975, when the Galole lost 70% of their stock, did a significant number of them turn to wage labor.

cooking oil was a substantial budget item, for ghee and milk yields had fallen significantly as a result of overgrazing around permanent settlements and the consequent removal of more stock to the distant cattle camps. Again, in both cases the Orma were better off in terms of trade against these commodities, although they have faced the same significant decline with regard to paraffin since the early 1970s that has been realized the world over.

Overall, it would be consistent with these data to conclude that at least some portion of the increased profits from exchange were being shared with the producers in spite of the ethnic monopoly existing in wholesale trade and transport.

Another way of presenting the data graphically is to plot each commodity price as a percentage of the price paid for the same commodity in a given base year. I have chosen 1926 both because we have a complete set of prices and because it was not an aberrant year in any regard. The plot that results (Figure 2.4) is not corrected for inflation; thus we can compare only the price divergence between cattle and other commodities for a given year, since this does control for inflation. This method allows us to get a better feel for the timing of the relative price changes. The real gains in livestock as opposed to other commodities began in the late 1950s. Of all the changes noted earlier, this would appear to coincide most immediately with the expansion of transportation, telecommunications, and the greater administrative presence in the area. Not all institutional changes can be expected to have immediate effects on transaction costs, because it takes all parties some time to adjust to the new conditions. Thus the expansion of credit systems as a consequence, in part, of the conversion to Islam may not have taken off until the 1950s, and this might also have contributed significantly to the increasing profitability of trade.

CONCLUSIONS

The history of trade in Tana River District provides some support for competing theoretical perspectives. In support of dependency theorists' notion that peasants do not generally benefit from trade, and may therefore trade only when coerced, we may cite the role played by colonial taxation in increasing commercial production in the 1920s. Similarly, we might cite the fact that trade was rather limited in the precolonial context, and the Orma appear not to have wanted to facilitate it. Finally, in this century several new plateaus of exchange have been reached only after some ecological calamity thrust people into dependence on the market (e.g., rinderpest in 1933 and drought in 1943, 1974–5, and 1984–5).

Table 2.1. Prices over time (in Kenyan shillings as paid and received by the Orma)[a]

Year	Cattle (age 5)[a]	Ghee (liters)	Wages (mo)[b]	Maize (kg)[c]	Rice (kg)[d]	Sugar (kg)[e]	Kaniki cloth[f]	Leso cloth	Paraffin (liters)[g]	Oil (liters)[h]
1923	10/00				0/17	0/55	2/50	4/00		
1924						0/55	2/50	4/00		
1925						0/55	2/50	4/00		
1926	20/00	1/65	18/00	0/12	0/24	0/55	2/50	4/00		
1927							2/50	4/00		
1928							2/50	4/00		
1929		1/32		0/09	0/34	0/67	2/50	4/00	0/59	0/98
1930				0/13	0/61		2/50	4/00		
1931		1/70		0/13						
1932				0/08	0/49					
1933	20/00		8/00	0/07	0/29					
1934										
1935				0/08	0/24					
1936			12/00		0/44					
1937	35/00	1/52								
1938	45/25									

Year								
1939								
1940					0/06			50/00
1941								
1942								
1943								33/00
1944	6/00	3/00	1/10		0/22		1/52	60/00
1945								
1946								
1947								
1948								
1949								187/45
1950			2/20					108/73
1951								
1952								
1953				1/61	0/55		5/49	162/00
1954					0/56	30/00		161/00
1955					0/41			164/00
1956					0/43			166/00
1957					0/46			180/40
1958								
1959								192/00

Table 2.1 (continued)

Year	Cattle (age 5)[a]	Ghee (liters)	Wages (mo)[b]	Maize (kg)[c]	Rice (kg)[d]	Sugar (kg)[e]	Kaniki cloth[f]	Leso cloth	Paraffin (liters)[g]	Oil (liters)[h]
1960										
1961				0/68					0/68	
1962										
1963	300/00									
1980	853/00	17/14	300/00	2/50	4/00	5/00	45/00	65/00	4/29	17/14
1987	1807/00	42/86	700/00	5/50	11/00	9/00	130/00	130/00	8/57	22/86

Note: In most cases, for the years 1923-63 the source is the Tana River Annual District Report or the Handing Over Report. Exceptions are noted below by commodity. All 1980 and 1987 data come from my household surveys in Wayu.

[a] It is assumed that the average age of cattle is 5.0, based on a report in the 1955 district record that only 9% of sales were immature and there was really no market for them. In 1980 the actual average age of sales was 4.94 years, while it was considerably lower in 1987. Because prices are strongly correlated with size of livestock, it was essential to control for the age factor in these later sales. Therefore, the average price used for 1987 was based on a pairing of average prices for the age structure of the sales reported in 1980. If anything, one would expect the average age of cattle sold in earlier years to have been higher than the 5-year average in 1980, which would mean that the figures for 1980 and 1987, based on lower aged sales, underrepresent the relative prices changes over time.

Prices in the years 1923, 1926, 1933, 1944, and 1963 were derived from Galole Orma elders. Elders also confirmed that, in one year (probably 1949), prices were far higher than either before or after. This confirms the district records that show extremely high prices in that year. The district records indicate a higher price for sales at Wayu in 1957 than for the district as a whole (231/= average for Wayu as opposed to 180/40 average for the whole district), which could mean that the figures for 1949-59 are biased on the low side. This would not affect other years, either earlier or later, since those reports come directly from the Orma at Wayu.

72

b Wages in 1936 and 1987 are for roadwork; earlier reports in the district records appear to be primarily for hired agricultural labor. When a range of wages was given in the colonial days, the top was taken, since the low wage usually included food.

The wage figure for 1954 is based on the salary of an Orma working for an Arab as a hired herder. At least in recent years, the salaries paid by Arabs for hired herders are similar to those paid for roadwork.

c Where only the price to the producer was reported in the district records, the retail price was assumed to be 80% higher, based on a report of both prices in 1953. Where prices differed for upper and lower Tana, the upper prices were used, for the residents of this area are the people with whom the Galole would have traded.

All prices come from the district records, with the exception of 1944, which is based on an Orma elder's recollection. Also, the Orma report that in the 1930s the prevailing rate of exchange was one *mzigo* (58 kg) of maize for an average goat. This works out to 0/11 per kilogram, which is quite consistent with the reports in the district records.

d Prices are for cleaned rice. Where only the unhulled price is recorded, 30% was added based on the differential reported in 1923 when both prices were recorded. See also note c for the handling of price differences between retail and wholesale and upper and lower Tana.

e Sugar prices before 1926 and for 1944 and 1950 are from Shambaro's recollections of his trading days.

f All *kaniki* prices are from Shambaro's recollections. However, the 1929 district records indicate that a "package" of cloth sold for 248/=. If such a package consisted of 100 pieces, this would be directly in line with Shambaro's recollections. Although the solid black *kaniki* were for a long time the standard cloth worn by women, they had been almost entirely replaced in 1987 by much more desirable printed cloths. Even *kanga* (called *leso* by the Orma), the norm in 1980, were less desirable in 1987 than the more expensive *apollo* and *wili*, imported from Somalia. The latter two were in wide circulation by 1987.

g The Galole Orma consumed no appreciable quantity of paraffin until the 1970s. Even in 1987, nomads rarely used it. No one cooks with paraffin; it is merely used for light, either in kerosene lanterns by wealthy households or in small lamps made from tin cans by poorer households.

h Orma consumption of cooking oil has increased in proportion to the decline in milk yields, which is related to home production of ghee. Purchases of cooking oil today are a substantial percentage of the average household budget.

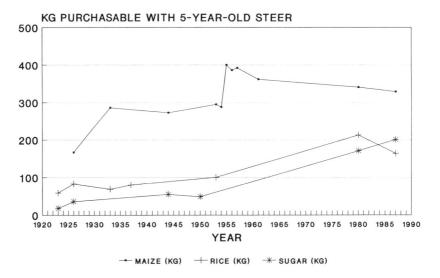

Figure 2.1.   Terms of trade: cattle, maize, rice, and sugar.

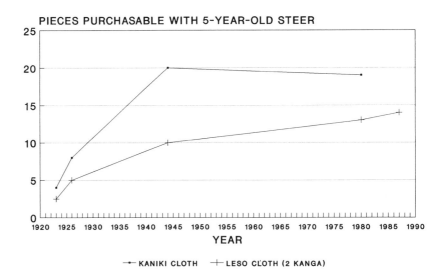

Figure 2.2.   Terms of trade: cattle and cloth. Note that Kaniki cloth ceased to be worn by 1987.

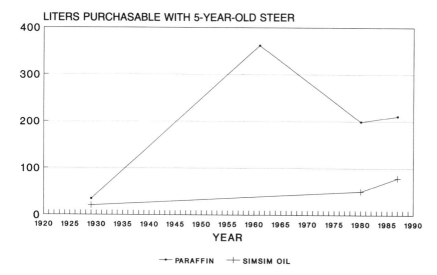

Figure 2.3.   Terms of trade: cattle, paraffin, and oil.

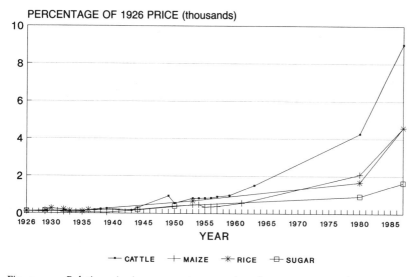

Figure 2.4.   Relative price increases: price per commodity as percentage of 1926 price.

Once trade did take off (especially after the 1950s), the quantitative data appear to support the neoclassical prediction that exchange could benefit both parties. Finally, there is strong evidence to support the new institutionalist notion that institutions make a difference. By reducing transaction costs, institutions made trade more profitable for traders and producers alike, which explains why people preferred greater dependence on the market.

One of the most dramatic demonstrations in this case study of the importance of institutions to exchange comes from the precolonial period. We saw that following the disruption of indigenous Orma social and political institutions in the nineteenth century, trade declined even below its already low levels. Ironically, this occurred at a time when the Orma were probably most in need of exchange and had lost the incentive they once had to keep the territory closed in order to protect their tributary relations with the hunters and gatherers. Nevertheless, the consequences of the loss of a political structure with which to negotiate and a warrior force with which to ensure safe transit, together with the resident sultan's encouragement of banditry, effectively shut down exchange temporarily.

The colonial era saw the development of many significant institutions that had a bearing on transaction costs. I have argued that conversion to Islam between 1920 and 1940 had significant implications for the extension of credit and the development of increasing specialization in marketing (in the form of middleman agents and shopkeepers). Next came the standardization of weights and measures in 1937, which had a significant impact on the grain trade. Finally, in the 1940s and 1950s there were considerable improvements in roads, transport, and telecommunications, which among other things greatly reduced the costs of transportation and information, thus increasing the profitability of exchange. As already noted, each of these changes also led in the short term to opportunities for monopoly rents. Each institutional change, while reducing transaction costs over previous conditions, also created opportunities for those in the right place at the right time. This meant that the increased profits from the reduced transaction costs were not necessarily immediately realized by the population at large. Rather, when traders were in a position to do so, they undoubtedly tried to monopolize those benefits for themselves as long as possible.

Even in the case of conversion to Islam, Shambaro happened to be in the right place at the right time. Other would-be traders who were not Muslims in those early years most likely would not have been able to work out such favorable terms with Arab agents. Shambaro's conversion helped to overcome the fact that he was dealing with a foreign ethnic group with which he would not otherwise have shared institutions capable of ensuring good-faith behavior. However, it was not long before the entire population of Orma was converted, and thus this window of opportunity was closed. Next, Shambaro may well have used his political connections to protect his position. Later, he lost no time in keeping up with the technology of the day and became one of the first to realize (and cash in on) the advantages of motorized transport. This undoubtedly facilitated his monopsony in the Galole area for some fifteen more years. Eventually, however, both Shambaro and his original supplier, who dominated the cattle trade from the 1920s to the early 1980s, lost ground to competition from other traders.

The expectation that people will obstruct free trade for the purpose of seeking monopoly rents gives this analysis a more neo-Marxist flavor. However, the realization that such efforts often break down (or at least reorganize) as economies increase and attract added competition is more consistent with neoclassical analysis. The mechanism by which monopolistic cartels break up is an example of the failure of collective action (Olson 1965), and this is an insight of rational choice theory. Another critical dimension in this process is the existing political structure. If one group has privileged access to the political process, they might be able to stave off competition longer than the simple economics of the situation might predict.

In each case of institutional change we can point to some windfall benefits for those in a position to take rapid advantage of the new circumstances. In all cases studied here, each advantage eventually eroded, and competition spread the gains from decreased transaction costs down to the producers until the cycle started anew. The ultimate measure is change in terms of trade over time, for which there were dramatic improvements for Orma producers between 1926 and 1987.

Nothing has yet been said about the distribution of these gains among households. Have all benefited equally, or have some even lost ground? This important question is the subject of Chapter 3, where we look at the economic effects of increasing commercialization on the same households over time.

3

Distribution of the gains from trade

The historical data for Tana River District point strongly to the fact that there have been gains from trade among the Orma over the course of the century, but it remains to be seen how these gains were distributed among households. Development analysts are rightfully concerned with the differential impact of economic growth on various segments of society. For example, the fact that Kenya experienced 6.4 percent average growth per year from 1965 to 1980 and 3.7 percent from 1980 to 1987 (Lele 1991; World Bank 1989), says nothing about how these benefits were distributed across ethnic groups and social classes. Data on these matters are hard to come by. For the 1970s and 1980s, however, we do have household economic data for the Galole Orma such that we can actually trace these effects over time, in some cases on the very same households.

One of the issues I address in this chapter is the evidence for proletarianization and the implications of this process for the economic well-being of the poor. Lenin (1956 [1907]) predicted that commoditization alone would lead to a differentiation of the peasantry into "kulaks" and proletariat, those who owned the means of production and those who had only their labor to sell.[1] Indeed, evidence on the Orma for the 1970s points in this direction.[2] But data for the 1980s indicate other trends that do not fit the scenario we usually associate with proletarianization. Rather, they appear to be more consistent with the rosier picture predicted by neoclassical economists, who argue that increasing specialization and division of labor (of which proletarianization is but one variety) ultimately lead to economic growth, and at least the potential for greater

---

1 Neoclassical economists have also found empirical data to support the fact that economic growth may lead to a worsening of the position of some members of society (see Adelman and Morris 1973, 1978).
2 See Guyer and Idowu (1991) for a discussion of economic differentiation, and see Cancian (forthcoming) for a comparison case study.

well-being for all. One thing that emerges from the 1980s data is that the poorest and middle sectors of the population are indeed reaping some of these benefits (for a similar finding see Attwood 1979).

METHODS AND DATA SET

The quantitative data presented in this chapter are based on two periods of field research among the Orma; the first lasted thirty-two months beginning in July 1978, and the restudy took nine months beginning in April 1987. Research methods over both periods included participant observation and informal interviewing by me and formal questionnaire surveying by native-speaking Orma research assistants.

Owing to the difficulties involved in drawing a random sample from a partially nomadic and scattered population, I elected to define a geographic sample and survey the entire population within the selected territory. The Galole Orma can be split into three geographic zones with market orientations around different centers. For the purposes of my survey I chose the central market center, Wayu, and attempted to survey the entire population residing within this 20-by-20-mile block (see Map 2.3). The data reported here are drawn from two household economic surveys of most residents within this 400-square-mile area. Of the 230 households resident in 1979, basic demographic data were collected for 174 (76 percent), while of the 214 households resident in 1987, basic data were gathered for 180 (84 percent).[3]

In most of the analyses to follow, wealth is a crucial variable. For the Orma, as for most pastoralists, wealth is comparatively easy to quantify, for it is held almost exclusively in livestock, which in turn represents virtually all of the privately owned means of production.[4] The land on which the Galole graze their cattle is state-owned, and use is for the most part communal. The Galole Orma are largely cattle pastoralists, but they also keep some small stock, which for the purposes of comparison were calculated at the rate of six small stock to one head of cattle in 1979 and five to one in 1987, following Orma exchange rates and international convention (FAO 1967).

---

3 A higher percentage of nomadic as opposed to sedentary households were missed in both survey periods; because many factors are correlated with form of residence, all sample means in the tables are weighted to reflect the proper distribution of the population along this critical variable.

4 By 1987 this was beginning to change. A few extremely wealthy households held some other property, primarily in the form of shops and rental housing, both in Wayu and in Hola, the district headquarters. However, these households fell into the most wealthy category on the basis of their cattle holdings even without consideration of these other productive assets.

In making comparisons of wealth among households, it is not appropriate to use absolute wealth, because household size varies considerably. As a result, the measure of wealth used in all of the analyses described here is wealth per capita, based on a strict definition of household membership reflecting established Orma patrilineal inheritance and virilocal residence patterns. In calculating household size, I have counted only those who share "ownership" of the herd or those who were born or married into the household and continue to live off the products of the herd.[5] Excluded are those who left the household to establish independent households or to become members of another household and retain no claims to patrimony in the herd (this includes independent married sons and brothers, as well as married daughters and sisters). Also excluded are hired laborers who have no "ownership" interest in the herd and other "immigrants" to the household such as foster children, who will not have claims to the herd for patrimony.[6]

In most cases the surveys on herd size were carried out just after *zakat* month, the time of year when the Orma count all of their herds in preparation for paying Muslim alms. By carrying out the survey at this time I was able to ensure that households knew the extent of their holdings. While there were inevitably those who reported incorrectly, the extent of a household's holdings was fairly common knowledge, and in particular the enumerator carrying out the survey was in most instances familiar with the individuals and their holdings. It is important to note that the government does not (nor did it ever) tax households on the size of their herds; thus there is less incentive to conceal animals than might be assumed. In addition, I lived in the area for three and a half years and gained considerable familiarity with the individuals and their herds. Furthermore, a detailed survey of herd structures containing many internal

---

5 This definition reduces the size of rich households in comparison with a definition based on number of residents, while it increases the size of poor households, who have more net absentees. Consequently, this definition has the effect of amplifying inequalities in wealth as compared with one based on residence. The data reported here should not be conflated with those in Ensminger (1984), since both the definition of household and the wealth divisions have changed. In Ensminger (1984) the wealth categories were divided into fourths, whereas here they are thirds. Also, the breaks in Ensminger (1984) were based on the total number of households regardless of the number of people in those households. In this study the break is based on the actual number of individuals it takes to make up one-third of the population for each wealth group. This results in a different number of households within each wealth category. Most notably, because wealth is correlated with household size, it takes fewer households in these analyses to make up the wealthiest one-third of the population.

6 See Netting, Wilk, and Arnould (1984) for a discussion of the problems involved in defining the term "household." Table 4.1, note *a*, also provides more detail on some of the numerical breakdowns of different definitions of household.

checks on consistency was carried out during both the initial survey and the restudy with a sizable sample of the same households; in most cases the figures were congruent.[7] Consequently, there is every reason to believe that the figures for both 1979 and 1987 are quite reliable.

At the same time that these data on current holdings were collected, households were asked to report their livestock holdings for the period just before and just after the droughts that struck much of Africa in the mid-1970s and mid-1980s. These droughts were so severe, and losses so high (in the range of 70 percent), that most people were able to remember the circumstances clearly four years later in the case of the 1979 survey and two years later during the 1987 survey. An aggregation of household reports of losses comes to 72 percent for 1975, which agrees roughly with the 80 percent loss estimate of the veterinary people in Hola who were in the district at the time. As I explain later, there is good cause to be suspicious of some of the predrought reports.

EVIDENCE OF PROLETARIANIZATION IN THE 1970S

The severe drought of the mid-1970s left a substantial portion (39 percent) of the Galole population living in market towns and heavily involved in commercial production. This tendency received further impetus from the 1985 drought, during which the Galole once again lost 71 percent of their herds; the number of permanently settled households rose to 63 percent. For the reasons noted in the preceding chapter, sedentarization among the Galole necessitates a commercial adaptation. Thus as was documented in the preceding chapter for the entire century, recent years have seen even more rapid conversion to commercial production.

To address the question of how increased commercialization has differentially affected the population, the data reported here are disaggregated into three groups based on wealth per capita of the household: the poorest third, the middle third, and the richest third of the population. Let us turn now to the data on trends in wealth per capita over time. Table 3.1 presents the data for 1974 through 1979, and Table 3.2 for 1983 through 1987. One must bear in mind that for both the 1970s and 1980s the pre- and postdrought data were collected several years after the fact.[8]

---

7 For example, herd statistics were elicited for ten age/sex categories of each species of stock by all locations – permanent village, nomadic camp, and up to four cattle camps. In some cases this involved a seventy-cell matrix, in which one could easily spot inconsistencies, such as between number of reported sucking calves and number of lactating stock.

8 It is important to note that Tables 3.1 to 3.3 do *not* take into account the fact that there was migration in and out of the area between the predrought and survey period in each case. Consequently, if the wealth of those emigrating is not consistent

Table 3.1. *Wealth (in TLU)^a for Galole survey households by wealth per capita of household,^{b} 1974, 1975, 1979*

	Poor	Middle	Rich	All^c
Number of households, 1979	57	55	51	163
Mean size of household, 1979	10.0	9.9	9.5	9.8
Mean wealth of household				
1974 (before the drought)^d	64.4	85.6	148.6	98.3
1975 (after the drought)^e	6.6	23.9	55.5	28.0
1979	10.5	42.6	106.6	51.9
Wealth per capita, 1979	1.1	4.2	10.1	5.0
Percent loss, 1974 to 1975	89.8	72.1	62.7	71.5
Percent gain, 1975 to 1979	59.1	78.2	92.1	85.4

^{a} One TLU (tropical livestock unit) is equal to one head of cattle. Sheep and goats are converted at a ratio of 6 to 1, reflecting prevailing exchange rates in 1979.

^{b} Households are divided into categories on the basis of wealth per capita for the poorest, middle, and richest thirds of the population.

^{c} These data do not take into account the fact that some households emigrated from the area before the survey of 1979; consequently, there is a selection bias in the data and they should be used cautiously. The means in each category are adjusted to reflect the true proportion of nomadic households in order to compensate for their underrepresentation in the 1979 survey.

^{d} Data for 1974 were collected from each household in 1979 by recall. These data should be treated with caution, because there may have been a tendency to inflate predrought holdings, and this tendency may have been more prevalent among the poor (see Table 3.2, note d).

^{e} Data for 1975 were collected from each household in 1979 by recall; they are probably more reliable than the 1974 data.

There are strong indications that the poor, especially, tended to exaggerate their predrought holdings (see Table 3.2, note d). Nevertheless, even discounting this evidence, the poor clearly lost ground relative to other households with respect to livestock holdings. Two processes appear to be at work here. First, the data indicate that the poor lost a higher percentage of their holdings during the drought. Second, their rate of postdrought growth was lower than that of the middle and rich households. While the extent of the first trend may be exaggerated owing to inflation

with the wealth of those immigrating for each period, there is a bias in these tables. This bias is corrected in all subsequent tables, but could not be corrected for the 1974 period because the earliest census was in 1979. In order for these tables to be compatible, therefore, the bias was not corrected for the later period either. See note 12 below for details on the corrections to succeeding tables.

Table 3.2. *Wealth (in TLU)[a] for Galole survey households by wealth per capita of household,[b] 1983, 1985, 1987*

	Poor	Middle	Rich	All[c]
Number of households, 1987	68	67	42	177
Mean size of household, 1987	9.5	10.4	15.7	11.2
Mean wealth of household				
1983 (before the drought)[d]	33.1	82.1	293.7	108.3
1985 (after the drought)[e]	5.4	17.2	103.5	31.2
1987	7.0	25.7	167.2	49.0
Wealth per capita, 1987	0.7	2.4	10.7	3.5
Percent loss, 1983 to 1985	83.7	79.0	64.8	71.2
Percent gain, 1985 to 1987	29.6	49.4	61.5	57.1

[a] One TLU (tropical livestock unit) is equal to one head of cattle. Sheep and goats are converted at a ratio of 5 to 1, reflecting prevailing exchange rates in 1987.

[b] Households are divided into categories on the basis of wealth per capita for the poorest, middle, and richest thirds of the population. Owing to the larger size of rich households, it takes fewer to make up one-third of the population.

[c] Unlike the other reports of wealth and income for the 1987 sample, these data do not take into account the fact that some households emigrated from the area before the survey in 1987. This is because it was not possible to correct for this selection problem in the 1979 data (see Table 3.1, note *c*), and therefore in order to make the figures comparable to those for 1979, the bias was repeated. The means in each category are adjusted to reflect the true proportion of nomadic households in order to compensate for their underrepresentation in the 1987 survey.

[d] Data for 1983 were collected from each household in 1987 by recall. There may have been a tendency to inflate predrought holdings, and this tendency may have been more prevalent among the poor. For example, we see in Table 3.1 that the mean wealth of the poor was 10.5 in 1979 and the percent gain over the previous four years was 59.1. Had this pattern held, we would have predicted holdings of 16.7 in 1983. However, poor households reported holdings of 33.1. Such computations for middle and rich households lead to projections far closer to actual reports for 1983.

[e] Data for 1985 were collected from each household in 1987 by recall.

of predrought holdings, there is good reason to believe that the pattern does in fact exist, as does the lower postdrought growth rate.

In Table 3.3 these data are presented as percentages of total wealth held by each sector of the population over time. Again, while the holdings reported in 1974 by the poor may be exaggerated, the trend is nevertheless clear: the relative share of wealth held by the poorest one-third of the population is declining. The most reliable data, those for the actual survey years, show substantial relative losses for the poor, from 6.6 percent of total wealth in 1979 to 3.5 percent in 1987. Furthermore, the middle

Table 3.3. *Percentage of total wealth (in TLU)[a] held by percentage of population, 1974 to 1987[b]*

Year	Poorest 33.3%	Middle 33.3%	Richest 33.3%
1974	21.6	28.7	49.8
1975	7.7	27.8	64.5
1979	6.6	26.7	66.8
1983	8.1	20.1	71.8
1985	4.3	13.6	82.1
1987	3.5	12.9	83.6

[a] One TLU (tropical livestock unit) is equal to one head of cattle.

[b] The wealth data for 1979 and 1987 are from actual surveys in those years. All other years were reported by households from memory. As noted in Tables 3.1 and 3.2, it is likely that predrought holdings were inflated for at least the poorest segment of the population; consequently, data for 1974 and 1983 should be treated with some suspicion. There is also selection bias in the data due to migration by some households out of the area between 1974 and the actual survey in 1979 and again between 1983 and 1987. This selection bias pertains only to Tables 3.1, 3.2, and 3.3, where it could not be controlled because of the use of the 1974 and 1975 data. It is controlled for in all subsequent analyses.

households are also losing; only the rich are gaining in *relative* terms. These findings are corroborated by similar trends among other Kenyan pastoralists (for the Ariaal, Fratkin and Roth forthcoming; for the Boran, Hogg 1980; for the Njemps, Little 1985a).

One must bear in mind that these tables do not necessarily indicate a permanent decline in *absolute* wealth. One expects herd size to be very low immediately after a drought and to grow rapidly in succeeding years. The 1979 data follow four years of rapid growth after the 1975 drought. Bearing in mind that fertility rates are low in the first year after the end of a drought, it is not inconceivable that by 1989 per capita holdings would have returned to their 1979 levels for the poor and middle households, while we would expect them to be significantly higher for the rich.

UNDERSTANDING THE PROLETARIANIZATION OF THE 1970S

Whether absolute wealth is increasing or decreasing for the Galole poor, the decline in their relative wealth still deserves explanation. What processes could account for a higher rate of loss than that experienced by middle and rich households during droughts and a lower recovery rate afterward, and how has commercialization contributed to this process?

Until about the 1940s, most Galole Orma were nomadic and lived primarily off the subsistence production of their herds. Although there were considerable differences in wealth among households, the quality of life between rich and poor probably did not differ substantially. In most years milk yields were generous, and having little market for their surplus production, the rich tended to share a considerable quantity of milk with those worse off. Poor households paired themselves with wealthier households, who were often in need of labor. Having little need to dip into their small herd for subsistence, poor households were able gradually to build a herd with the intent of eventually gaining self-sufficiency. Even today, poor households living outside market centers are able to avoid cutting into their productive capital more than are poor sedentary households. This is partly because more milk is available and partly because of life-style differences.

Market centers tend to attract sedentary populations and usually ones of high density. The result is that the area around the settlement rapidly becomes overgrazed and does not provide adequate grazing for all of the community's livestock. To maintain healthy herds, most households send a large proportion of their stock to remote cattle camps manned only by young men (usually aged fifteen to thirty). These camps provide excellent conditions for the livestock because the herders are unencumbered by household goods, children, the elderly, and the infirm. They move the camps frequently and over great distances to maximize access to grazing. The drawback is that the stock in cattle camps are inaccessible to the household for subsistence needs. In addition, because of the unfavorable grazing around permanent settlements, those milking stock that are left behind produce only about half as much milk for human consumption as do those outside the market centers. Households have little choice, therefore, but to convert to commercial beef production once they make the decision to settle.

In addition to the need to sell stock to meet subsistence needs, several other factors conspire to make it more difficult for sedentary smallholders (and to a lesser extent middle households) to get ahead in livestock production. Most of these factors are related to a lack of economies of scale in stock production, including limited access to cattle camps where grazing conditions are best, less access to veterinary services and medicines, less favorable terms of exchange in the cattle market, disadvantages in access to marketing and grazing information, and relative lack of labor. While rich households realize economies of scale in these factors of production, poor and middle households generally do not. For example, while a rich household might typically divide its stock into efficient cattle camps of fifty to a hundred head, poor households may have only ten head total, which does not justify a cattle camp.

Although wealthy households fairly easily agree to take a small number of other people's stock into their camps, the quality of herding afforded these stock is questionable. This becomes extremely significant during times of stress, when labor is at a premium. For example, in both 1975 and 1985, the largest cattle losses occurred not during the drought, but when the rains came at the end of the drought. The cattle were extremely weak and often sick, and tended to get stuck in the mud with the first heavy rains. Lifting a full-grown steer out of the mud is an arduous process. As one youth from the cattle camp put it to me, "If five of your stock and one of your relative's were stuck in the mud, whose would you lift out first?" It is not surprising, therefore, that poor households had a higher percentage of losses during both droughts and lower growth rates during good times.

Life-style differences also made it more difficult for poor sedentary households to build a herd. Even in 1978 Orma who lived in market towns talked about peer pressure to buy attractive new clothes in much the same way that people in urban environments worldwide feel drawn into nonessential consumerism. The nomads spoke quite analytically about their desire to avoid such expenses in order to build a herd. One nomad, surveying the crush of young men and women before him at a large Muslim celebration in a market village, commented that while almost every woman and child there had a new cloth for Id, that was definitely not the expectation in the nomadic villages. In 1987 nomads still eschewed the use of paraffin for light and sometimes made their own soap.

As one might expect, the Galole were well aware of these patterns, and one might ask why any poor households would wish to choose the commercial option associated with a sedentary life-style. Indeed, they consciously chose to be nomadic in order to refrain from interacting in the market, and their decision was perceived as a strategy to gain self-sufficiency in pastoralism. The following discussion with a nomad in 1980 illustrates this point:

Q: Why is it that some people choose to be nomadic while others choose to stay permanently in villages?
A: You have just asked the amount of milk we get from cows right now and you heard we get two cups and they get only one. We have to spend less money to buy food for children and those in the permanent village have to sell cows all the time to get money. They cannot build a herd. In the shifting village we spend less money than they do. The calves that survive this drought will grow big and we will have cows. In the permanent village the calves that survive will be sold.

Q: So why doesn't everyone shift?
A: We don't know! When we go to Wayu we ask people the same question.

One might well wonder why the sedentary poor were so foolish as to choose a strategy that would appear to rule out a future of self-sufficiency in livestock production. In part, the answer lies in the fact that once a considerable portion of the wealthy make the choice to settle and engage in commercial production, their would-be clients have no choice but to follow them.

The relative success of the wealthy market-oriented households is easy to explain. Their holdings were sizable enough that by hiring labor and using cattle camps they could overcome the otherwise detrimental aspects of coupling a settled existence with pastoral production. Many of them were also involved in the retail or stock trade, for which they also reaped substantial profits. Because the purchase of foodstuffs increased considerably during droughts, they tended to come out of droughts with lower net losses than other households. Their profits from trade also contributed to their higher growth rates in good times.

Although poor households knew that their prospects for a future in pastoralism were bleak if they stayed in town, there were just not enough stock remaining in the nomadic sector for all of the poor to stay there and share in the surplus subsistence of the wealthy, which was necessary until their own herds multiplied to the point of self-sufficiency.

For those so inclined, there might also have been no going back. Once a commitment to commercial production was made, the return to subsistence production would not have been an easy transition, certainly not in a short time. Over the years, as the Galole have become more involved in the market economy, they have come to favor different breeds of stock. Many stock are now selected for their ability to put weight on rapidly in the wet season, even though it is known that these breeds have far less resistance to drought and lower milk yields than former favorites. As a consequence, they are realizing higher beef prices, but with greater vulnerability in time of drought. This transition is the result of conscious breed selection, about which the Orma can talk specifically. A shift such as this evolves over a long time and cannot be reversed rapidly.[9]

Even this is not the whole story. Poor sedentary households reported their own version of being attracted to the "bright lights of the city." In particular, they cited the convenience of a settled life (especially if the family had elderly or infirm members) and the proximity of shops, school, dis-

9 This evidence contradicts Hyden's (1980) argument that small producers in Africa are powerful vis-à-vis the state because they retain the "exit" option, i.e., they can withdraw from commercial production and dependence on the state at any time and resort to subsistence production.

pensary, mosque, the chief, and transportation. Most significantly, in the 1980s many poor households were attracted by employment prospects.

In summary, there is no question that the Galole Orma are becoming a more economically differentiated society; by 1987 approximately one-third of the population dominated livestock production. Economies of scale are rewarding this group and may ultimately lead to their control of virtually all significant livestock production.[10] Surprisingly, this scenario has not led to the dire consequences for poor and middle households that we might at first be inclined to predict. I turn now to an analysis of what these trends have meant for the economic well-being of all segments of the Galole population.

FROM PROLETARIANIZATION IN THE 1970S TO ECONOMIC TRANSFORMATION IN THE 1980S

In comparing the changes in economic well-being of the population from 1980 to 1987, I again divide the population into thirds on the basis of wealth per capita. Most of these data are drawn from a two-village subset of the larger survey population. Numerous one-shot and recurrent panel surveys were conducted with this population both in 1980 and in 1987. Household data reported here include wealth, income, and expenditures; individual-level data are reported for height, weight, education, and vaccination history.[11]

To ensure that the two-village subset is representative of the larger population and to control for the self-selective effects that migration could have on these data over time, the wealth categories are based on the wealth of the original 1980 survey households both in 1980 ($N = 174$ of 230) and in 1987 ($N = 203$ of 230), regardless of their migration out of the survey area between these dates.[12] Most of the data reported here

---

10 Further evidence of a change in scale is provided in the data on household size. We see in Tables 3.1 and 3.2, for example, that the mean size of the wealthiest households rose from 9.5 in 1979 to 15.7 in 1987. In rural Nigeria, Netting, Stone, and Stone (1989) also found an increase in household size as a consequence of similar market incentives to increase the scale of production. For a further discussion of increasing household size see Chapter 4 on changing labor relations.

11 Other data collected in both time periods, but not reported here, include individual demographic statistics, health data, genealogies, extensive time allocation observations, food consumption, milk yields, and herd structures.

12 Of the 230 households living in the survey area in 1980, 125 were still resident there in 1987 and 119 of these were resurveyed (see Table 3.10). Over this period 89 new households moved in, of which 61 were surveyed. Given the recent nomadic tradition of the population and the relatively small size of the survey area, such a high rate of mobility is not surprising. However, it is potentially confounding of any analysis attempting to make statements about the nature of economic change over time. For example, if a disproportionate number of poor households

Table 3.4. *Comparison of mean wealth per capita (in TLU) for different samples by wealth of household[a]*

	1980 samples				1987 samples			
	Original 1979 sample		Two-village sample		Original 1979 sample		Two-village sample	
Wealth of household	n	Mean	n	Mean	n^b	Mean	n	Mean
Poor	58	1.17	16	1.45	80	0.64	39	0.66
Middle	57	4.01	11	3.96	72	2.05	30	1.98
Rich	59	11.51	25	11.70	51	8.15	21	8.08

[a] A TLU (tropical livestock unit) is equivalent to one head of cattle. Sheep and goats in 1979 were converted at 6 to 1, while in 1987 they were converted at 5 to 1, consistent with local exchange values.
[b] Given the significant differences in household size that existed between poor and rich households in 1987 (8.4 vs. 17.1 for the two-village sample), it takes far more poor households to make up 33.3% of the population.

are from panel surveys conducted among fifty-two households from a subset of two villages in 1980 and ninety households from the same two villages in 1987.[13] Of the fifty-two panel households in 1980, thirty-three were still resident in 1987, and thus a substantial portion of the data reported over time are for the same households. T-tests of the mean wealth per capita of the panel data samples for both 1980 and 1987 show them to be statistically identical in each wealth category to the larger samples from which they were drawn, thus indicating no bias on this most crucial variable (Table 3.4).[14]

emigrated, or rich ones immigrated, data on the resident population over time might well appear to show economic improvement when there was none. To control for this, the 1987 wealth groups were based on the wealth of the *original* 1980 sample households in 1987 rather than on the 1987 resident population. In other words, the wealth of all residents in 1987 is ranked relative to the 1987 wealth of the original 1980 sample, whether they continue to live in the area or not. These data on 203 of the original 230 households were in 125 cases based on actual surveys and in 78 cases based on the chief's and elders' estimates of the household size and livestock holdings of households that had emigrated. While such estimates are not perfect, given the relatively short distances that the house-holds had migrated and the continued contact with kinsmen, there is reason to be confident of their accuracy. In six cases where households that migrated were surveyed, their wealth per capita agreed fairly closely with the chief's estimates.

13 One could in fact consider these four villages, since both Wayu and Koticha are split into two settlements.
14 Although not statistically significant, there is a considerable difference in the mean

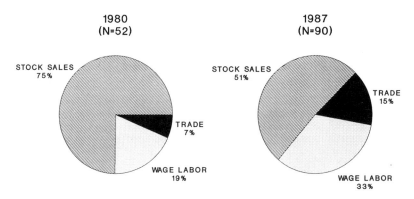

Figure 3.1.   Income by source for two-village sample, 1980 and 1987.

The combined effects of drought and transition to commercial production in the 1970s, which favored larger producers who could realize
necessary economies of scale, led to substantial and lasting economic
stratification among the Orma in the early 1970s. The poor fended as
best they could with help from wealthy relatives, government famine
relief, and limited employment prospects in the area. An increasing number of young men from recently impoverished households sought employment as hired herders of the rich, but there was not enough
employment to absorb all of the available labor. It was not until the
1980s that significant new employment prospects for the poor appeared,
reflecting an increasing economic diversification, as well as increasing
specialization and division of labor, or what might be argued to be the
beginning of true structural transformation (see O'Brien 1991).

Data on income by source demonstrate a significant increase in economic diversification over time. While stock sales made up 75 percent of
income in 1980 for fifty-two households in the two-village sample, they
made up only 51 percent in 1987 for ninety households in those villages
(Figure 3.1, Table 3.5). The contribution of wage labor to total income
increased from 19 percent to 33 percent, while that of trade rose from
7 percent to 15 percent. In Table 3.5 the data are broken down by wealth
group, which indicates that wage labor rose substantially as a major

of the two-village sample of poor in 1979 and that of the population at large
(1.45 vs. 1.17 tropical livestock units). The poor of the two-village sample in 1979
are richer than the poor at large. Since consumption is positively correlated with
wealth, this bias goes against the direction of the findings reported here. In other
words, had the poor sample in 1979 been more representative of the poor at large,
we would have expected to find an even larger increase in their consumption
between 1980 and 1987.

Table 3.5. *Percentage of income by source for two-village household sample by wealth of household, 1980 and 1987*

Income source	Poor		Middle		Rich		All	
	1980	1987	1980	1987	1980	1987	1980	1987
n/N	16	39	11	30	25	21	52	90
All stock-related	61.9	42.1	77.0	49.0	84.9	62.9	74.8	51.3
Stock sales	60.7	40.6	71.8	47.7	67.4	61.4	66.7	49.9
Stock products	1.2	1.5	5.2	1.3	17.5	1.5	8.1	1.4
All wage labor	33.2	52.3	16.7	32.7	6.8	14.8	18.6	33.2
Hired herder	14.6	19.8	3.4	9.5	2.7	5.6	6.7	11.6
Stone digger	16.4	13.3	12.3	16.8	4.1	4.1	10.8	11.4
Casual laborer	0.0	10.5	0.0	2.6	0.0	1.3	0.0	4.8
Traditional	2.2	4.6	1.0	0.3	0.0	0.1	1.1	1.6
Civil servant	0.0	4.1	0.0	3.5	0.0	3.7	0.0	3.8
All trade	4.8	5.5	6.3	18.2	8.4	22.4	6.5	15.4
Shop/kiosk	0.0	3.0	0.0	13.1	3.9	16.0	1.3	10.7
Stock trade	1.4	1.3	6.3	2.7	2.5	6.2	3.4	3.4
Nonstock trade	3.4	1.2	0.0	2.4	2.0	0.2	1.8	1.3

Note: Income does not include subsistence production or gifts from other households.

source of income for all wealth groups, but remained most significant for the poor (52.3 percent), while trade was increasingly important for the middle and rich households (18.2 percent vs. 22.4 percent, respectively).

One poor and particularly entrepreneurial man in his thirties described these changes as he saw them in 1987:[15]

The rich still have some stock. There are two types of poor people. Some, if they don't have stock, just beg. Some don't, they go here and there for casual labor. They slaughter and open a butchery. They do any kind of work. I myself am working. I am poor, but I am making a living.

According to what I saw after the drought, it taught people something very important. Since the drought, rich and poor are planning work. The work was there before, but since the drought people are really doing it. Many more rushed to dig stones because they saw that it earned money. I thought of opening a tea

15 This man was the first to open a tea kiosk in Wayu Boro. Despite the fact that his success led to competition from the opening of five more tea kiosks in a short period of time, he continues to support his entire family, including two wives, from the income he derives from his kiosk.

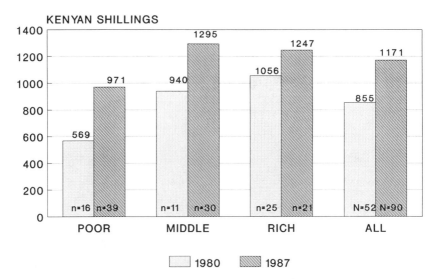

Figure 3.2. Annual income per capita for two-village sample by wealth of household (in 1987 Kenyan shillings), 1980 and 1987.

kiosk and many others have now followed. Even the rich are working now. They don't sleep. After the drought we have thought of many ideas to make money. The poor used to rest, but not now.

One interpretation of these trends is that they merely reflect the classic process of proletarianization associated around the world with increased production for the market. But as noted earlier, the poor population in 1980 had already lost the bulk of its livestock in the early 1970s. Nevertheless, the 1985 drought exacerbated both the relative gap between rich and poor and (at least temporarily) the absolute holdings of all households, but especially those of poor and middle households. These changes very likely compelled even more individuals to seek wage labor. Whatever the driving force, it remains to be seen what effect this diversification of the economy has had on the economic welfare of the population. Quite simply, is the population better or worse off in absolute economic terms as a consequence of trends in the 1980s?[16]

Figure 3.2 and Table 3.6 present the data on real per capita income over time for the two-village sample.[17] For all households the mean

16 By focusing on the absolute economic effects for which quantitative data exist I do not mean to imply that relative economic status does not matter.
17 Income is defined as all cash or other remuneration received for capital, products, or labor, but gifts from other households are *not* included. Subsistence production is also not included. In most cases income was received in the form of cash or

Table 3.6. *Annual income per capita for two-village household sample by wealth of household (in 1987 Kenyan shillings), 1980 and 1987*

	Income	
Wealth of household	1980	1987
Poor		
Mean	569	971
n	16	39
SD	413	562
Middle		
Mean	940	1295
n	11	30
SD	608	951
Rich		
Mean	1056	1247
n	25	21
SD	677	614
All		
Mean	855	1171
n	52	90
SD	83	77

Note: The exchange rate for Kenyan shillings in 1987 was 16 shillings to the dollar. Income does not include subsistence production or gifts from other households.

increase was 37.0 percent, while for the poor it was 70.7 percent, middle 37.8 percent, and rich 18.1 percent.

Data on household consumption show the same trend, but in a more exaggerated form (Figure 3.3, Table 3.7). Consumption data for the same households indicate even higher increases than do the income data; these average 83.3 percent (Table 3.8).

Increases in household consumption, even in real terms as presented here, do not necessarily indicate an improvement in economic well-being. For example, food accounts for a great deal of the increase in household consumption (see Table 3.9 for a breakdown of the household budget). While some of this may reflect an actual increase in caloric consumption,

cash credit at the shop; the major exception was cattle received for payment by hired laborers, and these were converted at prevailing exchange rates. Income from all family members is counted, including that of those living away from home.

93

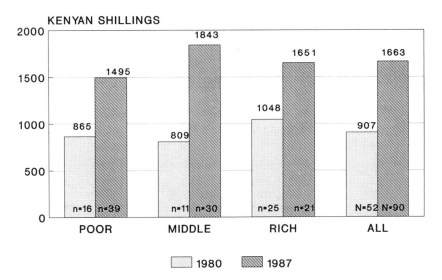

Figure 3.3. Annual consumption per capita for two-village sample by wealth of household (in 1987 Kenyan shillings), 1980 and 1987.

and therefore an improvement in nutritional well-being, much of it undoubtedly stems from the replacement of lost subsistence production with purchased food. The large increase in purchased food in 1987 may also have been due to the fact that 1987, although not a drought year, was a dry year; thus food expenditures were considerably higher than would ordinarily have been the case; but 1980, the year of baseline comparison, was also a dry year. Much of the higher food expenditures of households in 1987 can be attributed to the fact that herd size (and thus milk yield) was substantially lower than in 1980 owing to the relatively recent heavy losses of the 1985 drought. Increased sedentarization and resultant overgrazing had a similar effect. These factors also contributed to the dramatic closing of the gap between rich and poor per capita food expenditures. While rich households got much of their subsistence from milk in 1980, this was not true in 1987. My suspicion (unconfirmed) as to why middle households spent more on food in 1987 than either poor or rich households is that they had less milk than the rich, and thus had to purchase more, and although they had more milk than the poor, they bought more expensive foods.

Several other peculiarities of the years 1980 and 1987 inflated the relative food expenditures for 1987. Especially since 1985, Galole households have begun to farm much more extensively along the flood plain of the seasonal Galole River. Due to the dryness in 1987, the Galole did

Table 3.7. *Annual consumption per capita for two-village household sample by wealth of household (in 1987 Kenyan shillings), 1980 and 1987*

	Consumption	
Wealth of household	1980	1987
Poor		
Mean	865	1495
n	16	39
SD	363	632
Middle		
Mean	809	1843
n	11	30
SD	566	731
Rich		
Mean	1048	1651
n	25	21
SD	536	424
All		
Mean	907	1663
n	52	90
SD	69	65

Note: The exchange rate for Kenyan shillings in 1987 was 16 shillings to the dollar.

not flood and no homegrown maize was being consumed throughout the survey period, which resulted in higher than normal food expenditures. Finally, 1980 was a year of exceptional food shortages of all major food commodities – maize flour, rice, and sugar. In fact, from July to October 1980, food was frequently rationed and almost never were all three staples available at the same time.[18] This most certainly depressed food expenditures during that survey period, and to some degree the increased expenditures in 1987 probably actually reflect higher caloric intake.

18 It is worth noting that the national shortages in foodstuffs that Kenya experienced in 1980 fell especially hard on remote districts such as Tana River. Furthermore, it was the poor in this district who were the last to get access to supplies during rationing. There is little question that even the poor would have preferred to pay higher prices for maize flour to ensure supply rather than go without, as they often had to do that year.

Table 3.8. *Ratio of reported income to consumption and percentage of increase in income and consumption by wealth of household for two-village household sample, 1980 and 1987*

Wealth of household	Ratio of reported income to consumption		Percent change in income	Percent change in consumption
	1980	1987	1980-7	1980-7
Poor	0.65	0.65	+70.7	+72.8
Middle	1.14	0.70	+37.8	+127.8
Rich	1.00	0.76	+18.1	+57.5
All	0.93	0.70	+37.0	+83.3

Note: Because income does not include gifts between households, the ratio of income to consumption within wealth groups can be greater than or less than 1. Here it is lowest for the poor, which would be expected if they were receiving gifts from other households. For all wealth groups together, the ratio should be equal to 1.

More telling of the real trend in household consumption are the data on nonfood consumption, which increased 44.2 percent for all households, 34.2 percent for the poor, 95.4 percent for the middle, and 19.0 percent for the rich (see Table 3.9). These rates are more in keeping with the increase apparent in the income data, although there the poor fared better than the middle households, while here it is the reverse.

One pattern that emerges from the consumption data in Table 3.9 is the transformation of nonfood consumption patterns for middle households. While in 1980 their expenditures closely mirrored those of the poor, in 1987 they were virtually identical to those of the rich. These findings appear to give strong support to those of Cowen (1982), who argues that an identifiable middle class has emerged elsewhere in Kenya. Even more striking is the parallel between these findings and those of Collier and Lal (1986), who analyzed data from a much broader cross section of Kenya for the 1960s and 1970s. They also found evidence of significant improvement in the consumption patterns of poor and middle households. Also notable in the data presented here and consistent with Collier and Lal's findings is the narrowing of the ratio between poor and rich spending on nonfood items; in 1980 the poor spent only 67 percent as much as the rich on nonfood consumption, while this had risen to 75 percent in 1987.

The significant discrepancy between the absolute level of income and consumption reported, especially in 1987, warrants discussion. In Table

Table 3.9. *Consumption per capita by commodity for two-village household sample by wealth of household (in 1987 Kenyan shillings), 1980 and 1987*

Commodity	Poor 1980	Poor 1987	Middle 1980	Middle 1987	Rich 1980	Rich 1987	All 1980	All 1987
n/N	16	39	11	30	25	21	52	90
Total food	491	993	461	1162	487	982	480	1046
Sugar	175	213	169	238	188	223	177	225
Flours	111	422	99	467	89	374	100	421
Tea/ginger	63	90	60	98	71	100	65	96
Cooking oil	36	166	29	195	27	174	31	179
Rice	61	45	66	70	84	72	70	62
Other food	45	56	37	94	29	39	37	63
Total nonfood	374	502	348	680	561	668	428	617
Household	101	134	95	159	138	154	111	149
Clothing	149	159	173	248	287	239	203	215
Other nonfood	124	209	80	274	135	275	113	253
All consumption	865	1495	809	1843	1048	1651	907	1663

Note: The exchange rate for Kenyan shillings in 1987 was 16 shillings to the dollar.

3.8 the ratios of reported income to reported consumption for 1980 are compared with those for 1987. As defined, income and consumption should balance for the population as a whole, although not necessarily within wealth groups. This follows because these income data do not capture transfers between households, so one would expect the ratio for poor households, which derive a significant percentage of their income from transfers from rich households, to be less than 1, as indeed it is in both years. The considerable shortfall in income as compared with consumption for all households in 1987 is more difficult to explain. One possibility is that households were carrying more indebtedness over the 1987 survey period due to dry conditions and consequently unexpectedly large food purchases. Livestock sales, and the other incomes these generate, were also delayed because of the dry conditions and a foot and mouth quarantine at the two most lucrative markets, having the effect of decreasing income and increasing indebtedness.[19] Thus there are reasons to trust that the data are not as distorted as they would at first appear.

19 While the survey periods encompassed roughly parallel months of the year, cattle

Nevertheless, the possibility remains that, for whatever reason, income was (relatively speaking) overestimated in 1980, or that consumption was overestimated in 1987. This being the case, the most conservative approach would be to trust more in the increases in income over time than in consumption, since the bias would be against the observation reported here. Thus the evident overestimate of income in 1980 would make it even more difficult to document an increase in income over time, which is indeed what the data show. Consequently, even if there were a large error in the data, the evidence of a 37.0 percent real per capita increase in income may stand, while one would reject the larger 83.3 percent increase evident in the consumption data.

Another strong indicator of the economic situation among the Galole Orma over this period is the data on migration. While there has been substantial movement within the district, of the 230 households resident in 1980, only 2 were no longer residents of Tana River in 1987, and both of these were originally from outside the district (Table 3.10). The lack of any substantial out-migration is consistent with favorable economic conditions, at least relative to other areas.

Limited documentation of improved well-being comes from data on weight per height (Table 3.11), which is regarded as an accepted proxy for nutritional status (Tanner 1978). Although anthropometric data do not exist for the population in 1980, data on comparisons between the 1987 nomadic (bush) versus sedentary (town) populations may be taken as indicative of the longitudinal trend because there was a significant increase in sedentarization over the period (from 39 percent to 63 percent of the population). There is a statistically significant improvement for male adults (.318 to .333; $t = 2.39$; $p < .02$) comparing the mean weight per height of the bush and market town samples. However, there is no statistically significant change for male children (.170 to .181), adult females (.305 to .309), or female children (.188 to .187).

Two final pieces of data round out our picture of the effects of economic change on economic well-being. Table 3.12 presents data on education among the whole survey population. When I left the Wayu area in 1981, there was only one primary school serving the population of approximately 2,400. During my absence, a neighboring village had completed a substantial fund-raising project and in 1987 was in the process of constructing a high-quality permanent school building. Enrollment of school-age boys increased between 1979 and 1987 from 26 percent to 50 percent. Even more impressive, while only 4 percent of school-age

sales are tied to the rains, not to the calendar. When the survey period ended in 1987, the rains had not yet begun; consequently, cattle sales and related incomes had not yet covered outstanding debts.

Table 3.10. *Migration pattern of original 1979 Galole Orma survey households by location in 1987*

Location in 1987	n	Percent
Tana River District		
Galole survey area	125	53.9
Hola (district headquarters)	32	13.8
Garsen town and area	22	9.5
Bura town and area	15	6.5
Nomadic areas	23	9.9
Small towns	9	3.9
Other		
Left the district[a]	2	0.9
Unknown location	1	0.4
Deceased[b]	3	1.3
Total	232	100.1

[a] Both of the individuals who left the district were foreigners. One returned to his native Boran area and the other to Lamu.
[b] Households are counted as deceased only when they become absorbed into existing households upon the death of the head of household. More typically, the household continues to exist as a unit under the son or brother of the head of household.

girls were enrolled in 1979, that figure rose to 30 percent in 1987. The government also implemented the first adult literacy program in the area in 1983. The striking finding here is that it was the women, not the men, who were the keenest participants.[20] While twenty-six men in the survey reported some participation in the program, forty-seven women had participated. Far more striking is the fact that only one male adult from Wayu town was continuing his adult education, while thirty-one adult Wayu women (41 percent of those in the town where it was offered) were continuing.

Table 3.13 provides data on vaccination histories for children in the Galole area. At the time of my departure in 1981, only sporadic mobile vaccination campaigns had taken place. In the early 1980s, however, a major vaccination program through the permanent dispensary in Wayu

20 One reason women are so motivated to attend literacy classes is that they want to learn Swahili. Swahili is the language of the government bureaucracy (including the courts), of national political campaigns, and of trade. Women have learned that without fluency in Swahili they cannot take full advantage of their rights and opportunities.

Table 3.11. *Mean weight per height for 1987 resident Galole survey sample by type of residence, gender, and age category*

	Males				Females			
	Age 2-18		Age 19+		Age 2-18		Age 19+	
Type of residence	n	Mean	n	Mean	n	Mean	n	Mean
Market town	276	0.181[a]	163	0.333[b]	269	0.188[c]	196	0.309[d]
Bush	95	0.170	52	0.318	90	0.188	79	0.305

Note: Within age/gender categories a higher ratio of weight to height is generally indicative of greater nutritional well-being; women's ratios are typically lower than men's. Comparative ratios for Turkana pastoral nomads are 0.331 for adult men and 0.302 for adult women (Galvin 1985:232).

[a] There is no statistically significant difference between market town and bush male children.

[b] A difference-of-means t-test for market vs. bush male adults is significant at the .02 level.

[c] There is no statistically significant difference between market and bush female children.

[d] There is no statistically significant difference between market and bush female adults.

town (opened in 1953) was initiated. Several findings surface from the inoculation data. A fairly remarkable number of children have already been reached by the program. Second, the Orma appear to be very diligent about seeing vaccination series through to their completion, as evidenced by diphtheria–pertussis–tetanus (DPT) and polio vaccinations, which require two and three return visits respectively at specified intervals. Third, no discrimination against female children exists, such that males are more likely to be vaccinated than females.

Summarizing the distributional consequences of two decades, we are struck both by the decline in *wealth* of the poor and middle households begun in the 1970s and by the increase in *income* experienced in the 1980s. While commercialization is favoring larger economies of scale in livestock production and eroding the economic base of all but the rich in this form of production, it is simultaneously opening other economic opportunities. I turn now to a discussion of some recent policies of the Kenyan government that may have contributed to the trends apparent in the 1980s.

Distribution of the gains from trade

Table 3.12. *Education by gender for resident Galole sample, 1979 and 1987*

Amount of education	Males				Females			
	1979		1987		1979		1987	
	n	%	n	%	n	%	n	%
Some school	119	17	253	30	13	2	132	18
In school	82	26	158	50	9	4	84	30
Some adult education[a]	0	0	26	12	0	0	47	19
In adult education[b]	0	0	1	2	0	0	31	41

[a] Adult education was originally offered in Wayu and Wayu Boro. This figure represents the percentage of the population age 18 and above with some adult education for those two villages only.
[b] The adult education program was offered only in Wayu in 1987. These figures represent the proportion of the population age 18 and above continuing adult education in that village only.

EXPLAINING THE TRENDS OF THE 1980S

Three categories of economic policies implemented by the Kenyan government can be argued to have contributed to the economic changes observed among the Orma in the 1980s: structural adjustment, policies resulting in declining transaction costs, and decentralization of the central government.

Structural adjustment

Structural adjustment, often referred to as "getting the prices right," relates to the policies being widely implemented around the developing world that are intended to utilize government resources more efficiently (O'Brien 1991). These policies typically include currency devaluation and relaxation of price controls so that local prices are more consistent with world market prices; they also often mandate balanced budgets, which usually translate into declining government revenues for social services.

As Bates (1989), Lele (1991), and Lofchie (1990) have noted, Kenya has had a history of better economic management than most African nations. Consequently, as the World Bank and International Monetary Fund initiative on structural adjustment swept Africa in the early 1980s, Kenya was in the desirable position of requiring less drastic corrections;

Table 3.13. *Frequencies of vaccinations for Galole survey by gender, all children age 0 to 16 in 1987*

Vaccination	Sex	N	No vaccination		One vaccination		Two vaccinations		Three vaccinations		Four vaccinations	
			n	%	n	%	n	%	n	%	n	%
DPT	M	351	135	38.5	17	4.8	14	4.0	185	52.7	NA	NA
	F	333	124	37.2	20	6.0	14	4.2	175	52.6	NA	NA
Polio	M	351	133	37.9	9	2.6	13	3.7	26	7.4	170	48.4
	F	334	127	38.0	15	4.5	18	5.4	31	9.3	143	42.8

Table 3.14. *Terms of trade for the Galole Orma at Wayu (in Kenyan shillings), 1980 to 1987*

Commodity	1980	1987	% increase, 1980-7
Price to Orma producer			
Cattle: 1-2 years	366	787	115
Cattle: 3-4 years	753	1741	131
Cattle: over 5 years	988	2072	110
All cattle sales[a]	NA	NA	116
Price to Orma consumer			
Sugar (1 kg)	5	9	80
Maize flour (2 kg pkt)	5	11	120
Tea leaves (50 grams)	1/50	1/90	27
Simsim oil (700 ml)	12	16	33
Rice (1 kg)	4	11	175
Kanga cloth	65	130	100
Paraffin (700 ml)	3	6	100
All food	NA	NA	89
All commodities[b]	NA	NA	93

Note: The exchange rate for Kenyan shillings in 1980 was 8 shillings to the dollar and in 1987 it was 16 shillings to the dollar.
[a] Weighted by the proportion of sales in each age category.
[b] Weighted by the proportion of the household budget spent per commodity.

the Kenyan economy was never as badly out of alignment with market forces as were those of nations such as Tanzania and Nigeria. Nevertheless, in the 1980s the Kenyan government made changes in the government-controlled prices of key agricultural commodities and further devalued its currency. Given that Africa is the only continent in the world where food production in recent years has not kept up with population growth, the purpose of these policies was in part to provide incentives to agricultural producers. The policies are highly controversial, however, because they often involve proportional increases in food prices to consumers, and when incomes do not rise accordingly, at least the short-term consequences can be devastating for nonfood producers (see Campbell and Loxley 1989; Gladwin 1991).

The Orma are much affected by these pricing policies, because they are producers of meat and consumers of grain. The net effect of changes in the terms of trade for the Orma from 1980 to 1987, however, was positive (Table 3.14). This continues the trend noted in Chapter 2 for most of this century (see Table 2.1). The Orma's main cash-earning commodity for sale (cattle) yielded 116 percent more in 1987 than in 1980, while their total consumer price index rose by 93 percent and their food costs rose by 89 percent. The Kenyan shilling was devalued by 100 percent over the same period. The result was a net gain in purchasing power of about 23 percent for the Orma. While this is a substantial increase, it cannot in itself account for the 37 percent overall increase in income demonstrated earlier, let alone the 83 percent increase in consumption.

Policies that reduce transaction costs

Aside from raising the prices to producers, the profitability of trade can be increased by decreasing the costs of production. One set of costs often overlooked in traditional economic analyses are those associated with transactions themselves. One consequence of extremely costly transacting is the development of a high level of vertical integration, whereby one organization (often based on ethnicity) is involved in many different stages of production and distribution of a particular commodity. The cattle-trading monopsony that had existed among the Galole for most of this century was still intact in 1980; it was finally broken in the early 1980s.

Institutions that have the effect of decreasing transaction costs not only make trade more profitable, but may also increase competition in different sectors of the trade, thus affording the opportunity for those with less capital to break into one stage of the marketing process. Examples of such institutions are the simple notarizing of legitimate traders and property rights by third-party agencies, security forces that reduce banditry, banking facilities that extend credit and reduce the dangers of travel with cash, the regulation of weights and measures, courts that enforce contracts and property rights, and telecommunication and roads (which increase the flow of traffic and information). Such institutions have become more prominent in Tana River District in recent years, and one consequence is an increase in the level of Orma involvement in all aspects of livestock marketing. Between 1980 and 1987 many new livestock traders emerged, as did several new markets for stock. This had the effect of increasing producer prices as well as providing more diversification in the form of income from trading itself. One example dramatizes how seemingly small changes can have significant consequences.

Two new livestock markets opened to the Orma during the 1980s and paid approximately 30 percent more than the Orma's traditional coastal market.[21] Local traders reported that these markets were feeding the

21 In fact, for the period during which the survey was run in 1987, these two new

export trade to the Middle East, which could be directly related to the devaluation of the Kenyan shilling – a structural adjustment policy that makes exports more competitive abroad. Alternatively, the higher prices at the new markets could reflect the differences in supply and demand for beef between the Nairobi and coastal markets now that price controls have been rescheduled, also a structural adjustment policy. Both of the new markets are also located in the territories of traditional enemies of the Orma: the Kamba and the Somali. Livestock traders who are known to be carrying a large quantity of cash are obvious targets in these areas. For example, in the early 1980s four Orma traders were robbed and shot to death on such an expedition in Kamba territory. It remains to be seen, therefore, how much the government's efforts to increase security in the area through the posting of more police and civil servants has contributed to opening these markets by decreasing the transaction costs associated with trade. Similarly, the government now notarizes the ownership of livestock destined for market, and this has reduced the costs of exchange for those who might unknowingly buy and sell stolen goods and later be subject to claims by the rightful owner. In short, it is possible to argue that a great variety of policies discussed here have contributed to increased incomes from trade.

The increased competition of two new cattle markets has also had enormous secondary consequences. By breaking the virtual monopsony of the coastal trader, more local Galole have been able to get involved in livestock trading. Consequently, more of the money from such trade is staying in the district and helping to fuel the development of many service industries. The opening of six tea kiosks in Wayu is one example. Another example of increased specialization and division of labor is the purchase by wealthy households of handicrafts that they previously produced for themselves. Similarly, specialized traders in tobacco, *miraa* (a root stem chewed for its amphetamine qualities), and animal skins have developed.

A primary insight of the NIE is that the state can realize economies of scale in the provision and regulation of institutions such as those described earlier, further reducing transaction costs (North 1981). As more economically efficient state institutions reach farther into peripheral areas such as Tana River District, the costs of transaction decline and are shifted from local traders and producers to the state. Consequently, the relative profitability of trade increases, and more actors are pulled into exchange. This was the pattern among the Orma in the 1980s. This transformation is reflected not only in the fact that local income per capita from trading

markets were quarantined because of foot and mouth disease. Had they been open, it is likely that income would have been higher than reported here.

activities more than doubled over the period (see Figure 3.1, Table 3.5), but also in the fact that the more commercial sector of the population, comprising those living in market towns as opposed to nomadic villages, grew from 39 percent to 63 percent of the total. Thus, not only did the percentage of income coming from nonstock sources increase from 26 percent to 48 percent per household, but the absolute number of those involved in substantial wage labor and trade increased by 70 percent as well.

Decentralization of the central government

Another significant change in government policy had some dramatic effects on transportation, information, and other transaction costs in the district during the mid-1980s. The Kenyan government launched a major administrative decentralization initiative in 1983 referred to as District Focus for Development (Government of Kenya 1983).[22] Among other things, this involved upgrading the level of civil servants in all ministries in the rural areas. This was not intended to be an expansion of the civil service, but rather a re-posting of civil servants out of urban areas and into the rural areas where they could be most effective. Among the Orma in 1987, this affected the schools, the dispensary, the district development office, and the veterinary office; indeed, across the entire administration, both the number and the qualifications of civil servants in Tana River District government ministries were increased in the mid-1980s. The mid-1980s brought many new civil servants to Wayu, the center of Galole. For instance, while in 1980 a veterinary officer rarely visited the remote Galole area, in 1987 one was actually permanently posted there. A more qualified health officer was brought in to oversee the local dispensary and two assistants were added to the staff, thus tripling the number of health personnel. The number of schoolteachers increased severalfold over this period, and the adult education program was initiated. The number of administrative police in the area was increased fourfold, thus contributing to greater security in an area continuously plagued by bandit attacks. Significant improvements in roads and bridges were also undertaken.

To some extent, the improved economic circumstances of the Orma can be attributed to increased government expenditures, which have created some employment for the Galole. For example, the few Orma with secondary education are employed as clerks and schoolteachers. The government has also employed Galole on construction and road-building

22 See Chapter 6 for a more detailed account of this program and its affects on the Orma's relations with the state.

projects. However, much of the increase in construction employment can be traced to increased trade and commerce rather than to government building. For example, a local stone quarry in Wayu supplies building stones for construction to the district headquarters. Many poor and some rich households have members who earn considerable incomes there. While some stones are used for government buildings, most are used in the construction of new shops and private residences in the district headquarters.

Although it is not possible to measure the precise contribution of each of the government policies to the economic trends reported here, it seems fair to conclude that on balance they have improved the environment for exchange among the Orma and, in so doing (at least in the 1980s), have led to significant improvements in economic well-being, even for the poorest sector of the population.

Interest rates

As final support for the thesis that the 1980s brought some positive economic changes to the Orma, we can look at interest rates for this period. North (1990: 69) notes that "the level of interest rates in capital markets is perhaps the most evident quantitative dimension of the efficiency of the institutional framework." Interest rates are calculated for this period on the basis of the differential between the price the Orma receive for cattle when they sell them to the shopkeepers from whom they take credit and the price they receive from independent traders who pay them cash. The results are quite dramatic. While in 1980 the shop-keepers paid 631/= on average for a 4.0-year-old head ($n = 18$), the traders paid 1001/=, yielding a difference of 37.0 percent for one season, or the equivalent of 87 percent interest annually.[23] In contrast, in 1987 the shops paid on average 825/= for a 1.7-year-old head ($n = 65$), while the traders paid 874/=, yielding a difference of 5.6 percent, or the equivalent of 12 percent interest per year.[24] This represents an enormous drop in the cost of consumer credit, about which the Orma were themselves quite aware.

The poor have shared a great deal in these savings. This is dramatized by the fact that while in 1980 the poor received 85.3 percent ($n = 17$) of the price received by the rich for stock of equivalent age, in 1987 they received 95.3 percent ($n = 53$). These two changes alone undoubtedly

23 In order to control for age of stock at sale, which of course strongly correlates with price, the trader sales were paired by age with those to the shops.
24 The average age of cattle sold in 1987 had declined dramatically owing to the recent drought of 1985. There is also an increasing tendency for Orma to sell immature cattle to fattening ranches in the south.

account for some of the improvement in income for poor households between 1980 and 1987.

CONCLUSIONS

The longitudinal Orma data for the 1970s and 1980s enable us to see fairly clearly how the transition to increasing commercial production is differentially affecting the population. As noted in the preceding chapter, this process has been well under way through the entire century, but has witnessed especially strong bursts in recent decades. It is definitely clear from the distributional data of the 1970s and 1980s that the relative gap in wealth has increased. The evidence on absolute wealth is not as clear, but it is very likely that absolute wealth declined for poor and middle households, at least during the 1970s. The surprising findings are the numerous indicators of improvement in economic well-being for these poorer households in the 1980s.

All of the data appear to point to increases in scale of livestock production. For example, the wealthiest one-third of the population has increased its household size by 65 percent, thus facilitating the maintenance of larger herds under one management. It is also evident, however, that the economic imperative driving this transformation is rendering poor and middle households far less competitive in livestock production.

Unlike the usual scenario associated with increasing commercialization and proletarianization, here we find that new economic opportunities for the poor and middle households have brought some positive changes in economic well-being. Among these we can cite increasing real income and consumption, more favorable terms of trade, better education and health care, improvement in nutritional status for men, lower interest rates, and less discriminatory pricing policy against poor households. Many of these can be related to government policies such as structural adjustment (as it affects the terms of trade between beef and grain and the demand for Orma beef abroad), policies that reduce transaction costs and therefore increase profits to traders and/or producers, and more effective central government.

Given the commitment to commercial production now evident among the Orma and the obvious movement toward larger scale in livestock production, it is not surprising that pressure is being brought to bear on many Orma institutions – social, political, and economic. Among these, labor relations, property rights in common grazing, and political organization in the form of the council of elders stand out. In the next three chapters I examine each of these institutions in turn to see how the considerable transformations in production and distribution (including power) have precipitated changes in these key institutions.

4

Agency theory: patron–client relations as a form of labor contracting

Both specialization and division of labor are increasing among the Orma. Poor households derive a significant portion of their income from sources other than the sale of their herds. Rich households, in contrast, are increasingly taking advantage of larger economies of scale in livestock production. The effect of these increases in scale on labor relations is the subject of this chapter. While neoclassical economists and Marxists alike would be inclined to predict a movement toward purely contractual wage labor to create these larger economies of scale, we find instead the persistence of more informal methods of increasing the labor force. This chapter draws on a new institutional perspective, principal–agent theory, to explain the persistence of patron–client relations and other forms of labor contracting even in the context of a highly market-oriented economy (for an interesting critique of this use see Bailey 1991).

A consideration of institutional constraints enables us to explain the conditions under which paternalistic relations will be preferred to strict market wage contracting and also to understand the replacement of the former with the latter over time, especially with the introduction and expansion of state institutions. While I am not arguing that this theory explains all aspects of patron–client relations, it can account for many of them, including some that may not at first glance appear to be part of the economic realm.

The particular form of patron–client relationship I shall consider is that between herd owners and their herders.[1] Among the Orma, these relationships exist on a continuum from related individuals who are neighbors and who share herding duties to individuals of absolutely no

---

1 See Beck (1980, 1991) and Bradburd (1980, 1990) for discussions of hired herders among Middle Eastern pastoralists. There are considerable similarities between Beck's observations and those noted here. See Little (1985b) for a discussion of East African hired herders.

relationship who herd for a household on more or less contractual terms. In the past, household imbalances between stock and labor were resolved primarily by coresidence in nomadic camps and common herding and sharing of subsistence production. As sedentarization increased and a larger number of stock had to be kept in cattle camps, such informal relations became more formalized and individualized. Young men from poor families began working away from home and exclusively for their wealthy patrons. These ties were usually of long duration and were reinforced by marriage bonds and terms of endearment. Many such relations still exist among the Orma, but even more specifically, contractual relations have evolved. These may be quite short term and involve more specificity of duties and compensation, even to the point that salaries are contracted per month in cash.[2]

It is in the ability to distinguish and predict the likelihood of one form of contracting over another that the new institutional approach excels (see Alston, Datta, and Nugent 1984: 1122). Assuming that the actual value of the goods and services exchanged is equivalent, neoclassical theory cannot differentiate between a labor relationship based on a pure wage contract and one based on a patron–client relationship. In the latter case, work and rewards may not be clearly contracted in advance and the relationship between parties may be couched in such language as "I treat him like my son; he is no different from my own child; I paid his bridewealth for him, and now I look after his wife and child while he is in the cattle camp." Assuming equivalent values, to the neoclassical economist the patron–client "contract" is identical to the pure wage contract. To the new institutional economist, as to the anthropologist, they are decidedly different.

PATRON–CLIENT RELATIONSHIPS

Foster (1963: 1281) defines patron–client relations as follows:

Patron–client contracts tie people (or people to beings) of significantly different socioeconomic status (or order of power), who exchange different kinds of goods and services. Patron–client contracts are phrased vertically, and they can be thought of as asymmetrical since each partner is quite different from the other in position and obligations.

Patron–client relations represent an enigma for both the economist and the anthropologist. While they almost invariably involve considerable exchanges of goods and services, they do so in the context of a relationship based on strong moral sentiments couched in a language of paternalism

---

2 Very rarely do Galole Orma employ fellow Galole on a cash basis. Commercial ranches and Arab herd owners, however, typically use this form of remuneration.

and voluntarism. These exchanges do not look like market exchanges. This point has rendered them elusive to the economist and has often hindered the anthropologist by obscuring the degree to which they *are* fundamentally economic relationships.

Among those writing on patron–client relations, there are considerable differences of opinion over who, if anyone, is perceived to be the net beneficiary in the exchange. Those who emphasize the benefits to the patron focus on the "exploitative" aspects of the relationship; those who focus on the benefits to the client characterize the exchange as "generalized" (see Eisenstadt and Roniger's typology, 1984: 33); and those who view the exchange as a market equilibrium are associated with an "individual exchange" perspective.

Those characterizing patron–client relations as exploitative (Leeds 1974; Li Causi 1975; Michie 1981) consider the patron to be in substantial, if not complete, control over the terms of the relationship, which work to the detriment of the client and into which he or she may need to be coerced. The patron is analogous to a monopolist who takes advantage of the client in an unfair exchange. Alternatively (Li Causi 1975), the relationship is assumed to exist merely to mask class exploitation.

Those subscribing to the "generalized exchange" model (Eisenstadt and Roniger 1984; Mauss 1967; Sahlins 1972; Scott 1976) emphasize the benefit that accrues to the client in the relationship. For Scott (1976), the utility is a guaranteed subsistence, and the beneficial nature of the relationship from the point of view of the client is captured in the title of his book, *The Moral Economy.*[3] Eisenstadt and Roniger (1984) also emphasize the beneficial aspects of the relationship for the client, but they see the benefits chiefly in psychosocial terms; that is, the client is made more secure by the relationship in an otherwise insecure world. Clientage is beneficial because it relieves tension.

Finally, there are those who view the relationship as one of individualized exchange, following Blau (1964) and Homans (1961). These theorists are inclined to see the relationship between patrons and clients as one of market equilibrium in terms of the goods and services exchanged.

While the new institutional approach has more in common with this last position than with either of the other two, the individualized exchange approach suffers from the same failings as pure neoclassical economics. One must ask the obvious question: If the relationship is merely one of labor supply and demand, why is it not transacted in more "tidy" contractual terms? Why must ritualized kinship and moral sentiments

---

3 To Scott, a moral economy is one in which there is an ethos guaranteeing minimum subsistence to all members of society.

enter into the transaction? For what reason does this form of contractual relationship exist at all, when the market could conceivably handle the exchange in an impersonal, clear-cut manner, as indeed does better characterize some Orma herding relations?

The work of new institutional economists on principal–agent theory and contractual choice between, for example, sharecropping and wage labor sheds light on this problem.

TRANSACTION COSTS AND AGENCY THEORY

Agency theory (Alston 1981; Alston and Higgs 1982; Fama 1980; Fama and Jensen 1983a, 1983b) is a specific application of transaction cost analysis and forms a major field of study for new institutional economists. Agency costs arise as the division of labor intensifies in a hierarchical nature. Whenever an individual (identified in the literature as a "principal") engages another individual (identified as an "agent"), to whom some decision-making authority is granted, a potential agency problem exists (Jensen and Meckling 1976: 308). Agency costs stem from the fact that the interests of principals and their agents may diverge and consequently there are transaction costs for the principal involved in monitoring the behavior of the agent. Jensen and Meckling (1976: 308) put it this way:

If both parties to the relationship are utility maximizers there is good reason to believe that the agent will not always act in the best interests of the principal. The *principal* can limit divergences from his interest by establishing appropriate incentives for the agent and by incurring monitoring costs designed to limit the aberrant activities of the agent.

Agency theory has also been used to examine contractual choice between wage labor and sharecropping in agrarian societies (Alston et al. 1984). In their study of agrarian contracting in the southern United States, Alston et al. (1984) argue that fixed-rent and sharecrop contracts reduce the need for direct supervision of labor, and it is therefore not surprising that such contracts are preferred to wage contracts by those farmers who have fewer supervisors (Alston and Higgs 1982: 351).

Alston and Ferrie (1985, 1989) have used the insights of agency theory to explain paternalistic relations in southern U.S. agriculture. Similarly, my intent in this chapter is to treat the patron–client relationship as a special form of contractual relationship that reduces agency costs to the principal. Further, I wish to speculate on the conditions under which one might find this relationship rather than some other form of contract and, by so doing, provide an explanation for the frequently noted decline in patron–client relationships with incorporation into the institutional structure of modern nation-states (see Michie 1981 for a review of this literature).

GALOLE HERDING RELATIONSHIPS

Almost all East African pastoralists make extensive use of cattle camps. These camps afford ideal conditions for herd mobility in order to maximize access to grazing and water resources. Because the cattle camps are unencumbered by household members, including the elderly and infirm, and are left in the care of agile young men who often travel with nothing more than a spear, milking gourd, and hide for sleeping, their mobility is uninhibited. The stock are also far out of the control of the head of the household, who often is the owner of the majority of the herd; thus a potential agency problem exists. Cattle camps among the Orma (as among most East African pastoralists) easily roam 100 miles from the residential village, sometimes moving daily. Supervision is difficult, and there is an inevitable conflict of interest between the absentee herd owner (the principal) and the on-site, day-to-day decision maker, the herder (or agent). Indeed, this problem is a favorite subject of discussion among Orma elders, who spend endless hours developing strategies to overcome this problem.

Orma use of cattle camps is consistent with the practice of many other East African pastoral societies.[4] Generally, herds are broken into the milking herd, which is kept at the primary residence (whether sedentary or nomadic), and the *ureni* herd, or the cattle camp, consisting of immatures, dry female stock, steers, bulls, and milking stock for the use of herders in the cattle camp.[5] Given that 60 percent to 100 percent of a household's livestock may be kept at these remote cattle camps, the risk to the household's economic resources is potentially enormous.

One former herder from the cattle camps, who herded for his extremely rich father, described the training and practice of herders this way:

In the old days when there was no school, a ten year old could go [to the cattle camps]. They did no work, but learned everything by practice – cleaning the gourds, herding calves, and walking with big boys. By the age of fifteen they could do everything if they were good, even carry a calf from the bush. By the time they were twenty they could start scouting, take responsibility, and make

4 The Orma, however, are more sedentary than most pastoralists. Consequently, the grazing conditions around permanent settlements are worse, making it necessary for more animals to be kept in cattle camps.
5 Owing to extreme overgrazing in large settled communities, by 1987 the Orma were having to send even their milking stock to cattle camps. The Orma also keep separate camps for sheep and goats. Most of the discussion related to cattle camps can be assumed to apply as well to sheep and goat camps.

decisions. Each cattle camp has its head and all cattle camps that stay together have one head over all. The head of all cattle camps [that stay together] is usually the eldest boy or the most experienced.

The agency problem among Galole herders

Cattle herding under the conditions that pertain in East Africa is a risky venture. Common dangers that befall Orma herds but can be mitigated by careful husbandry are the following: weight loss or death due to drought conditions or failure to move stock to the best grazing areas, weakening of calves due to overmilking, failure to vaccinate stock against endemic diseases, attack by wild animals (especially lions and wild dogs), loss of stock in thick bush, attacks on stock by farmers if cattle are allowed to encroach on farms, exposure to disease if herders take stock into tsetse-fly-infested areas, and death following the first rains after a drought, when the stock are in a weakened condition and easily get stuck in the mud.

While careful husbandry can reduce these risks, it is hard work indeed. As has been pointed out to me on numerous occasions by herd owners, it is not easy to lift a 600-pound steer out of the mud. It is backbreaking work and takes the effort of at least four men with poles to support the underbelly of the animal as it is righted. Herd owners use this example to dramatize the difference between the care a herd owner would provide for his own animals and that commonly provided by a hired herder. They maintain that in the absence of the herd owner, or at least his son, a hired laborer would not make the effort to lift stock stuck in the mud, as happened to a large number of weakened stock in both 1975 and 1985, following the first rains after a severe drought. There is ample evidence among the Orma that a principal–agent problem exists in the cattle camps.

Solutions to the agency problem

Given the great risks involved, one would expect pastoralists to be extremely reluctant to engage hired laborers. Indeed, Sperling (1984, 1987) finds that the Samburu avoid this practice for precisely this reason. The Samburu relieve labor shortages over the long term by practicing polygyny (thereby producing their own labor force) and, over the short term, by borrowing the children of close relatives for years at a time or by herding cooperatively with other members of their settlement. The Orma also engage in all of these practices.

We see in Table 4.1, in fact, that the large increase in household size between 1979 and 1987 for rich households (from 10.9 to 15.5 based

Table 4.1. *Labor transfers for market households over time by wealth of household, 1979 and 1987*

	Poor	Middle	Rich	Total
1979				
Number of households	32	22	29	83
Cattle equiv. per household	9.6	41.4	140.3	63.7
Household size (owners)[a]	9.4	9.2	10.9	9.9
Household size (residents)[b]	8.4	9.3	13.7	10.5
Hired herders per household	0.0	0.1	1.2	0.4
Immigrants per household[c]	0.4	0.6	3.0	1.4
Emigrants per household[d]	1.4	0.6	0.3	0.8
Net immigrants[e]	-1.0	+0.1	+2.8	+0.6
1987				
Number of households	53	35	31	119
Cattle equiv. per household	6.8	19.8	140.0	45.3
Household size (owners)	9.4	10.1	15.5	11.2
Household size (residents)	7.6	9.7	17.9	10.9
Hired herders per household	0.0	0.0	1.1	0.3
Immigrants per household	0.4	1.3	4.2	1.7
Emigrants per household	2.3	1.7	1.7	2.0
Net immigrants	-1.9	-0.4	+2.5	-0.3

[a] In most analyses in this book, "household size" refers to those who share in "ownership" of the herd, or those who were born or married into the household and continue to live off the products of the herd. Excluded are those who have left the household to establish independent households or to reside as members of another household and retain no claims to patrimony in the herd (this includes independent married sons and brothers, as well as married daughters and sisters). Also excluded are hired laborers who have no "ownership" interest in the herd and other "immigrants" to the household such as foster children, who will not have claims to the herd for patrimony. This definition closely parallels that used by the Orma themselves. See Netting et al. (1984) for a comprehensive discussion of the problems associated with defining households.
[b] Unlike the "ownership" definition of household, these figures refer to the population that actually resides in the household or one of its satellites—nomadic camp, cattle camp, or sheep and goat camp.
[c] Immigrants to the household are those who reside with the household (see note b) but who do not qualify as "owners" (see note a).
[d] Emigrants from the household are those who are "owners" within the household but reside away from the household.
[e] Due to rounding, net immigrants is not exactly equal to immigrants less emigrants.

on ownership and from 13.7 to 17.9 based on residence) was achieved by increasing the size of the owner unit, that is, those with rights to the herd, rather than by taking in more nonowner residents (such as foster children and hired herders).[6] An increase in the size of the ownership household can be achieved not only if fertility and polygyny rates are higher, but also if fewer sons split off and more joint families stay together on the death of the father. Thus the increase in the number of owners in rich households (4.6) actually exceeds the increase in the size of rich resident households (4.2); net immigration to rich households by "non-owners" actually declined slightly (0.4).

Many Orma households still find themselves in need of additional labor. This can be explained in part by the fact that the Orma are more sedentary than most East African pastoralists; by 1987 fully 63 percent of households were permanently settled in the Galole area. Sedentarization requires a greater dependence on the use of cattle camps because settled villages afford far inferior grazing conditions than do nomadic villages and much more stock (often even milking stock) must be kept in the cattle camps, often for far longer periods of the year. Also, there may be greater inequality in the distribution of wealth among the Orma than among most other East African pastoralists, thus creating a greater labor shortage in the wealthiest households. Among the wealthy Orma, a high portion of young men are in school, are employed with cash incomes, marry early and settle down in permanent villages, or are kept out of the cattle camps by their mothers, who now often prefer to have their sons near them rather than in the distant cattle camps (see Ensminger 1987, 1991).

The result is that the wealthiest one-third of market households employed on average 1.2 hired laborers in 1979 and 1.1 per household in 1987 (see Table 4.1), about 80 percent of whom herded in the stock camps. Of the hired herders in 1979, 46 percent were relatives (sister's sons and daughter's sons together make up almost half of this group). Significantly, 54 percent of hired herders had no relationship whatsoever to the household.[7] It should be noted, however, that the Orma still place an exceedingly high premium on having at least one close relative of the family in the cattle camp. This should preferably be a son, but at the very least a sister's or daughter's son, who can act as a supervisor. One elder described the need for relatives in the cattle camp this way:

We cannot depend only on hired labor. Even if you have no son old enough to be in the cattle camp, your own son, no matter how young he is, must be there.

6 See Netting et al. (1989) for another African case of increased household size in response to economic incentives favoring larger economies of scale.
7 These ratios did not change significantly by 1987.

He sends information even if he cannot order around the others. Every household must have one son in the cattle camp. If people don't have children they must get someone to whom they are related – a brother's son or sister's son. But these ones must be supervised. You need counterchecking.

In agreement with Sperling's report (1984, 1987) of Samburu attitudes, the Orma believe that a close relative is more trustworthy as a herder than is a nonrelative. Given the extent of Orma dependence on hired labor, it appears that there are not always enough competent relatives available. It is for this reason, I would argue, that they develop and nurture paternalistic relationships even with youths to whom they may have no kin relation.

The usual herder contract among the Orma stipulates that the herder will receive food, clothing, and one female head of stock per year. These conditions are negotiated at the outset, but really make up only the minimal wage contract. Employers make use of all sorts of incentives to sweeten the arrangement if the herder is perceived to be doing a good job. For example, in any given year an employer will commonly make gifts of clothing above and beyond the norm, they may be generous in their gifts to the youth's parents, they may allow the herder to pick the head of stock he will receive as annual payment, and they may give a second animal per year in the form of Muslim alms (*zakat*).[8]

The ultimate gesture of a herd owner is to pay the man's bridewealth after many years of loyal service. If the herder remains employed after the marriage, the owner will extend his care to the herder's wife and children. Long before this point is reached, the relationship between owner and herder will clearly have made the transition to one resembling that between father and son. The Orma talk fondly of such relationships in paternalistic terms, and most wealthy households can point to two or three individuals for whom they have paid bridewealth in the past decade or so.

In the following account, an elder who is a long-term employer of hired laborers describes how one knows who the good laborers are and, having found them, how one shapes and rewards their behavior with incentives:

If [a hired herder] is bad he is just bad natured. The good ones are good natured. The bad ones cannot be made good. Such people you pay and get rid of. If he has not completed 12 months he gets no pay and is fired.

To best train boys who will herd for you, you should not give them permission to come to the [sedentary] village all the time. If they get used to the village they will be no good. Sometimes you see them come to the village when they aren't

---

8 See Scott (1985: 193), who reports a similar use of *zakat* to induce better performance among wage laborers.

supposed to be here. As soon as he arrives the employer begins to fight with him. The boy should stay only one night here. If you treat them like this they will be afraid and won't come back here. If according to you he was not angry with you for sending him back, then you reward him. These are the ones you want – the ones who are respectful and don't get angry with you. To reward him you give him clothes. You allow him to select his own cows for his salary (this makes him very happy because he knows the best cattle). Sometimes people even employ married laborers. With these ones you can take care of the family. Even our own children can go to the cattle camp after they marry. The employer must look well after the family while the boy is in the cattle camp or he will refuse to go. The family must be given enough milk and food.

Now the ones who herd well get a salary of 1 cow as well as 1 cow for *zakat* [Muslim alms]. Instead of giving *zakat* to someone else, the herd owner gives it to the boys in the cattle camp. I myself paid the bridewealth of two boys who herded well for me in the cattle camp. Ali Mohamed [a pseudonym] worked 5 years and married Galole Shure's [pseudonym] daughter. After he married he stayed with me another 6 years. I don't even remember how much I have paid to him. I even gave bridewealth from my own daughters to that man. I have never met the parents of that boy; he is a Wardei [descendant of an Orma who was captured by the Somali during the wars of the 1860s], but he did good work. All the boys doing well in the cattle camp get similar treatment from people. It is not only me. All the other people have ways of helping them. Those who don't work well don't get this treatment.

The costs to a herd owner of not finding good workers for the cattle camp are legendary. In the following account an elder describes the problems associated with long-distance management:

The ones doing the best work in the cattle camps are in their parents' camps and not herding for pay. Those are their cattle. The employees – there are so many things they don't do. First, they don't want to herd. There are young boys who are supposed to help them and they leave all the work to the young boys. The hired herders just pass the time and demand to be paid. They may leave a child to herd 7 or 8 days and give them no rest for even a day. There are so many like this these days. Second, they don't check the cattle when they arrive at the end of the day – they don't look for lost cattle. Third, they may leave the cattle camp and go visit a nearby village and say they are looking for a lost cow, but come back and say they couldn't find it. If cattle are lost they must be found immediately or they will never be found. So the owner loses his cow. Nowadays, people have noticed. If someone has lost a cow the boy won't get paid. This is the answer. Others decide to pay the salary even if the herder has lost a cow, but then they fire the boy. Others tell the boy to find the cow and if he does, then he will be paid. Then sometimes the boy goes and never comes back. These are the problems. Not everyone is like this. Some who herd for pay do a very good job. The owners trust them.

It is, of course, difficult to evaluate whether the respect for elders and the quality of herding are actually on the decline, as elders universally assert. While one has the distinct impression that these elders' grandfathers had the same complaints about *them* in their youth, one should not dismiss such complaints out of hand. Even herders from the cattle camps, though they would never admit to not working as hard as previous generations, did admit that they started in the cattle camps at an older age (due to schooling, among other things) and therefore had less knowledge than previous generations. They admitted to being more dependent on the elders for critical decision making regarding herd movements and strategies than was the case in the past. It is entirely possible that the employment prospects that have resulted from economic growth in the area have given young men a more cavalier attitude toward such grueling work and lessened their deference to their elders. As one elder put it, "These young men think that even if all the cattle die they can make a living for themselves."

It is exactly these problems that perpetuate the paternalistic nature of some herding relationships, and the increased compensation that goes with them. For example, one family has managed to maintain such relationships across generations. In this case, the former hired herder still lives next to the man for whom he herded, even though the former herder is now a man in his fifties of modest independent means with three wives. This hired herder not only had his bridewealth paid for him, but was also sent on the hajj. His own sons now herd for the wealthy elder, as their father did before them.

The conversion of Orma wage employment into a paternalistic relationship provides numerous benefits to both sides of the exchange. From the point of view of the patron, the arrangement ensures the quality of herding that is necessary to avoid potentially huge losses due to negligence. The fact that the "actual wage," as opposed to the "contracted wage," is not determined until after the quality of herding can be properly evaluated – which may ultimately take years – works considerably to the advantage of the herd owner and significantly reduces agency costs. In this way the owner is able to tailor the wage to the actual performance of the herder.

Meanwhile, the herder is protected from default by the owner because the latter has a reputation to protect. If it is perceived that an owner treated a herder unjustly – for example, if his loyal performance warranted the payment of his bridewealth, but the owner did not so volunteer – the owner will have tremendous difficulty attracting high-quality herders in the future. As one elder put it, "The herd boys know who the 'bad' old men are."

One notorious example concerns a wealthy elderly man whom many Orma considered disagreeable. He was known to be antisocial and remained nomadic in part because of his inability to get along with people. During the drought, the herders who worked for him sold some of his cattle and ran off with the money – leaving Orma territory completely. Ordinarily, repercussions would have followed – members of the lineages of the young men would have felt compelled to repay the stolen stock in order to maintain the good name of the family. Normal practice would have dictated that they take corporate responsibility.[9] In this case there was no such sentiment. Public opinion sided with the herders; they were judged (even by the elders) to have been justified because they had been treated so poorly by the old man.

Although the small sample sizes make it impossible to confirm this quantitatively, the elders were convinced that other "scrooges" also fared extremely poorly during the drought. The elders believe that the cattle of these men died in larger numbers out of neglect, and many were in effect stolen by hired herders. Not coincidentally, three elders who are highly respected, are considered good managers, and have reputations for treating their hired herders exceptionally well fared far better in the drought. As one elder put it:

The drought was what gave the boys the chance to cheat. The cattle left this area. People here had to be taking care of their families here [in the permanent village]. Usually we frequently visit the cattle camp – that helps a lot. People can check and see if a cow is missing. There is less supervision during a drought.[10]

Because the cattle were so far removed from their owners, many herders had the opportunity to settle the score, so to speak, with the "bad" old men. The prospects of employment outside the district also meant that the young men could violate accepted behavior with impunity, as long as they had no intention of returning to Tana River District.

Such behavior did not characterize the vast majority of hired herders, for whom the hope of future rewards, although not specifically negotiated, provided a clear incentive to perform well in herding activities in the absence of direct supervision. Over the long haul, it is obvious from milk yields whether cattle have been well cared for in the camps; it is also apparent whether morbidity and mortality of the stock are within the bounds expected, given existing conditions.

For a herder who performs up to standard, the rewards in the form of additional payments may well exceed the equivalent of three or four times the standard herding contract of one cow per year. In addition, the herder receives many benefits from the patron that are harder to quantify. He may have privileged access to information, both political

9 As we shall see in Chapter 6, such responsibility is also on the decline for other reasons.
10 In the 1985 drought the cattle had to move exceptionally long distances from Galole permanent villages. This made monitoring extremely difficult, far more so than had been the case in the 1975 drought.

and concerning livestock trading, he may be extended credit, and he may enjoy other privileges associated with the status afforded elites in the society – such as better dress, better nutrition, and access to better health care. Also, his poor relations, especially his mother and father, will have someone to whom they can turn in times of need.

Finally, the terminology used to characterize these relationships, something close to "father–son" relations, undoubtedly has some impact on the normative behavior both parties bring to the exchange. To the extent that each party expects the other to act as if in the closest of lineal relations, there are assumptions about responsibility, which may in practice turn out to be more "real" than "fictive," not merely because both sides stand to gain economically from the relationship, but because both sides are taken in by the ideology.

Up to this point, I have discussed only the question of how agency costs are reduced through the use of paternalistic labor relations rather than pure market wage contracting. Supervisors, of course, also reduce agency costs, and whenever possible the Orma like to have at least one son in the cattle camp. The head of the household and other sons may also visit the camps regularly to monitor activities there.[11] It is a straightforward extension to predict that those households with fewer supervisors in the cattle camps (see Alston and Higgs 1982) will tend to favor more paternalistic relationships with their herders over the "cheaper," but less reliable pure wage contracts. In this sense, therefore, the patronage arrangement creates a multitiered labor market. Indeed, as already noted, the cattle camps have always recognized a hierarchy of authority, with each camp having a leader and each group of camps an overall leader. Thus the variable wage rate allows for compensation to reflect productivity and responsibility, while wages nominally appear to be equal, since only one cow per year is contracted in advance for all hired herders. The "client-sons" become supervisors in much the same way as do true sons.

THE AGENCY PROBLEM AND THE STATE

What changes can we expect in labor relations if state institutions, as they reach farther into the periphery of developing nations, gradually reduce transaction costs, including those involved in the agency problem? The Orma are well aware that in the most recent drought (1984–5) some of their herders in the cattle camps sold a large number of livestock and claimed that they had died from the drought. Only one of these individuals was actually prosecuted; others guilty of serious infractions either

---

11 It is reported that such supervisory trips to the cattle camps by family members have increased since the drought.

ran away from the territory permanently or were forgiven. If legal institutions became sufficiently developed to provide a greater deterrent to future transgressions of this sort, however, we would predict a decline in this particular agency cost. Similarly, movements currently under way to have chiefs verify the ownership of cattle before sale could close another avenue of deceit. The development of basic infrastructure such as roads and telecommunications also reduces agency costs by lowering the costs of monitoring labor in the cattle camps. Any technology that facilitates travel and the conveyance of information enables owners to monitor herders more easily. Finally, veterinary advances that improve the health and reduce the vulnerability of livestock to disease lower the level of vigilance necessary in herding and thereby reduce the total losses associated with agency costs.

All of the preceding examples give a hint of the direction in which developments may be moving in East African pastoralism. Each reduction in agency costs lessens the need for paternalism in herding contracts. Under these conditions, one would predict that these developments would lead to a gradual replacement of paternalistic relationships with more straightforward wage contracts.

It has been widely reported in the literature that patron–client relationships break down with the introduction of state institutions (see Michie 1981 for a review of this literature). If state institutions offer some efficiencies over previous institutions, and thereby decrease transaction costs generally and agency costs specifically, a decline in paternalism is perfectly consistent with the theory presented here. The data from the Orma indicate that agency costs have not yet been reduced to the extent that patron–client relations can be abandoned.

The change likely to reduce agency costs most significantly would be a decrease in the distance between cattle camps and permanent villages. To achieve this, the large herd owners would have to effect a change in property rights. This would necessitate the creation of large territories close to the permanent villages for the exclusive use of villagers' cattle camps. As we shall see in the next chapter, such a dismantling of the commons is already under way. High agency costs, which so far perpetuate patron–client relations, are one reason for the lobby to hasten this process.

5

Property rights: dismantling the commons

The economic growth documented in Chapters 2 and 3 has brought dramatic changes in Orma property rights.[1] In the past, Ormaland was owned communally. Sedentarization and other pressures associated with economic growth have now eroded the viability of the commons.[2] Although in the past the commons were regulated to prevent overgrazing, the Orma have recently had less success in this regard. Today, various groups are staking claims to large portions of that land for their exclusive use. The roots of these changes in property rights lie in the economic and political changes brought on by economic growth.

Economic growth has increased the gains from dismantling the commons while also making it harder to reach agreement about how to distribute those gains. Sedentarization has increased the costs of maintaining common grazing, and growing economic diversification within

---

1 This chapter is based roughly on a paper written with Andrew Rutten (Ensminger and Rutten 1991). I wish to acknowledge the major contribution Andrew Rutten has made to my thinking on the issues addressed in this chapter. He, of course, bears no responsibility for the liberties I have taken in revising our earlier work.

2 Economic growth is defined here as change in the total output of society, regardless of the distribution.

   Another hypothesis for many of the changes described in this chapter is that population pressure, rather than economic growth, has been the driving force. Indeed, population pressure can lead to many of the same changes in property rights noted here, and for many of the same intermediate reasons (e.g., increasing land values). In this particular case, however, a strong argument can be made that economic growth in itself accounts for much of the change. The 1980 human population for the Galole Orma area under study was approximately 2,232, while the 1987 population was approximately 2,414, representing an increase of only 8.2% over seven years. Population growth was greater than this, however, and resulted in a net emigration to nearby large towns. The livestock population is actually the more significant variable, and this population declined over the period from 1980 to 1987 (by approximately 24%) due to the severe drought of the mid-1980s.

the society has created interest groups that want very different property rights. At the same time, the replacement of local government by national government has changed the balance of power within, as well as among, groups and made available third-party enforcement. Technology, transportation, and telecommunications have also reduced the transaction costs of monitoring and enforcing more exclusive rights.

The Orma, like most African pastoralists, developed a complex system of property rights. Land tenure consisted of shared grazing open to the entire ethnic group. Until recent times, overgrazing was prevented by territorial expansion and control over access to water. Unlike grazing land, wells, which were redug seasonally at select locations in dry riverbeds, were not owned in common, but by the person who first dug the spot and his patrilineal descendants. Without access to water, common grazing land was unusable. As the Orma began to settle, these controls became insufficient and the Orma had to develop new methods of preventing the overuse of land, which they did by institutionalizing restrictions on access to the commons near sedentary villages. These institutions functioned quite effectively in the absence of third-party enforcement until the mid-1980s.

By the mid-1980s, the broad support for these institutions began to break down owing to the diverging interests of some commercially oriented sedentary livestock producers and others (cf. Johnson and Libecap 1982; Libecap 1989). This trend was compounded by other groups' pressure on Ormaland. The more sedentary producers have been aided by their ability to use the national government's policies in favor of sedentarization to enforce more restrictive property rights against the more nomadic subsistence-oriented producers. The result has been a gradual dismantling of the commons to the benefit of the sedentary producers.

THE THEORY OF PROPERTY RIGHTS

The expansive literature on property rights developed as part of the NIE highlights many of the key issues in the Orma case. Libecap (1989: 1) defines property rights as follows:

Property rights are the social institutions that define or delimit the range of privileges granted to individuals to specific assets, such as parcels of land or water. . . . Property rights institutions range from formal arrangements, including constitutional provisions, statutes, and judicial rulings, to informal conventions and customs regarding the allocations and use of property. Such institutions critically affect decision making regarding resource use and, hence, affect economic behavior and performance. By allocating decision-making authority, they also determine who are the economic actors in a system and define the distribution of wealth in a society.

Property rights

New institutional economists have argued that effective property rights are essential to economic success (North and Thomas 1973). When property rights are not completely specified or enforced, people may be giving up gains from cooperation. But contrary to the assumption of many economists, this does not mean that incomplete property rights (e.g., commons) need be irrational. There are good reasons why property rights are not always perfectly specified or enforced (Barzel 1989). Most important, property rights may be incomplete because the transaction costs of specifying, monitoring, and enforcing them are high. Goods have many characteristics; to be complete, rights would have to be established and enforced over every valuable characteristic of a good. Even in the most developed societies this does not occur, nor would it make economic sense. It is costly not only to determine which goods are valuable enough to warrant exclusionary rights, but also to police compliance and punish offenders. Because of these transaction costs, property rights are never completely specified and enforced; the degree to which they are depends a great deal on the forgone losses of not restricting access, as well as the effectiveness of informal controls and the economies of scale provided by state or private monitoring and enforcement.

Some of the assumptions of new institutionalists are similar to those of proponents of the "tragedy of the commons" (Hardin 1968; Hardin and Baden 1977). In his 1968 article, Garrett Hardin suggested that common ownership carries with it the threat of the "tragedy of the commons," for it is in the interest of each producer to use as much of the common resource as possible, with no concern for the long-term effects on that resource. Thus in the case of pastoralists, the coupling of private ownership of livestock with common ownership of land gives each herder an incentive to overgraze the land and ultimately leads to environmental degradation. Yet the historical viability of pastoralism and any number of common resources elsewhere indicates that the "tragedy" is not inevitable. People are capable of changing institutions as need arises.[3]

As a common resource begins to deteriorate, perhaps through population growth, people have an increasing incentive to incur the costs of restructuring their property rights. Examples of such restructuring abound in the literature: Netting (1972, 1976, 1982) observed that Swiss meadows were protected by the development of informal monitoring systems; Acheson (1975) found the development of de facto property rights in fishing grounds to prevent the overfishing of Maine lobsters; Blomquist and Ostrom (1985) and Ostrom (1990) reported on a solution to a common-pool problem involving an underground water basin in Los

3 Hardin does, in fact, acknowledge this possibility.

Angeles County; and Behnke (1985) described a case of spontaneous range enclosure in Sudan analogous to the situation described here.[4]

NIE theory can reconcile the economic assumption that incentives are important with the empirical observations of anthropologists that common property is not necessarily problematic. Economists and other tragedy theorists see commons as economically undesirable, if not downright disastrous, because they fail to model all of the constraining resources (such as water) and do not take account of the transaction costs involved in alternative forms of ownership.

Some property rights analysts (Demsetz 1967; cf. Williamson 1985 on contracts) also make the assumption that competition forces property rights to change in the direction that enhances economic growth. Like others (see Binger and Hoffman 1989; North 1981, 1990), I argue that the role of politics and ideology may well set a different trajectory for change in property rights. Political choices depend on the political structure, which determines the division of political power; how choices are made can determine which choices are made (Riker 1980, 1986). Political power may allow some to create property rights that protect monopolies and diminish overall economic performance (Bates 1981). Alternatively, people's preferences (stemming from their ideology regarding the just distribution of rewards in society) may preclude property rights that allocate property to those best able to maximize yields. Politics and ideology are precisely why institutional change does not necessarily enhance economic performance. The question of the economic desirability of different property rights is complex, however, because property rights that distribute rewards more equitably may in fact lead to greater output than those that appear in the absence of transaction costs to maximize net output. Equality increases output when the greater legitimacy afforded by a more equitable distribution reduces "cheating" sufficiently that the overall performance is greater. For such reduction to occur, the savings in transaction costs (from reduced negotiating, monitoring, and enforcing) must exceed the losses in underutilized potential. Ideology greatly affects economic performance in the property rights domain, as elsewhere.

The new institutional approach is especially useful for analyzing the path of institutional change. For example, it enables us to explain why common property systems worked so well in the past but are now giving way to alternatives. A new institutional analysis goes a long way toward explaining the nature and timing of these institutional changes.

---

4 For more recent anthropological examples of commons situations see Acheson (1988), Baxter and Hogg (1990), Feeny, Berkes, McCay, and Acheson (1990), McCabe (1990), and McCay and Acheson (1987).

Property rights

WHY PROPERTY RIGHTS CHANGE

Libecap (1989: 16), following Demsetz (1967: 350), identifies four factors that motivate individuals to contract to change property rights: shifts in relative prices, changes in production and enforcement technology, shifts in political parameters, and changes in preferences. In the Orma case we see evidence of each of these motivations. Economic growth caused a change in relative prices; better roads, telecommunications, and transportation allowed for better monitoring and enforcement of boundaries; the greater presence of external pressure and the Kenyan state dramatically transformed the political environment; and quite possibly, all of these factors together put pressure on existing ideologies (and preferences) concerning fair distribution of property.

Since property rights must be tailored to particular economic circumstances, changes in circumstances will change their effectiveness. Such changes provide an incentive to some to change property rights. For example, an increase in the relative price of beef may raise the costs of overgrazing associated with a commons because the forgone earnings from the lost production have increased. Similarly, increasing population pressure increases the value of land and therefore the costs of land degradation.

Changes in the technology or institutions of monitoring and enforcement, such as roads, transportation, and courts, may also provide incentives to change property rights by altering the transaction costs. Thus where a lack of roads once made it impossible to monitor exclusionary property rights in land, better infrastructure may significantly reduce the costs and open privatization as an alternative to common tenure. Similarly, in the absence of courts to punish offenders, the enforcement of restrictions on access might not have been possible.

Even in the absence of changes in relative prices or the technology of enforcement, a change in political institutions may alter the balance of power in the society such that an interest group succeeds in making property rights more beneficial to themselves. Such motivations and consequences are, of course, completely independent of the effects on economic performance for the society as a whole.

Politics is the process by which the desires of the members of the group are turned into collective choices. The political structure determines how much influence each member has over the outcome. Political problems occur only if there is disagreement among individuals over policy; when everyone agrees, the collective choice is obvious. Changing property rights is likely to cause extensive disagreement. Property rights are never neutral in their economic effects, and changing them creates winners and losers. Inevitably, there will almost always be disagreement over which property rights ought to be chosen. As we shall see in the Orma case, the issue of property rights is so critical that it may even have propelled a change in the political structure.

Because the process of changing property rights is inherently political, property rights do not automatically adjust to changing economic circumstances. To understand why they do not adjust spontaneously nor necessarily facilitate economic performance, it is necessary to examine how economic growth changes both the effectiveness and adaptability of property rights.

Economic growth decreases the capacity of the political system to resolve conflicts over property rights in a variety of ways. Increasing specialization and division of labor bring with them increasing economic differentiation, with each group potentially wanting the property rights that favor them. Growth also creates winners and losers. Losers may turn to the political system to reverse their losses rather than revamp their economic strategies to adapt to the new conditions. They may even find ideological backing, for theirs is a plea to return to a previous status quo, which may still be supported by the prevailing ideology.

Growth changes the political structure as well. Especially in developing nations, one change is the expansion of national government at the expense of local government. With improvements in transportation and communication, national governments have been able to increase the scope of their authority. The coalitions that control national politics are often very different from those controlling local governments.

The economics and politics of property rights say nothing about what property rights people want. The economist's usual assumption is that people will want those property rights that maximize net output. Otherwise, the reasoning goes, people will be forgoing gains; capturing these gains will provide a powerful incentive for the restructuring of property rights. This argument ignores the role of ideology in determining property rights.

Ideology shapes preferences over property rights by allowing the possibility that people consider more than their own narrow gains when evaluating different systems of rights. In particular, people may be interested in ensuring that economic rewards are distributed fairly within society.

What are we to conclude from this? The complexity of the world makes it hard to design property rights that promote economic performance while fulfilling societally desirable dictates regarding distribution. Because they are costly to negotiate, monitor, and enforce, it is likely that property rights will not be complete, but will focus on a few valued characteristics where compliance is easily enforced. Such shortcuts are particularly sensitive to changes in the relative cost of not complying with the restrictions on those characteristics. When property rights, for whatever reason, result in large economic losses, the losses create an incentive to change them. Whether and how these property rights are changed will depend not only on the economic incentives, but on the political structure and ideological perspectives. Each of these theoretical points comes into play in the complex process of changing property rights currently under way among the Orma.

THE HISTORICAL ORMA SOLUTION TO THE COMMONS PROBLEM

Although the limited historical accounts of the Orma that exist for the past few centuries provide few precise details of land tenure practices, there is every reason to believe that land was held in common and stock owned individually, as was the case among most East African pastoral groups until recent decades.

Given the arid ecology and relatively low population density of pastoral lands, common property makes economic sense. These regions are characterized by erratic and unevenly distributed rainfall. Climatic conditions demand large areas of land to support livestock. Common property eliminates the large expenses that would be incurred to monitor and enforce private rights to the huge parcels of land necessitated by the ecology. These benefits do not explain how traditional systems avoided the tragedy of the commons, nor why some of them are now succumbing to the tragedy phenomenon. What is needed is a model of common property that explains when common property will be tragic and when it will not (see Barzel 1989).

From the earliest accounts, it appears that the Orma relied on military expansion to reduce overcrowding of commonly held grazing land. In the absence of shortage, which continual expansion afforded, no commons problem existed. The Orma were, of course, not alone among pastoralists in adopting this strategy. Among others, the Somali and the Maasai were known to be expanding their territories at the time of the British pacification efforts in the late nineteenth century. In fact, these three groups eventually met in military adventures over Orma territory.

Until the 1860s, the Orma were exceptionally successful militarily. Although originally from Ethiopia, the Oromo expansion beginning in the 1500s made it as far as northern Tanzania, all in less than a century. Their fierce military posture also discouraged attempts by foreigners, including the usually aggressive Arab coastal traders, from penetrating their territory (Lobo 1984: 66; New 1873: 161). Beginning in the 1850s and intensifying in the 1860s, the Maasai and the Somali, also in an expansionary posture, made serious attacks on the Orma from the south and the north, respectively.

As long as the Orma were successful militarily, they had less need to develop mechanisms for regulating grazing. Moreover, the defeats of the mid-nineteenth century so decimated both the Orma and their stock, that repopulation, even of their much reduced territory, took a long time. Once again, therefore, pressure on the commons was not an issue in the first half of this century.

But ease of expansion was not the only reason that the commons failed to become tragic in the first half of this century. Another explanation lies in the oversimplification of the tragedy scenario itself. In the tragedy model the only inputs into the production of livestock are livestock and land. When land is free, so the theory goes, pastoralists have an incentive to overuse the land by increasing the number of livestock they put on it. In fact, land is not the only factor whose availability constrains production. Raising livestock requires several inputs besides land, notably water and labor. As a result, pastoralists do not necessarily have an incentive to use more and more land simply because it is free. Generally, they will do so only if the expected value (including insurance) of doing so exceeds the cost. While the marginal cost of land is almost nothing, the marginal value may be even lower. Whether it is depends on the cost of the other inputs needed to produce livestock.

Stocking levels will depend in part on the cost to the pastoralist of each of the inputs. Moreover, the marginal cost of inputs depends on property rights. If property rights can be established over one of the other inputs, then the cost of using it can be raised enough to make it uneconomical to overuse unowned inputs such as land. Indeed, it may be cheaper to establish and enforce property rights over these other inputs than over land. When this is so, then it may be economically sensible to structure property rights so that land is free.

Such protective mechanisms are found in most pastoral areas. Among any pastoral group, several sorts of rights in property are likely to coexist. Some resources belong to individuals, others to lineages, and still others to everyone; some are usufruct, some leasehold, and some freehold. While tragedy theorists assume that in the absence of strong states to enforce collective decisions to preserve the environment, individual greed will inevitably lead to disaster, this is not necessarily the case. In fact, most pastoralists have rules that govern the use of resources during emergencies, such as droughts and epidemics. Taken together, these make it seem unlikely that the tragedy model, based on the oversimplified assumptions of individual freehold rights in livestock and common rights in land, applies to real pastoral systems.

Not surprisingly, the resource that is the subject of many complex rights is water. Without water, even free land is worthless to a pastoralist. In arid regions, access to dry-season water is easily controlled, since there are often only a limited number of sources. Among most East African pastoralists, dry-season water sources are often not owned in common (see Gulliver 1972: 37 for the Turkana; Helland 1980 for the Boran; and I. M. Lewis 1961: 34 for the Somali).[5]

Among the Orma, wells are owned by the individual who first dug the spot and his patrilineal descendants.[6] This does not necessarily mean that it is easy to refuse access to water, for there is a strong ideological sentiment against such refusal, especially if stock are in dire need. However, there are technological and ecological limits that give real legitimacy to well ownership and exclusivity. Along the Galole River, relatively few spots are known to be extremely reliable wells. During periods of peak demand, these wells are tightly scheduled for use by their owners, and often they are in operation round the clock on a fixed time-sharing schedule worked out among the well partners who share responsibility for maintenance. Others have to be turned away. Those who do not have access to water are effectively excluded from the grazing that surrounds the well. Galole cattle generally stay on a daily watering regime, thus barring use of land more than one day's round trip from the nearest well, roughly ten miles. In other words, wells definitely act as a limit on the use of the surrounding grazing area.

Given the effectiveness of the institutional structures developed by the Orma to handle the control of water, it is not surprising that institutions also evolved to handle grazing emergencies such as drought and quarantines due to disease outbreaks. In such cases the council of elders met to set specific policies, which were then enforced by the population at

---

5 Some herders control inputs other than water. For example, in those areas where the livestock of different owners are allowed to mingle, owners need to be allowed access to the annual roundup. In other areas, where production is commercialized, access to the market is controlled (Dennen 1976).

Botswana provides striking evidence of the efficacy of ancillary controls (Hitchcock 1985; Peters 1984). In Botswana, development planners noted that a lack of water limited the number of cattle that could be raised. To solve this problem, they began a program of sinking boreholes. As anticipated, this dramatically increased the amount of water available to pastoralists and led to an increase in the number of cattle they raised. It also had the unplanned effect of causing a destructive overuse of land. Yet this was the predictable consequence of relaxing the constraint – the limited access to water – that was keeping the value of land low. Thus the failure of the borehole program was not a tragedy of the commons, but a tragedy of making common what was previously private property. Ironically, many of the boreholes eventually fell into disrepair, themselves the victims of a tragedy of the commons.

6 Orma lineage rights over water are similar to those found among the Boran (Helland 1980: 65), from whom the Orma separated several centuries ago.

large. Presumably, offending parties were brought before the elders' court or dealt with by the withdrawal of communal cooperation and insurance. In the TRD Annual Report (1950: 12) we see evidence of the efficacy of these institutions:

The Oromo [Orma] have their own water tight customs in regard to grazing control and dry season grazing. These Customs are rarely transgressed and it was not found necessary to interfere.

And again in 1954 (p. 17):

The light and irregularly distributed long rains led to a hard season from July to November, but this was not so hard that they [the Orma] were unable to weather it with little or no loss, by organizing themselves to make intelligent use of the available water and grazing. (It is curious that the Orma, whose tribal organization on all other matters is almost non-existent, should on this one point have the ability to work out and operate quite complicated grazing controls.)

To my knowledge, no specific details of the "complicated grazing controls" used in the 1950s were recorded by the colonial administrators.

The combination of territorial expansion, regulation of wells, and crisis restrictions on grazing served the Orma well until the 1960s. At this time, however, they came to face increasing problems of land pressure. These problems took the form of both external encroachment by the government and other ethnic groups, and internal pressure from higher population levels, greater stocking rates due in part to successful inoculation campaigns, and increased sedentarization, which tended to distribute the growing population poorly.

EXTERNAL ENCROACHMENT ON ORMA TERRITORY

The nationalization of government has increased outside encroachment on Ormaland. Part of this increase comes from the activities of the national government itself. A variety of development projects are land intensive, and in Kenya, as elsewhere, pastoral lands are a natural source of land for these projects. In addition, the national government prohibits the Orma from defending their territory militarily. As a result, the Orma are increasingly susceptible to encroachment, especially by Somali pastoralists.

The Orma have lost a large amount of territory to development projects and reserves. The most notable of these are irrigation schemes along the Tana River (including Hola, Bura, and the Tana Delta Rice Project), game reserves (including Tsavo, the Tana River Primate Reserve, and Kitui Reserve), non-Orma commercial ranches (especially Galana), and group and cooperative ranches. The Orma have been relatively powerless to stop any of the encroachment on their territory for agriculture, irrigation, commercial ranches, or game reserves. All of these land uses are considered more economically productive by the government and therefore have been given national priority over pastoralism in this and other parts of Kenya. Even if the Orma had powerful representatives in Nairobi, it is unlikely that they would be able to stop these encroachments.

The Orma have had relatively more success in drawing the attention of the government to encroachment by other pastoral groups. In particular, they have taken advantage of the hostility between Kenya and Somalia to push for the removal of the Somali from their territory. For example, in 1980 there was a severe influx of marauding bandits believed to be Somali (commonly referred to as *shifta*).[7] The Orma took advantage of the situation to attempt to rid their territory of all foreign ethnic groups: Somali, Wardei, and even Boran. Accusations that each of these groups were harboring foreign bandits in their settlements were rampant at the time. Following attacks by bandits on Orma villages, there were retaliatory raids on Somali settlements, which constituted the equivalent of ethnic warfare. Ultimately, however, the Orma were no match militarily for the Somali. Consequently, when the Orma were inundated by a large number of Degodia Somali in the drought of 1980, they had no recourse but to turn to the government for help in ordering these outsiders out of their territory. The government of Kenya did take action on their behalf and permitted the Orma chief to assert the chief's act, which allows the chief to order any foreign stock out of his location (the smallest recognized territorial political division) and to refuse any other livestock permission to enter.

Before this resolution, the Orma had also attempted to force the Somali out by making it difficult for them to get access to water. The Orma complained that the Somali and Wardei residing in the northern part of Orma territory at this time refused to acknowledge Orma ownership of wells and merely used (and destroyed) them at will. When chastised for this behavior, the Somali responded that the Orma did not own the wells, since "only God can own a well." This was probably a strained effort to appeal to a common institutional structure in the form of Islam, which is shared by all of the ethnic groups.

This state of affairs represented the breakdown of the Orma's primary institutions for regulating common pasture. The first was the military option, and the second the control of dry-season grazing indirectly

---

7 The application of the term *shifta* to these bandits should not be confused with the political movement of the same name in the late 1960s.

through ownership of wells. At this point the Orma had little choice but to resort to a higher authority, for the Wardei and Somali made it very clear that they did not consider Orma institutions binding on them.

The experience with the influx of Somali and Wardei had several consequences for Orma property rights. More than ever before, the Orma realized the vulnerability of their situation and began taking steps to solidify it. This they did by cultivating the sentiment of national Kenyan officials against the Somali. They also took steps to guard their territorial claims more directly. For example, in one remote nomadic area far from any shops, villagers were reported to be afraid to shift for fear that if they vacated the area the Somali would move in. Thus a strong incentive to sedentarize developed in order to establish more recognized rights to land.

This crisis was eventually resolved when the rains came at the end of 1980. The Somali temporarily left Galole territory, but the Orma were much changed by the experience. Furthermore, the Somali returned in even larger numbers during the drought of the mid-1980s.

The external threats to Orma property rights have the potential of being more costly to the Orma than internal threats. Consequently, the effect of the external threats should not be ignored in consideration of the internal dynamics of change that ensued. However, when weighing the relative causative effect of internal versus external pressures on the commons, one must bear in mind that the dismantling of the commons began in the early 1960s, long before the recent wave of Somali encroachment on this area. Nevertheless, while the processes of economic growth and Orma settlement would ultimately have precipitated a change in property rights on their own, the Somali crisis may have aided in overcoming ideological resistance to the distributional consequences of the system that resulted. With this in mind, I turn now to the internal situation, which may be more theoretically instructive for changing property rights in other contexts.

INTERNAL PRESSURE ON PROPERTY RIGHTS

When a small number of Galole Orma began to sedentarize in the Wayu area in the late 1940s and early 1950s, there were at first no detrimental consequences to either the ecology or the well-being of their livestock. No alteration in the common tenure system was necessitated at this time. By the 1960s, however, the population was great enough that the people were beginning to feel some pressure on local resources.

While we often think of sedentarization as synonymous with a transition to farming, this was not the case for the Orma. Although the chief did some experimentation with large-scale commercial agriculture in the

1960s, wide-scale farming along the seasonal Galole River did not develop until the 1970s. Even today it is at best an opportunistic strategy,
since it depends on river flooding. Therefore, as more and more Orma
settled, many continued to maintain large herds, eventually causing extensive erosion.

Settling is incompatible with East African pastoralism because rainfall
tends to be highly localized. Ideally, pastoralists must be as mobile as
possible in order to pursue the rains and grazing and to match population
density with resource availability. The wealthy sedentary households
solve this problem by keeping only small milking herds in the village and
sending sons and hired herders to take the majority of their stock to
remote and highly mobile cattle camps. As the settled population grew,
however, even milking herds became too much. By 1987, a much smaller
number of milking stock were being kept in the village, and some wealthy
herders refused to keep any because the grazing conditions were so detrimental to the stock.

The Orma were attracted to settlement for a variety of reasons. For
those with commercial interests, settlement greatly facilitated access to
information, transportation, and buyers and sellers. For others, the attractions were some combination of school, mosque, dispensary, shops,
arable land by the river, presence of wealthy kin, employment, and relative ease of settled versus nomadic life-style. Whatever their reasons for
settling, all households were forced to depend on purchased foodstuffs
for a great deal of their subsistence, for access to milk (the dietary mainstay) was greatly reduced with sedentarization; all were forced into a
highly commercialized production strategy – they sold stock and purchased grain.

As stocking pressure increased over the entire territory, there was nothing to stop nomads from using the lush grazing in the settled area, thus
leaving insufficient grazing for the sedentarists' milking herds during the
dry season. Early in the 1960s, the sedentary elders, including the resident
government chief, proclaimed that a small area around the permanent
village of Wayu was off-limits for wet-season grazing to any stock but
that owned by the local villagers. The Orma term for the area was *laf
sera*, or roughly "prohibited land."[8] While the restriction applied to the
wet season, the intent was to protect dry-season grazing. There were two
reasons for this. First, the amount of dry-season grazing was limited to
that which was not eaten in the rainy season, and second, ownership of
wells already served to a certain extent to limit access during the dry
season. The elders explained that this restricted area was "like our ranch,"

---

8 It is interesting that *laf sera* is borrowed from the term the Orma elders used to
apply to the quarantine zones established during disease outbreaks.

and "we used it to store our grass" for the dry season. The impetus for this change was the permanent villagers' need to protect the dry-season grazing around their settlements. The only way they could do so was to prohibit nomadic herders, who could go elsewhere, from using the only resources that were within the reach of villagers' herds. The fact that villagers could continue to use as much as they liked of the remaining commons (which they used extensively for their remote cattle camps) was seen by them as irrelevant.[9]

In the 1960s and 1970s the restricted area was not large enough to represent a serious threat to the nomads. Conflict was relatively easily avoided. Incursions were not serious enough to jeopardize the resource base of the settled households.

Over the years, the settled villagers gradually increased the restrictions on this grazing area by limiting the period recognized as "dry season" and by increasing the size of the territory to include all grazing lands within a day's walk from the center in every direction. By 1985 the restricted area was substantial and was out of bounds to outsiders year round. As always, nomads still had the option of settling at any time and enjoying access to the restricted grazing, but there were costs. All settlers were obliged to send at least some of their children to school and to contribute to *harambee* (self-help) fund raising (the primary means of taxation).

Significantly, by 1985, enforcement of the new property rights had shifted from decentralized enforcement to third-party enforcement by the state. Up to the early 1980s, trespassers were reported to the elders by herders and sanctions worked through traditional Orma institutions controlled by the elders. The chief (a state civil servant) never arrested herders for trespassing on the restricted grazing. By the mid-1980s, the chief was commonly using his police to arrest both Orma and Somali encroachers. Typically, offenders were detained briefly and fined. It is difficult to overstate the support of the sedentary population for this policy. Usually, when the chief visited settled villages along the Galole, it was the first issue raised by the inhabitants, rich and poor alike, and much emotion accompanied the pleas of herders for the chief to act quickly against territorial incursions. Nevertheless, while the majority of the settled Orma supported the chief in this policy, the Orma nomads clearly did not, and some settled households were sympathetic to the nomads' cause.

In order to understand the breakdown of the elders' ability to enforce restricted grazing, and thus the need for third-party enforcement by the state, it is necessary to analyze the increasing differentiation that occurred

---

9 Orma tradition follows that of the Boran in favoring milking stock (*hawicha*) over cattle camp or fallow stock (*ureni*) (see Hogg 1990: 10).

among the Orma during the 1970s and 1980s. Much of this can be related to economic growth and the divergent economic interests that resulted.

Over the 1970s and 1980s there were significant changes in relative prices that favored the commercial production of livestock and increased the value of land around permanent settlements. As noted in Chapter 3, between 1980 and 1987 the returns to livestock production in Ormaland increased by 116 percent, while overall inflation was 93 percent. The increasingly favorable terms of trade probably induced more people to engage in exchange. Because sedentary households had better access to transportation, markets, and price information, increased commercialization tended to result in increased sedentarization. As the sedentary population increased (from 39 percent of the Galole population in 1979 to 63 percent in 1987), so too did the value of land, leading to the desire for more restrictions on land around the permanent settlements.

Growth has dramatically increased diversity, with some Orma becoming commercial producers, traders, farmers, and wage laborers, others remaining more interested in subsistence pastoral production. One result is that there is less agreement about what form of property rights is appropriate. A growing share of pastoral output is being sold on the market, not kept for domestic consumption. The needs of commercial beef producers are very different from those of subsistence-oriented nomads. As a result, the two groups want very different property rights systems.

The emergence of a commercial sector can be traced directly to the changes associated with economic growth on the national level. One such change is the increase in the relative and absolute size of the urban population in Kenya. Since city dwellers cannot grow their own food, their food needs must be met by the commercial production of those who remain in agriculture. The growth of international tourism on the coast of Kenya has also greatly increased the demand for livestock in the Orma's traditional coastal market. Growth has also resulted in improvements in infrastructure (roads, telecommunications, public transport, government, and banking facilities), even in pastoral areas. Moreover, the spread of stores, along with the increased use of money and credit, makes it possible for pastoralists to use the proceeds from their sales. The cumulative impact of these changes is to make it economic for some pastoralists to specialize in producing for national and international markets.

Nevertheless, not all Orma are equally interested in producing for the market. Those who have appropriate access to stock, skill, and labor, or a preference for decentralized political authority, still migrate and avoid dependence on the market for subsistence foodstuffs as much as possible. This is widely believed to be the best means of building a herd, since the pressure on sedentarists to sell their "productive capital" is constant. Some of the factors related to settlement and commercial involvement include facility with the language of trade, kin relations with traders or other well-off sedentarists, access to credit, job opportunities, arable riverine land, a household age structure that makes movement difficult, infirmity, which makes access to health facilities important, desire for education, and fear of losing land that is not permanently settled. The fact that nomads and sedentarists have very different land tenure needs makes it increasingly difficult to reach agreement over property rights.[10]

Changes in the relative costs of maintaining distant cattle camps also lead to increases in the demand for land by sedentarists. As the demand for education increases, not only does the direct cost of labor increase as the pool of available young men decreases, but the transaction costs (agency costs) may increase as well. As sons' labor is replaced by that of hired herders in the remote cattle camps, the quality of herding may decline, leading to significant losses. Such labor problems are less exaggerated among hired herders resident in the settled village, where they are under the watchful eye of the herd owner on a daily basis. Thus a movement developed in 1987 to increase the restricted area around settled villages to accommodate the cattle camps of the residents.

The timing of the initiative to greatly expand the restricted grazing zone may also have been affected by the drought of 1985, which killed 70 percent of the Orma's livestock. By choosing a period when stocking rates were far lower than in recent years, the burden on those excluded from the restricted grazing was less in the short term than it would otherwise have been. Among other things, because the immediate cost to the nomads would be less, it would be more difficult for them to mount resistance. By the time the nomads' herds regained their former size and the loss of land began to really hurt, thus motivating action, the precedent would have been firmly entrenched and quite possibly even formally recognized by the national government.

In addition to efforts to expand the restricted grazing, a group of wealthy herders from Wayu have renewed their interest in acquiring government backing to set up a private ranch on the western border of the now-restricted territory. If successful, this would represent a movement even closer to privatization than that which exists currently. While all nomads are free to settle and by so doing automatically have access to the currently restricted zone, the ranch would be open to members

---

10 I in no way wish to suggest that until recently pastoral societies were undifferentiated. Rather, I am arguing that differentiation has *increased* in the economic realm and that the outcome is less agreement regarding property rights.

only and thus completely exclusionary. It would also represent the only such ranch in the Galole area.

The alienation of Ormaland to irrigation schemes, game reserves, and a variety of ranches has also drastically reduced Orma access to dry-season water sources such as the Tana River. As the number of places where access to alternative water sources declines, the relative value of land around the sedentary villages, which have their own water supplies, increases. Finally, the social and economic services available in the sedentary villages in the form of schools, mosque, dispensary, transportation, shops, police, and administration all increase the relative benefits of settlement and thus the value of land in the area.

These changes in relative prices have increased the differences in economic interests between the sedentary and nomadic herders and possibly persuaded some sedentarists to overcome their ideological misgivings about restricting access to the commons. Over the years, settlers have used two forms of ideological reasoning to justify more restrictive property rights. Initially, the Orma appealed to custom, which gave preference to the needs of milking herds over those of *ureni,* or cattle camps (cf. Hogg 1990 for the Boran). Conceivably, even the nomads could have accepted this, especially given that the costs to them were initially small. Later, the sedentarists argued that they had sedentarized in order to send their children to school and therefore they had to prohibit nomadic herders (who could go elsewhere) from using the only resources that were within the reach of villagers' herds. This explanation appealed to the national "ideology," since compulsory primary schooling was the law (though not seriously enforced) as of the late 1970s. The sedentarists knew, therefore, that by so arguing their case they could claim the backing of the national government.

By 1987 the situation had changed such that neither of these claims to ideological legitimacy was tenable. First of all, for some years the children of many households excluded from the restricted grazing were already going to school. Second, the initiative in 1987 for an extension of the restricted grazing zone to encompass an area large enough to accommodate the cattle camps in the dry season could not be supported by custom, which gave preference only to milking herds. Thus a new ideological rationalization was formed – the sedentarists proposed expansion of the restricted zone as the most effective strategy to counter the Somali threat to their territory. Together with similar initiatives in other villages along the Galole River, this movement threatened to provide a nearly continuous restricted zone east to west across the entire Orma frontier. Such a change would probably force all Galole nomads to sedentarize. While this proposal was still in the negotiation phase in late 1987, the fact that it was even seriously considered by a substantial number of sedentarists is highly significant. It indicates either that norms regarding acceptable distribution of costs and benefits across society had changed considerably over the years, or that the wealthy sedentary households felt confident that their will would prevail in the face of significant ideological objection.

Evidence of just how far ideological and majority sentiment had shifted was presented by one of the assistant chiefs from an area still inhabited by many nomads. In a conversation with the chief regarding a proposed extension of the restricted grazing, he asked, "But what about the shifting villages?" The chief responded that people in Wayu did not seem to worry much about the shifting villages anymore. The chief said that maybe the sedentarists wanted everyone to settle down. The assistant chief agreed that it was good if they all settled down, but added that if Wayu people were not going to look after the interests of the shifting villages, it was the chief's responsibility to do so.

The difference in interests between sedentary commercial pastoralists, rich and poor alike, and those of more subsistence-oriented nomads does not capture the full extent of the economic differentiation now prevalent in Orma society. Were this the only differentiation, it is possible that decentralized enforcement sanctioned by the sedentary elders would still be working. Within the sedentary community serious cleavages also developed, some clearly economic and others less clearly so. Most notably, a number of wealthy sedentary households, many of which settled only recently as a consequence of the 1985 drought, had close family members who were nomads and whose interests they supported. Many long-term residents also still practiced a divided strategy, with part of the household sedentarized and part nomadic, and thus had mixed interests. In addition, a limited number of wealthy shopkeepers and poor tea kiosk owners did considerable trade with both the nomads and the Somali and supported them politically. Clearly, the lines of conflict in this dispute were not based on class interests so much as economic interests and kin loyalties.

For most Orma, the external threat to grazing experienced in the form of Somali encroachment precipitated a crisis that may have greatly facilitated the ability of the sedentarists to overcome ideological resistance to changing property rights. While some change would have been necessary even in the absence of the external threat, it might not have come as fast, nor have taken the form that it did, had historical circumstances been different.

What state enforcement offered over decentralized enforcement was the advantage of harsher sanctions (thus greater protection for the now more valuable land) and less need for near unanimity in support of the new property rights. The presence of the state makes it possible for a smaller group to implement changes in the institutional arrangements, such as property rights, which favor them. There is little doubt in anyone's mind (except perhaps that of the idealistic assistant chief just cited) that collective decisions backed by the state are favoring commercial producers at the expense of subsistence producers. The fact that over a brief period between 1980 and 1987 close to half of the nomadic population settled is but one indication of this reality.

CONCLUSIONS

The relation between economic growth and property rights is complicated. Growth changes the costs and benefits of different systems of property rights and the distribution of those costs and benefits. Property rights are not always restructured only in response to these purely economic considerations; the long-run viability and desirability of property rights also reflect ideology and politics. Ideology, which includes notions about fairness and justice, influences the relative assessment of different systems of rights. In addition, perceptions of fairness affect people's willingness to comply with any particular system, and thus the transaction costs of that system. Which property rights are actually chosen depends on how rights are chosen, as well as which rights are desired. Many, if not most, property rights are chosen collectively, by means of a combination of formal and informal political institutions. The extent to which different groups can affect the choice of property rights depends on the political institutions used to make choices.

The interaction of economics, ideology, and politics in the evolution of property rights is illustrated by the case of the Orma. The timing of the move away from common to more restrictive property rights among the Orma is not coincidental. Economic growth created a situation in which new property rights were necessary, desired by some factions, and more affordably enforceable than they were previously. Since the 1960s, the Orma, like many other pastoralists in Africa, have faced increasing overgrazing. Reductions in overgrazing often require an alteration in property rights.[11] However, those who benefited from different systems did not agree on what rights to adopt. The disagreement was driven largely by the commercial producers' desire to protect their holdings.

As the Orma were fighting over property rights, the central government

11 As noted by Ostrom (1990), and well illustrated by innumerable successful commons cases, including those cited here, greater privatization and transfer to the state are *not* the only options for preventing the tragedy of the commons, although these were the outcomes in this case. Of course, neither privatization nor state control necessarily means that environmental degradation will abate; in numerous cases they have actually exacerbated the problem (see Feeny et al. 1990).

of Kenya was getting closer and closer. Those who had most contact with the government were in a favored position to use the new institutions of the nation-state to their advantage. The costs of enforcing more exclusive control of pastoral lands would previously not have paid the gains from such change in property rights. Once the costs of enforcement could be at least partially shifted to the central government, however, it was certainly in the interests of some Orma to do so. The presence of a large population of ethnic Somali probably did not dramatically alter the final outcome of this situation, but it may have considerably forced the issue, such that lingering ideological resistance to a solution so costly to the nomads was more easily overcome. Thus by 1985 most Orma agreed that it was legitimate for the state to use force against their own members. It was common practice for the chief to use his police to arrest encroachers on the restricted grazing, Orma and Somali alike, and this policy was considered legitimate by the vast majority of settled Orma (63 percent of the population).[12]

The issue of who pays for the enforcement of new rights is especially important for understanding these processes in developing economies. Central bureaucracies of developing nations are reaching deeper into remote areas. As they do so, forms of property rights that could not be economically enforced locally may become economic, because enforcement is subsidized by the central state, as was the case here. This implies nothing about the effect on economic performance of new property rights, their ecological soundness, or their equity. Economic growth not only creates economic winners, but also tends to create political windfalls in the form of privileged access to the central state. Those with better access to the state may be able to manipulate enforcement agencies to their own ends, thus creating new property rights favorable to them. In the next chapter I examine the process by which the property rights crisis contributed to state incorporation.

---

12 In almost all cases, violators of the restricted grazing were duly warned and given a chance to leave the area. Arrests were made only after herders refused to comply.

6

Collective action: from community to state

As we saw in the preceding chapter, the analysis of economic change in the case of property rights is inseparable from the analysis of political change. In this chapter I look in greater detail at political change. I argue that in the aftermath of increasing economic growth and resultant economic diversification among the Orma, there was a breakdown in community and a failure of collective action. This precipitated a major change in constitutional authority from rule by a collective council of elders to the modern nation-state of Kenya. One of the proximate crises that led to this change was the need for new property rights that the elders were incapable of enforcing without third-party institutions such as the state. The elders ceded authority to the state in part in return for enforcement of those new property rights. The lessons from this case study of state incorporation speak also to the issue of state formation, and more generally to the relationship between economic growth and the breakdown of communities and the institutions that support communities, in this case marriage, lineage, clan, gerontocracy, patriarchy, and patron–client relations.

Most of Africa was colonized close to a hundred years ago and achieved independence under sovereign states in the past thirty years. Yet to this day, many ethnic groups in Africa remain considerably autonomous in their political behavior. In particular, many ethnic groups do not consider state use of force against their members to be legitimate. For many Africans, matters involving the sanctioning of their own people are still often resolved internally by councils of elders or other indigenous institutions.

States are defined in part by their monopoly over the use of legitimate force (Taylor 1982: 5; Weber 1947: 156); thus one could argue that those peoples who fail to accept the state's legitimacy in this domain are less than fully incorporated into the state (Cohen and Middleton 1970). In this most important sense, such societies can be considered

143

"stateless." I have in mind not the revolutionary hot spots of the African continent, where the question is more one of *which* state a people recognize, but rather those peripheral and least developed areas that only minimally recognize state authority and jurisdiction. My use of "statelessness" here is also consistent with Colson (1974: 15), who differentiates "minimal" or "diffuse" government (following Mair 1962) from states, "when the organization of public affairs is left either to the community as a whole or to specialized categories who hold a collective office," rather than to an "organized executive with a hierarchy of offices." If, as Hyden (1980) has argued, it is necessary for the state to "capture" these areas before development can take off, it is well worth analyzing the process by which "capture" occurs. The case of the Galole Orma is instructive.

Among the changes I observed in 1987 were an accelerating dismantling of the common grazing system, a breakdown of gerontocracy and clan exogamy, and the frequent refusal by young women to accept arranged marriages and by widows to accept prescribed levirate marriages. I shall argue that all of these changes were related to the most dramatic change of all, the increase in authority of the government-appointed chief (a state civil servant) at the expense of the council of elders. One measure of this change was the frequency with which the chief used force (police and the courts) in the administration of his duties; this represented a considerable departure from previous practice. What is more, although the chief who took over in 1983 was an educated young Orma man and might have been expected to execute his duties in a different way than the previous, illiterate and elderly Orma chief, it appeared that what I was witnessing was not just the result of transition in personnel, but a fundamental change in the institution itself. This was supported by discussions with the elders, who made it clear that while they did not approve of everything the young chief was doing, they largely supported the increasing transition of authority to the state and supported the chief's use of force against their own people. This support implies that the shift away from local autonomy is not merely an exogenous change forced on the Orma by the state, but reflects a need (perceived at least by some segment of the population) for change in local institutions.

In order to understand these profound changes among the Orma it is helpful first to consider the nature of social order in stateless societies. Next, I examine the actual processes by which economic growth eroded the success of social order and collective action among the Orma. Finally, I examine the conditions that may independently have made the state a more attractive option, at least to some.

SOCIAL ORDER IN STATELESS SOCIETIES

In his *Community, Anarchy and Liberty,* Michael Taylor (1982) is concerned with the manner in which societies maintain social order in the absence of a state.[1] Taylor's work provides many insights relevant to the Orma case. He argues convincingly that "community" is a necessary condition for social order in a stateless society. For Taylor "community" pertains to societies with common values characterized by interactions among people based on reciprocity and direct and many-sided relations. Community, he argues, cannot exist without considerable equality. According to Taylor (1982: 66), social order is maintained in stateless societies by a combination of (1) structural characteristics of the society (such as rules of reciprocity, marriage, descent, and residence, which lead to cross-cutting ties that may check potentially disruptive behavior);[2] (2) processes of socialization that instill common values; and (3) threats and offers, or negative and positive sanctions.

Taylor discusses the conditions under which states develop. By arguing that stateless societies can perpetuate equality indefinitely, Taylor (1982: ch. 3) rules out the inevitability of inequality, on which Marxists rest their case for the development of the state. As Taylor sees it, the state develops under specific conditions of stress in areas where fissioning is not an option (cf. Carneiro 1970; R. Cohen 1975). Stress comes in the form of ecological pressure or external attack. Under these conditions, leadership is strengthened (cf. Service 1975) and given the authority to use force.

In many respects Taylor's theory agrees remarkably well with the facts of the Orma case, even though here I am concerned with the process of incorporation into an existing state rather than the development of a primary or secondary state. Orma institutions had long maintained social order under conditions of "community," although not necessarily with the level of equality that Taylor assumes. Nevertheless, the mechanisms by which the Orma elite (specifically the council of elders) managed to orchestrate consensus for collective action operated much as he describes – through cross-cutting ties, common values, and threats and offers. Furthermore, the mid-1980s, which brought local legitimization of habitual use of force by the state, did coincide with severe ecological stress in the form of a drought and was associated with an invasion of Somali, much as Taylor would predict.

1 For a fascinating legal case study of how U.S. cattle ranchers resolve disputes and maintain social order without using the courts or the state, see Ellickson (1991).
2 Here Taylor acknowledges the influence of Gluckman (1956).

Upon closer inspection, however, Taylor's theory does not completely account for the Orma case. First, ecological pressures and the threat of external aggression are endemic to the Orma homeland. Historical accounts and Tana River District annual reports document regular droughts, human and livestock epidemics, famines, and constant skirmishes with the neighboring Somali throughout the course of the Orma's more than 350-year residence near their current location. Given the close proximity of the Orma to Arab city-states on the coast of Kenya for most of this period, followed by British colonial domination from 1895 and independent Kenyan rule in 1963, one must ask why it was in the 1980s, and not during any number of earlier droughts or Somali invasions, that the Orma took the dramatic step of legitimizing the use of force against their people by an "external" state power. Why at this particular juncture did existing Orma institutions fail to maintain social order among the Orma? Second, while I believe Taylor correctly notes that stateless societies can maintain a high degree of equality over time, it does not necessarily follow that inequality never develops in the absence of the state, nor that it is insignificant in the development of some states. Finally, attention must be given to the issue of "supply" of institutional options. While various models of state organization have been available to the Orma for hundreds of years, these states have also evolved, and what the state organization of the 1980s had to offer may have been far more attractive than anything previously available.

The first step in my analysis will be to consider why the autonomous Orma social order failed. Accepting Taylor's analysis of the role of social structure, values, and threats and offers in maintaining social order, one must ask what forces undermined these components of the social order. One clue comes from Bailey's (1965) analyses of council decision making. He finds that in societies without separate implementing bodies and relatively weak sanctioning ability (as was characteristic of the Orma), rule tends to be by consensus rather than majority. This stems from the fact that the members themselves are responsible for implementation, and when decisions are not unanimous, it is easy for dissenters to shirk in implementation. Thus statelessness does not mean the absence of enforcement, but the decentralization (or privatization) of enforcement (Eggertsson 1990: ch. 9; Taylor 1982). Instead of relying on third-party specialists to enforce collective agreements, the citizens of stateless societies must rely exclusively on one another.

For decentralized private enforcement to work, ordinary citizens must want to enforce collective decisions.[3] They must also have the means to

---

3 This does not mean that enforcement must be unanimous or that members of society are equally involved. For example, there may be differences related to age, gender,

do so, and they must know who has broken the rules, and thus must be punished. When people deal with the same individuals over and over, they can punish offenders by refusing to deal with them in the future.[4] Moreover, in small groups it is relatively easy for them to determine who cheats and who does not (Hechter 1987).

Consensus rule does not, of course, mean frictionless negotiation, nor that the entire community plays an equal role in decision making. Certainly in the Orma case "unanimity" and "consensus" were arrived at through a great deal of negotiating and positive and negative sanctioning. It is likely, as Kuper (1971: 19) suggests, that on many occasions only a handful of people really made key decisions and managed to convert others. Such decision makers were typically heads of powerful lineages, recognized loosely as the council of elders (*gasa* – referring to the large shade trees under which the elders typically met). Through the mechanisms Taylor describes, especially social structural cross-cutting ties and positive and negative sanctioning, the few were able to win the support of the many. Thus when village meetings of the whole occurred, the gathering was not a forum for policy generation, but rather a public demonstration of acceptance for the prenegotiated policy. What defines the system as "consensual" rather than "majority" or "dictatorial" is not the relative proportion of people making the decisions, but rather the means by which decisions are implemented and enforced. The characteristic of Orma social order until the early 1980s that leads one to categorize it as consensual was that it relied more on compensation (offers) that ensured self-enforcement than on brute force (threats) or third-party sanctioning.

Disputes did, of course, arise and here the council of elders played a more formal role as an adjudicatory body. Disputants brought their conflicts to the elders, whose decision was binding on both parties and often required the payment of compensation. Social pressure to abide by such rulings was intense. For those who would not join the consensus, migration remained a viable option. By leaving, the detractors served to preserve the unanimity of those remaining behind.

A significant difference between rule by the council of elders and rule by the state, therefore, lies in the degree of consensus necessary for policy making. The state has the capacity to substitute force for negotiated compliance. In order to understand the breakdown of autonomous social order, it is necessary to consider the factors that have made consensus

wealth, economic strategy, and political status. Nevertheless, it is a characteristic of decentralized enforcement that the enforcing group is quite broadly distributed throughout the society.

4 This conclusion is supported by recent work in game theory in which players deal with each other repeatedly (Axelrod 1984; Taylor 1982, 1987).

formation more difficult. I suggest that the changing nature of the Orma's economic relations with the outside economy, including the increase in trade, specialization, and division of labor, has played a significant role in frustrating internal consensus formation by creating a diversity of interests and undermining the informal institutions through which elders worked to achieve compliance.[5]

THE FAILURE OF COLLECTIVE ACTION AMONG THE ORMA

The use of force by the state, sanctioned by the majority of elders, represents the crossing of a critical threshold in the transfer of authority to the state. It amounts to an admission by the elders that their institutions are no longer capable of maintaining social order. The decision of the elders to transfer authority to the state may also be thought of as itself a form of collective action, albeit of a higher or "constitutional" order.[6]

In the preceding chapter, I discussed the circumstances surrounding the need for new property rights. While that discussion explained why more restrictive property rights were favored, it did not account for why the elders chose not to work through existing political institutions, but rather to cede authority to the state in order to accomplish this objective. This "constitutional" change resulted from changes in "relative prices," in this case the cost of achieving consensus under the old rules relative to the benefits offered by state incorporation. More permanent inequality in the distribution of wealth and greater diversification of the economy increased the costs of achieving consensus and made it far more difficult to maintain social order by working through existing Orma institutions. Finally, the state offered several distinct political advantages over the council of elders, including to the elders themselves. Whereas virtual unanimity was needed to effect a policy change through the council, action by the state might demand a majority or even less. Thus while the elders previously had to "buy" the compliance of every dissenter, they would now be spared many of these costs, and many of the new costs of enforcing more restrictive property rights would be borne by the state.[7]

---

5 See Epstein (1962: ch. 6), who attributes the breakdown of consensus in a village in India to many of the same causes.
6 Kiser and Ostrom (1982) define a "constitutional" change as a change in rules governing future collective decisions.
7 I do not mean to suggest exclusively material transactions here. Labor exchanges and political support on other issues (possibly in the form of silence) may be substitutable. Nevertheless, gifts of livestock for bridewealth (among other things) were and are common exchanges that camouflage myriad patron–client and political relations.

The Orma suffered severely from two droughts in 1974–5 and 1984–5, during each of which they lost approximately 70 percent of their herds. The effect of the 1975 drought, in combination with a marked increase in sedentarization and dependence on the market, was to generate greater inequality in the distribution of wealth than had previously existed (Ensminger 1984). What is more, by 1987, despite another 70 percent overall loss of livestock in 1985, households came out in rank order close to where they were in 1979 following the 1975 drought losses. This may indicate that something resembling an elite group of livestock owners has developed, which can be quite confident of maintaining their position even through a drought.

The persistence of stratification over time has several implications for the maintenance of traditional clan, lineage, and affinal ties. To the extent that redistribution of resources among such groups, especially following times of drought, represents something of an insurance system, secure households have less need of continuing the practice. Before stratification became "permanent," those who were wealthy at any given time faced a higher risk of being wiped out in a drought or raid than do the wealthy of today. It made sense for them to invest in such relationships for insurance purposes, since they might well be on the receiving end at a future date. The wealthy households of today, however, have less prospect of ever being on the receiving end of these relationships. Also, the wealthy now have attractive alternative options for investing their surplus resources – they may trade livestock, build a shop, pay school fees, or invest in real estate in the district headquarters (see Anderson 1978).[8] This recent "portfolio diversification" is another reason why the rich are better protected against catastrophic losses. The high returns available on these alternative investments raise the opportunity costs of investing in social relationships. This does not mean a total collapse of the "moral economy," since many wealthy households still support poor dependents, for both insurance and humanitarian reasons. It is nevertheless true that changes in relative prices have reduced the volume of such transfers.[9] By 1987 the percentage of poor households that were living primarily off subsidies from wealthy relations or patrons had declined. Most poor households were less dependent on income from patrons than they had been in 1979. Another reason for a decline in transfers from rich to poor is that direct livestock production makes up a smaller percentage of the

---

8 This argument is very similar to the point made by Bates (1989, 1990), who argues that institutions such as lineages help to spread risk. As risks decline, in the Orma case because greater portfolio diversity reduces vulnerability to drought, the need to invest in risk-spreading institutions such as clans and lineages also declines.

9 Owing to increased employment options, the poor also have less need of support than in the past.

total economy than was previously the case. The 1980s brought a tremendous increase in economic diversification to the area.

Economic diversification has also had a significant effect on kin relations. By 1987 young men were capable of greater financial independence than they had been under a purely pastoral system in which fathers controlled the livestock and, indirectly, young men's access to wives. This decline in control by parents has had many consequences. Only fathers with a large number of livestock manage to hold their sons together, and even few of these are completely successful. For the rest, early independence of sons is now the norm. Independent young men can attract young wives, thus further reducing the control of elders over the younger generation. Increasingly, daughters are asserting their own will in marriage and divorce, refusing to accept arranged marriages, marriages to nomads, and prescribed levirate marriage. The extent to which young men and women are determining their own future in love marriages without respect for the institutions of their elders is also evident in the breakdown of clan exogamy, which occurred between 1981 and 1987, by which time intraclan marriages were common enough to not even occasion a comment.

The rise in divorce rates among the Orma followed a steady and substantial decline in bridewealth (a pattern seen elsewhere and well documented by R. Cohen 1971). The Orma themselves have not failed to notice this correlation. One young married man described the change this way:

The old men don't want any divorces. These days if we quarrel with our wives we divorce them. Previously we did not divorce a woman because we might have paid 30 cattle and would have to pay it again to get another. If you divorced in Wayu Boro you would have trouble getting another wife from here in Wayu Boro. Now it is easy to find women. But the old men are upset about this. These days the young men themselves can pay for their own marriages and don't need to consult the old men.

The weakening of all these institutions – gerontocracy, patriarchy, patron–client relations, clan, and even marriage, is important because it was through these institutions that the elders wielded authority and achieved compliance in political matters. In Taylor's (1982) terms, these make up two of the three components for maintaining social order in stateless societies: the social structural basis for cross-cutting ties and the institutions through which positive and negative sanctions are manipulated. When the strength of these institutions is diminished, so too is the ability of elders to form a consensus for their economic and political agenda. For example, as divorce rates increase, the "value" to the elders of marriage alliances decreases. One way of summarizing all these trends is to say that the costs of engineering a consensus have increased.

A further obstacle to consensus formation is the fact that economic diversity has also led to competing economic interests. While almost all households have some livestock interests, most now also have interests in trading, agriculture, government jobs, or wage labor. Among those with trading interests, most are involved to some degree with nomads, and a few do considerable business with the Somali, thus having an interest in their continuing presence in the territory. Thus, no consensus about policy regarding restricted grazing, or even the Somali invasion, has emerged, although there is clearly majority support for more restricted grazing and a total ban on the use of Orma wells by the Somali.

The most dramatic evidence of the elders' failure to achieve consensus regarding property rights was the behavior of several households, which allowed the Somali to use their wells (even inside the restricted grazing) in return for payments of sheep and goats. This seemingly insignificant breach of the norm by a small number of households opened Orma grazing to thousands of Somali livestock and threatened the entire Galole area.

It was this type of impasse that led the elders time and time again in 1987 to fall back on the chief and his police to arrest violators of the restricted grazing and send them to court. What the chief and the state had to offer was a separate implementing and enforcement body capable of acting on the decision of the majority. On numerous occasions the police were sent out to arrest Orma and Somali alike for infringing on the restricted grazing. The situation among the Orma in 1987 is aptly summarized by one senior member of the council of elders:

In the old days, even if the elders lied, they lied together. Even if they made a mistake, they made it together.

Yes, we need the chief, because we cannot agree. I can refuse the Somali my well, but my neighbor may not.

What the elder describes here is a classic failure of collective action, and the elder himself recognized it for exactly this when he added, "These are people who only mind their own welfare, not that of others. It is good for the people to take action against the likes of these ones."[10]

One explanation for the sale of well rights to the Somali is that some households actually had more to gain than to lose by the Somali presence in the area, but this is not the only explanation. It is possible that some

10 This conflation of the "people tak[ing] action," but "need[ing] the chief" to do it, implies to me that the elder perceived the chief to be acting on behalf of the population at large, not merely a small interest group. In fact, he was referring specifically to a meeting that had already been called at which the population later authorized the chief to ban the Somali from Orma wells and arrest any Orma who violated the rule.

of the households who sold rights to their wells did so only because they anticipated such action by others and reasoned that if the Somali were going to invade the area due to the defection of their neighbors, they might as well get something out of it for themselves. Given the minimal resistance that surfaced before a ban on such behavior, I suspect the latter accounted for much of this behavior. Even some of those who sold well rights to the Somali seemed pleased with the policy, as long as it was completely enforced.

Another factor may well have contributed to the elders' failure to engineer collective action. In his classic work on the subject, Mancur Olson (1965) gives considerable attention to the importance of community size in the success or failure of collective action. Consistent with Taylor's arguments, it follows that the larger the community, the harder it is to acquire information about who is complying and who is not. The reasoning here is that few wish to run the risk of being a sucker and working for the common good while others do not, and yet continue to enjoy the benefits of their own contributions. The larger the group becomes, the harder it is to monitor the behavior of others and the greater the likelihood that free riding will occur. As noted, the size of the sedentary community has increased considerably in recent years. This increase in size and the presence of many newcomers with fewer cross-cutting ties among old-time residents may well have contributed to the recent failure of the elders to maintain control.

Finally, in a fascinating account of the conditions under which collective action *is* successful, Wade (1988) concludes that the key ingredient for success is a high benefit or cost. He studied cooperative behavior in a controlled environment with forty-one villages along one irrigation canal in India. He found that the villages with the most to win or lose as a result of the failure of collective action were the most likely to cooperate. This finding would seem to run counter to the evidence from the Orma if we consider the cataclysmic consequences of not cooperating to control the Somali threat. However, one could view the decision to cede authority to the state as a collective decision in itself, albeit of a higher, or "constitutional," nature. The same forces that determine the success or failure of collective action within the context of existing institutions may also govern that of a constitutional nature, that is, decisions regarding the rules for making future collective decisions. In this sense, consistent with Wade, one could argue that only such an enormous cost as represented by the Somali invasion or serious environmental degradation could have moved people to make a constitutional change, especially one that might otherwise have been viewed by most as something akin to abdication.

Up to this point, I have focused on the changes among the Orma that decreased the attractiveness of alternatives to state incorporation, primarily the status quo, or consensus rule by the elders. But the state is also an actor in this process. I turn now to a discussion of the benefits that the state offered to various subsets of the Orma population and the role these played in the transition.

PREDATORY VERSUS CONTRACT THEORIES OF ORMA STATE INCORPORATION

Modern theorists of the state (Bates 1983, 1989; Ferejohn 1986; Levi 1988; North 1981) have adopted a theory that combines elements of both conflict (predatory) and contract theories, while avoiding the serious defects of those perspectives.[11] They agree that elites and special interest groups manipulate the state for their own benefit, but they do not view the state as completely controlled by a dominant elite that uses the state to achieve its ends without restraint. Rather, they view the state as an actor in an exchange or bargaining situation where limits are placed on extraction by competition (for a detailed discussion of these issues see Knight 1992). The democratic political process may ensure some degree of competition (leaders may be voted out of office), or in the absence of democratic political institutions, the prospect of revolution places the ultimate constraint on rulers. In the developing world, peasants may also choose the "exit option" (Hyden 1980) by retreating to subsistence production. Alternatively, the "weapons of the weak" may be effective (Scott 1985).

This perspective in no way assumes that the parties begin the exchange on an equal footing; differences in initial bargaining power may be great. But according to these scholars, states are neither all good nor all bad. Not all of these theorists subscribe to the notion that states arose because people perceived the collective economic benefits afforded by cooperation (Service 1975). However, neither do they deny that collective benefits *may* be the result of statehood. One must separate state origins from the consequences of statehood. Furthermore, when people choose to support the state, they may do so because it is the most desirable alternative among a group of poor choices, not necessarily because they believe in the state's moral validity. I turn now to the data from the Orma case, which I argue are consistent with this modern theory of the state held by many new institutional economists.

In support of the predatory aspect of the theory, there is ample evidence

---

11 See North (1981: 21), who also finds the two theories "not inconsistent." See also Eggertsson (1990: 323), who notes that "transaction costs blur the distinction between the contractual and predatory model."

that the Kenyan state is more likely to support the interests of the sedentary elite over those of the nomads. Thus it is perfectly conceivable that the recent change in political institutions could have been engineered by a small interest group with much to gain. There is no question that a change in the institutional structure could have a great effect on the outcome of many economic policies, property rights among them, and thus have profound consequences for distribution. Furthermore, although the powerful men who previously dominated the council of elders might appear to be losing local political control, it is possible that they expect to continue to control decision making through the state and, furthermore, at less cost to themselves. Thus they might have concluded that they had more to gain than to lose by this transition. The mere fact of no longer needing unanimity, but at most majority, reduces their costs of engineering policy.

Perhaps the most important consequence of decentralized enforcement, as exists in stateless societies, is that it limits the range of possible political decisions. Anyone who is not happy with a collective choice can refuse to implement or enforce it (Bailey 1965). As a result, choices that favor one part of the collectivity at the expense of another without acceptable compensation are unenforceable. Thus the need for broad support limits the degree of politically induced inequality. I would not go as far as Taylor (1982), however, who argues that this implies equality in stateless societies. After all, it is possible that people will accept unequal outcomes, as long as they are the result of fair play within accepted rules; however, it does seem unlikely that people will accept inequality that is based on manipulation of the political system.[12] Thus, ceteris paribus, decentralization implies that inequalities in stateless societies are less likely to be based on political decisions, whereas the state opens the door to more politically induced inequality. This could well be one of its attractions to those in a position to control the political process.

This having been said, it is important to note that even modern states do not rule by formal constraints and third-party enforcement alone. In fact, as North (1990) argues, much enforcement of contracts and property rights must come from informal constraints and self-imposed enforcement. In many contexts people will not break the law even when they know they can get away with it, because they believe in its legitimacy and justice. Thus the degree of ideological support that exists for property rights and other institutions will greatly affect compliance and, therefore, economic performance. For this reason, it is often in the interest of those

---

12 I believe that Dahl (1979: 167) was attempting to capture this phenomenon when she described the Boran (the closest ethnic relatives of the Orma) as having an "ethos of egalitarianism," despite considerable differences in wealth among them.

attempting to dominate decision making to act cautiously and bring others around to their perspective even when they have the government's police forces at their disposal. A loss of ideological support cannot be entirely compensated for by substitution of third-party enforcement.

The changing balance between indigenous political institutions and national governments has other implications. One is to increase the importance of national-level politics. Those who determine what policies the state enforces will be able to get decisions that favor them. National government also opens the door for the state to decide policy without considering the desires of local residents. However, for the same reason that a minority may not realistically wish to substitute force for ideological legitimacy by imposing a totally self-interested policy, the state may acquiesce in some degree to local interests.

Acceptance of the national government also increases vulnerability to its urban bias (Lipton 1977). For the Orma this translates into the passage of a variety of laws that are inconsistent with the continued viability of the more nomadic and subsistence-oriented households. Some of these policies, such as the creation of game preserves, irrigation schemes, and private ranches, may benefit outsiders at the expense of local groups. Others, however, favor some members of the local group at the expense of others; for example, compulsory schooling laws penalize nomads more than sedentary producers, and taxes are used primarily to fund social services consumed disproportionately by the sedentarists.

For all of these reasons, one can certainly find support in the Orma case for incentives that would have motivated one segment of the population to promote this political transition to serve its own interests at the expense of others.[13] This view is entirely consistent with standard rational choice theory and the NIE. But while it sounds superficially similar to a simple class analysis of state domination, the Orma case is far more complicated than that. To begin with, the Orma interest group in question is not identifiable as a class. Some wealthy sedentarists did not support the new property rights or transition to the state, because they had too many kinship ties of affection and business dealings with the nomads.[14] More confounding yet, many nonelite sedentarists and

---

13 It is also conceivable that even more powerful interests controlling the state at a higher level have designs on Ormaland and have merely duped the Orma elite into cooperation.

14 My analysis is consistent with the contributors to Evans, Rueschemeyer, and Skocpol (1985), who eschew the classical Marxist notion of class as an analytic category and focus instead on conflict *among groups within classes*. These authors also see the state as an autonomous actor and as an entity subject to capture by groups, including the factions within any class. For further discussion of the similarities and differences between positions like mine and those of neo-Marxists

most women did support the transition, and the explanation of their position has to do with what the new Kenyan state had to offer over available alternatives. While these other groups would not have had sufficient power (or necessarily the motivation) to propel the transition of authority, the benefits offered to them may certainly have reduced their resistance or opposition to the transition. I turn now to a discussion of the benefits offered by the state to these other interest groups, most prominent among which is the prospect of alternative employment through education and expansion of the local civil service. These changes are in turn related to decentralization of the national government.

The combination of a substantial loss of land in the past half century, healthy population growth rates, and a commercial environment that favors larger economies of scale has brought home to the Orma the fact that not all families can be sustained by pastoral production.[15] Even in 1980 poor families had no illusions about regaining self-sufficiency as pastoral producers. When I asked one poor resident if he thought he would be able to move back gradually into cattle pastoralism by building up his small herd of sheep and goats, his response was laughter and a resounding no. In 1987, by contrast, even wealthy households were expressing concern that the future did not necessarily assure even their children a life as pastoralists. As a consequence, elders increasingly looked to education and alternative economic prospects for their children.[16]

The increased value with which the Orma view education is obvious in many respects. Two senior and highly influential elders who vehe-

see Bates (1983: 134–47), Levi (1988: 185–204), North (1986), Przeworski (1985), and Roemer (1982).

15 One should not lose sight of the fact that the state (both colonial and present day) has also been a force in altering the benefits and costs of the different choices now available to the Orma. In particular, by taking large tracts of land from the Orma, the state has played a key role in undermining local institutions through increased population pressure. Similarly, economic growth policies have increased the job prospects and bargaining power of young men, thus undermining the gerontocracy and similarly weakening local institutions. Greater commercialization has also increased the economic resources and bargaining power of large commercial producers and left the stock-poor with a radically different set of choices.

16 It is worth noting that women perceived the value of education earlier than men. In fact, in the late 1970s women were constantly pressuring their husbands to keep their sons home from herding and the cattle camps in order to further their education. This can be explained in part by the differences in property rights and inheritance norms between men and women. Men own most of the livestock and therefore have a vested interest in using their sons to herd. Women have a lesser stake in the herd, but depend almost exclusively on their sons for support in old age. Consequently, women have a greater stake in the sons' long-term economic prospects, which they consider to be better served by education. In Ensminger (1984, 1987) I discuss other reasons women wish to keep their sons at home.

mently opposed education up to the early 1980s come to mind. Because of the prominence and respect of these elders, few other householders in their respective villages voluntarily sent their children to school. The drought of the mid-1980s, which highlighted the vulnerability of pastoralism, turned many elders, including these two, into ardent supporters of education as a means of providing alternative sources of livelihood for their children.[17]

Schools in Kenya depend on a combination of local and national support. Typically, schools are actually built by self-help (*harambee*) contributions from local citizens. The state provides teachers and supplies and may eventually take over the maintenance of the infrastructure. In the mid-1980s, Orma fund raising for schools escalated.[18] It is undoubtedly a testament to the enthusiasm of the population that enormous sums were raised between 1985 and 1987, right after a drought that wiped out 70 percent of the resource base.[19]

The new cooperation that evolved in this period between the population and the government was not entirely driven by changes among the Orma. The Kenyan government itself had undergone a substantial transformation during this period, at least as perceived by the local population. These changes at the top also made the government more attractive to the Orma.

On July 1, 1983, the Kenyan government launched a major govern-

17 It is not clear whether the 70% losses experienced in the 1975 and 1985 droughts were in fact higher than those in past droughts. The Orma are not in agreement on this point, although there is a tendency for the eldest among them to view the recent losses as lower than those of severe droughts early in this century. However, there is, in fact, good reason to believe that losses would be higher today. In the past the Orma bred their cattle for high milk yields and low loss of weight during the dry season. Today they breed them for rapid weight gain during the rains in order to maximize market value; unfortunately, the same breeds that put weight on rapidly when the rains come also lose weight most rapidly when the dry season arrives and are the most vulnerable to death during droughts. In other words, the Orma have opted for a far more risky strategy in their cattle breeding. One of the reasons many can now afford to take such risks is precisely that they have alternative (and more stable) sources of income from trade, wage labor, and real estate.

18 Those familiar with Kenya and the fervor with which education has been pursued by most ethnic groups for several decades may be surprised that this passion has come to the Orma at such a late date. Pastoral populations generally have lagged far behind agriculturalists in their desire for education. This can be attributed in part to the combined effects of high demand for child labor, especially that of boys for herding, and the obvious incompatibility of nomadism and schooling. For a further discussion of pastoral education see Gorham (1977, 1978), Nkinyangi (1981), and Roth (1991).

19 The role of the new, young and educated chief should also be noted, for his foremost initiative in the mid-1980s was to promote education.

mental decentralization initiative described in what has come to be known as the "Blue Book" or, officially, *District Focus for Rural Development* (Government of Kenya 1983). In the 1970s much lip service had been paid to attempts to decentralize the government bureaucracy (Oyugi 1983; Rondinelli, Nellis, and Cheema 1984: 30), but unlike these earlier attempts, what happened in 1983 had an impact in the rural areas, at least in Tana River District. The difference may have been due to President Moi's political motivations and consequent commitment to the initiatives, which resulted in far greater attention to the undertaking than had previously been the case.[20]

One objective of focusing on district development was to move the center for much development decision making closer to the respective recipients. It also meant that initiatives for rural development were expected to come more from below than they had before.

Between 1980 and 1987 there was a dramatic increase in the Orma's commitment to local fund-raising initiatives. Much of this can be attributed to the newfound desire for education discussed earlier, but it was more than this. While numerous fund-raising efforts were imposed on the Orma between 1978 and 1981, they were almost invariably fund-raising drives for projects in different districts. Typically, the provincial commissioner or the district commissioner (always from outside the district) would organize *harambee* fund-raising drives in support of projects in their home districts. The pressure put on local chiefs to raise funds for such distant projects was enormous. Chiefs were typically assigned a quota for collection. By 1987 this practice had changed dramatically among the Orma. From the beginning of "district focus" in 1983 up to the end of 1987, not one collection for projects outside the district was undertaken in the Wayu area, although the chief acknowledged that receipt books for external collections were still piling up in his office. The difference was that the Orma could now argue that collections for other districts were incompatible with the ideology of district focus. Over and over one heard the words "district focus" spoken with a nationalistic-like fervor among the Orma. For the first time the local community had a pride in supporting its own development. Needless to say, contributions increased substantially.

Local fund-raising drives in rural areas such as Tana River District are a major means of taxation in Kenya. The Orma pay no official income taxes to the central government, although there are taxes on commercial transactions such as livestock sales. Many of the funds for basic social services must come from the initiative of local communities, although

20 For more details on "district focus" see Barkan and Chege (1989) and Leonard (1991).

Table 6.1. *Structure of 1987 harambee tax contributions in Galole by wealth of household*

Wealth of household in cattle	Type of contribution	Value of contribution in Kenyan shillings
200+	Large sanga male	2,500/00
80-200	Hawicha female	1,500/00 to 2,000/00
50-80	Cash	1,000/00
30-50	Gabicha male	500/00
1-20	Cash	100/00 to 150/00
No stock	Cash	10/00 to 20/00

the government makes substantial contributions as well. These funds are collected in a highly formalized manner, however, and the system is quite close to an income tax, albeit a relatively regressive one. For example, the elders, together with the chief, agree on appropriate levels of payment for each household based on their wealth in livestock. For a major school fund-raising drive in 1987, for example, the tax rate schedule was as shown in Table 6.1. If a household resisted paying, the chief exercised such sanctions as were at his disposal; the compliance rate was very high.

As we saw in Table 3.12, the effect these drives had on school enrollment was impressive. In 1981 there was only one primary school serving the population of approximately 2,400. By 1987 the village that in 1980 had been most adamantly opposed to education was in the process of constructing a high-quality permanent school building. A temporary school was already operating there with overflowing classrooms. While total school enrollment in the Wayu survey area in 1977 was forty-six students, only seven of whom were girls, the estimated enrollment was 324 in 1987 for roughly the same population. Fully 34 percent of those in standard 1 in 1987 were girls. The chief noted that the addition of new classrooms was essential to his being able to put pressure on households to send their female children to school.

In addition to the positive effect that district focus had on local development initiatives, there were many signs that central government expenditures had also increased, consistent with a national policy of using decentralization to achieve a more equitable distribution of resources among districts (Leonard 1991: 206). For example, an adult education program was initiated for the first time, as was a major child inoculation effort (see Table 3.13).

Another government initiative, road building, had considerable import for the quality of life of the population, since food shortages were common during the rainy season, when roads were typically washed out in this flood-prone district. In particular, two seasonal rivers cut across the only supply road to the Galole survey area. A bridge being constructed over one of these in 1987 was paid for completely by government funds. The government was also in the process of paving the main road in and out of the district, along which all food and other supplies traveled.

Another of the most beneficial outcomes of the bureaucratic decentralization was the effort to upgrade the level of civil servants in all ministries in the rural areas. This was not intended to be an expansion of the national civil service, but rather the posting of civil servants out of urban areas and into the rural areas where they could be most effective – no small accomplishment in any African bureaucracy.[21] From the schools, to the dispensary, to the district development office, both the number and qualifications of civil servants in Tana River District increased in the mid-1980s. While it is hard to measure the consequences, one had the sense in 1987 that the local government bureaucracy ran more smoothly than it had in 1980.

The mid-1980s brought many new civil servants to Wayu, the center of Galole. For instance, while in 1980 one almost never saw a veterinary officer even visit the remote Galole area, in 1987 an officer was permanently posted there. The government also built an impressive house for the local nurse, who attended at the dispensary. The better accommodations allowed for the posting of a far more qualified health officer. An assistant nurse was also brought permanently, ensuring that the dispensary would remain open when the main nurse went on leave or left to collect medicine. The number of administrative police in the area increased fourfold, contributing to greater security in an area continuously plagued by bandit attacks.

Perhaps the most significant activity of the government during this period was the provision of famine relief during the 1985 drought. Famine relief had been functioning intermittently in the Galole area since colonial times, but households noted with considerable appreciation that the effort in 1985 was one of the best organized and most responsive. While the initial shipments could certainly have been used two months earlier, once begun, they were both sufficient and timely, and continued for more than a year at a significant level. The local chief's correspondence files clearly document the government's responsiveness. Maize sometimes arrived as quickly as five days after the request was communicated. There is no

---

21 To most Kenyans, posting to districts like Tana River, where electricity and piped water are lacking even in the district headquarters most of the time, is considered punitive.

question that the effort was more responsive than that during the 1975 drought.

These government initiatives contributed in a small way to the population's gradual acceptance that their prosperity and future quality of life were becoming increasingly tied to the state. More and more hope lay in the development of education, and this was clearly viewed as a joint effort with the government.

It is also notable that two areas of serious grievance against the government abated considerably in the 1980s. During the first period of my fieldwork, it was common for the "antipoaching unit" (a paramilitary unit) to terrorize the population with random beatings in their sweeps through the area. Bribery was also rampant in the district headquarters and provided a serious impediment to small livestock traders. By 1987 both of these problems had been significantly reduced. I would caution, however, that this could as easily reflect a cyclical perturbation as a permanent change in the state's behavior. Nevertheless, both changes certainly diminished the adversarial attitude toward the government, at least in the short term.

I turn now to the subject of gender, particularly the bargaining among the elders, the state, and women that accompanied the movement toward national incorporation. In one very important respect, the council of elders specifically, and all male elders in general, would appear to have lost a great deal in the transition of authority to the state. Like many African societies, the Orma deferred to the elders for the resolution of disputes. Even as recently as the early 1980s, the elders heard most noncriminal disputes and virtually all disputes involving women. Of these the most common were those between husbands and wives and often involved wife beating and threats of divorce.[22]

Dramatic changes in the handling of domestic disputes accompanied the increased role of the state among the Galole in the early 1980s. By 1987 divorce had increased substantially, primarily at the initiation of women, who now consistently took their cases to the chief rather than to the elders (cf. Lovett 1989: 26). Although the chief convened elders to hear such cases, by carefully selecting individuals, typically from among

---

22 Only the most extreme domestic disputes were brought to the elders, since social practice demanded that a wife go first to her husband's father. Failing resolution there, she went to her own father or brother. Most of the time both households had an incentive to resolve the dispute, so as not to risk divorce, which if granted might necessitate the transfer of cattle. In the past divorce was rare among the Orma. Given that wife beating, including a wedding-night ritual, was institutionalized, one can appreciate that women were expected to put up with a great deal before the families resorted to divorce.

the junior elders, and by controlling the agenda, questioning, and summation, the chief almost always managed to achieve the outcome he sought, which the women quickly found to be more receptive to their desires.[23]

Women were turning to the chief in increasing numbers for other domestic cases as well. In the mid-1980s the chief heard the first cases in which widows were permitted to refuse to be inherited in levirate marriage by their deceased husband's brother. The first case in which a widow was allowed to refuse to be inherited and to keep control of both her children and her deceased husband's livestock was heard in 1987. Increasingly, widows were choosing to live on their own, even in some cases when they were not past childbearing years.[24] This challenge to the patriarchy did not go unnoticed by the elders; they complained about it considerably. During an interview, a senior and highly respected elder told me in no uncertain terms that while much of what the new chief was doing was for the good, the elders, not the chief, should handle all domestic cases, especially those concerning women. Indeed, dissatisfaction over this aspect of the political transition seemed so great that one could wonder if the benefits offered by the state were worth this heavy cost to the elders. Surprisingly, however, shortly after the interview, the same elder showed up at the chief's door himself, with his own daughter in tow. He wanted the chief to hear her case for divorce! The interests of the elders themselves in perpetuating patriarchy are complicated by the fact that most husbands have not only wives, but also daughters and sisters, and they know well that the latter's interests (at least to date) have been better served by the chief and the national courts than by the council of their fellow elders.

Just as in the case of women's new rights in civil cases and over property, the elders have reason to be ambivalent about women's role in politics. One of the key initiatives in the decentralization plan associated with district focus was to bring the locus of decision making closer to the rural areas. In theory, it is fair to assume that those most excluded from the upper echelons of power would be benefited by efforts that succeeded in moving the level of real decision making down the power hierarchy. It remains to be seen whether district focus will succeed in this, one of its stated objectives. In theory, however, one would expect

23 This is a perfect example of the fact that political choices depend on the political structure as well as on what people want (Bates 1981); how choices are made can determine which choices are made (Riker 1980, 1986). Those who control the agenda may well control the outcome.

24 Nevertheless, female-headed households were still relatively rare in 1987, accounting for only 10 of 211 survey households (4.7%).

women and nonelite men to be positively affected by such a change. The closer the political process gets to the rural village, which Galole women rarely leave, the more potential women and nonelite men will have to make a real contribution.

There are very small signs that this is beginning to happen. Between 1980 and 1987 there was a noticeable increase in the presence of women at village meetings (local *barazas*) organized by the chief. While most women even in 1987 played only a limited role in these public forums, they were at least getting access to information, which is a necessary step in the direction of exercising power.

It is also mandated by the government that women be included on the local development committee. In some respects, the increased power and position of the committee, charged with initiating projects, makes it the centerpiece of district focus (Leonard 1991: 204). This committee meets in the chief's office in the small village of Wayu in the heart of Galole. To my surprise, upon checking the minutes of meetings held in the mid-1980s, I found that women had in fact been committee members. Of twenty-five people present at one meeting, nine were women. At that meeting, when the members were asked to propose projects, the women spoke up in favor of a local nursery school and more resources for the dispensary. Both motions were acted on by the committee. In my discussions with the husbands of several of the women pioneering these political roles, I found them for the most part to be supportive, some even enthusiastic. This, of course, could change if the men perceived the women to be supporting causes not in the husbands' interests.

In conclusion, there is ample evidence to indicate why one sedentary interest group with significant cattle holdings strongly supported a change in property rights and a transfer in authority to the state. But the state has also offered benefits to other groups in recent years, including nonelite sedentary men and women. Because of the increasing attractiveness of the state, at least as the best alternative among a group of poor choices, state incorporation has met with less protest than might otherwise have been the case. Indeed, were this not true, it is unlikely that the transition would have been as smooth as it has been, or as effective in reducing transaction costs. One of the contradictions in the predatory theory of the state is that unrestrained domination undermines legitimacy and erodes voluntary conformity with informal institutions.[25] This in turn raises the transaction costs that the interest groups wish to reduce by controlling the state in the first place. Thus we do not have to attribute altruistic motives to those who resist the worst abuses of their privileged

25 See Levi (1988) for a discussion of quasi-voluntary compliance.

access to the state. There may be distinct benefits associated with keeping the majority behind significant political developments. At least to date, the Orma situation points more to this conclusion – larger economic and political gains for some than others, but enough to go around to maintain considerable support for most of the local initiatives of the national government.[26] This interpretation is consistent with much modern theory of the state that favors a bargaining or exchange model over either a pure predatory or pure contract perspective.

CONCLUSIONS

It is logical to assume, as does North (1981), that states can realize economies of scale in the provision of institutions. As these institutions reach farther and farther into the periphery, they may gradually reduce transaction costs and make even more attractive the gains from trade and increasing specialization and division of labor. This changing economic environment ultimately has the potential for profoundly affecting the societies it reaches. The gains from trade are rarely shared equally, however, and may result in a previously unknown degree of wealth inequality.

Increasing specialization and division of labor place yet more challenges before communities that heretofore may have maintained social order largely through consensus. Such consensus, supported by common values, social structures with numerous cross-cutting ties, and positive and negative sanctions, may be increasingly more difficult to realize under new conditions of inequality and economic diversity. Among the Orma, these difficulties led to a failure of collective action regarding a change in property rights over land. Ultimately, actors who had benefited from the new opportunities, and those who stood to gain handsomely by a re-definition of the rules of the game, campaigned for changes in existing institutions, including the transfer of authority to the state. Local ideology did not prevent this change, both because the threat in the form of resource degradation was so great and because other cross sections of the population stood to gain from the transition for a variety of other reasons. The farther the reach of state institutions, the greater may be the temptation in times of stress to opt for incorporation, including the legitimization of state force. As Service (1975) and Taylor (1982) have suggested, the same principle applies to the formation of an independent

---

26 This, of course, says nothing of the motivations of those who control the Kenyan state at the center and who play a large role in framing the set to which Orma choices are confined.

state. A society may for similar reasons opt to grant one of its own leaders the authority to use force.

It is certainly true that many institutional developments resulting from state intervention in recent years have brought benefits to the Orma. Among these one can count famine relief during the 1985 drought, which was on the whole quite responsive. Education, health care, job prospects, and infrastructure development also reinforced the desirability of the state (at least for most of the sedentary population). For women the main attraction was an alternative legal system offering more favorable judgments in domestic and property disputes. The clear losers on most issues have been the nomads.

What remains to be seen, of course, is whose interests will determine the state's agenda in Ormaland in the future. While current policies regarding restricted grazing can be said to have the support of the majority of Orma in the area, it is clear that a small group of elite who own most of the livestock benefit from this policy more than the rest. Were the interests of that small minority at odds with the majority, whose will would prevail? Alternatively, now that the use of force has been legitimized and institutionalized, what will happen if the interests of those controlling state power at the center differ significantly from the interests of the Orma, elite and nonelite alike?

7

Conclusions: ideology and the economy

Sometimes individuals have a vested interest in changing institutions. Their motivations may fall anywhere along the continuum from purely ideological to purely materialistic. But institutional change usually creates both winners and losers. Winners have an obvious interest in promoting such change; losers have an interest in resisting it. In this volume we have seen how these conflicts played out in the process of market formation in an African society. The case study highlights many aspects of a theory of institutional change that has been adapted from the new institutional economics. In particular, we saw that changes in relative prices played a larger causative role in institutional change than is usually acknowledged in anthropological studies. One could argue that this finding is to be expected, given the economic focus of the subject matter, and therefore may not be generalizable to other forms of institutional change. But we also saw that changing relative prices worked their way through all of society – ultimately touching ideology and intimate social relations.

Reaching this conclusion is not to say that a simplistic economic determinist approach takes us far. Changing relative prices in combination with competition do not act as a filter that screens out all economically inefficient ideologies and institutions. Among other things, consistent with a more Marxist orientation, we have also seen that the preexisting distribution of power within society is crucial in determining who has the resources to subsidize the often costly campaigns necessary to change institutions. While such change may be in the direction of increasing economic benefit to the powerful parties who initiate the change, there is no reason to expect that these interests will be consistent with increasing economic output for the society as a whole. The new institutional literature on transaction costs teaches us that there are good reasons why those in a position to exert pressure on institutions to serve their ends more effectively may not always find it worthwhile to do so. Changes that undermine ideological legitimacy may reduce economic performance so much that the perceived gains are not realized.[1]

A new institutional approach has been used throughout this volume to look at the relationship among the elements spelled out in Figure 1.1, particularly changing relative prices, institutions, organizations, bargaining power, ideology, and economic performance. While those writing in the NIE tend to be associated with one set of these relationships, this study has examined a large variety within one society.[2] Special attention was given to the effect of changing institutions on transaction costs from the 1920s to the 1980s. The analysis also considered the effect of preexisting political structures and bargaining power on the distribution of the benefits from declining transaction costs. In Chapter 4 on labor relations, institutions were taken as given and we examined the nature of the organizations to which they gave rise – in this case, forms of labor contracting. High agency costs led to the development of particular forms of labor relations as a means of overcoming these costs. Finally, in the case of property rights and political institutions, we examined how the actual institutions themselves changed as a consequence of changing relative prices. We considered not only property rights and formal political institutions, often the subject of new institutional analyses, but also the transformation of key social institutions among the Orma, including gerontocracy, clan exogamy, and marriage. Again, changes in bargaining power played a key role in these developments; as windows of opportunity opened, even young men and women were able to manipulate new political and legal institutions to their advantage.

Although changing relative prices are often given insufficient attention by anthropologists, they are not the whole story. In this chapter I address the areas least explored in this book, but potentially the most fertile for new institutional anthropologists – the relationship between ideology and changing relative prices. While this issue has been touched on in several chapters, far more remains to be understood. Anthropologists have done much research on ideology already, but rarely has it been combined with attention to changing relative prices so that we can answer the questions: Which ideologies are most resistant to changing relative prices and why? What role does the "moral economy" play? And finally, where does ideology come from?

1 I use "legitimacy" here specifically in the sense of "moral validity," and not in the sense of "compliance" or "acceptance" (see R. Cohen 1988).
2 For example, property rights theorists take relative prices, ideology, organizations, and bargaining power to be exogenous, while they examine the effects of different social and political institutions on economic performance. Similarly, those writing about principal–agent relations focus on the endogeneity of organizations, as does Oliver Williamson (1985) in his examination of firms.

Making a market

The evidence for economic determinism

Within anthropology, there is disagreement between those who see ideology as a prime mover of change and those who see it as reflective or derivative of the status quo, especially economic relations.[3] I have defined ideology as the values and beliefs that determine people's goals and theories of how the world works. This definition of ideology leaves unresolved the degree to which ideology determines social action (Bloch 1977) or results from the social action that "precedes and gives rise to the norms that symbolize and sanction such action" (Silverman 1968: 2; see also Asad 1979). Also unresolved is the degree to which ideology "is consciously manipulated for the purpose of building authority" (Apter 1964: 23).

Anthropologists have long debated the direction of ideological causality in social change, and yet the issue is as contentious as ever. Asad (1979: 612), for one, takes strong issue with the extent to which anthropologists tend to locate ultimate causality in the ideological or mental realm:

Thus anthropologists have presented the basic social objects in their texts ("social structure") in such a way that they inevitably propose for ideology an essential and determinate function – so that ideology is not only written in as the basic organizing principle of social life, the integrated totality of shared meanings which gives that society its unique identity (its culture), but also changing ideologies are said to be essential to basic transformations.

Similarly, Silverman (1968: 18) strongly objects to the tendency to locate the cause of economic change in ethos. Rather, she views agricultural organization as the key, from which values are merely derivative. To her the policy implications of this error are profound:

A theory of change that gives priority to ethos can have unfortunate consequences. It may lead to programs for change that concentrate on values, with inadequate treatment of the agricultural base. Worse, it may lead to minimizing efforts at change because people are believed to be hopelessly enmeshed in an ethos. It is misleading for the social scientist to regard values as the foundation of a society, it can be tragic for the planner to do so.

In the same piece, Silverman clarifies her stance (p. 3) by noting that "this causal order is not entirely one-way, for to some extent the orga-

---

3 Sahlins (1976) is one of the foremost proponents of the former position, while Harris (1979) represents the latter.

nization of agriculture in a given form depends upon certain conditions of social structure. Nevertheless, there are priorities of causation."

The evidence from the Orma case study is largely consistent with the position argued by both Asad and Silverman – namely, that ideology more often gives way to pressure from changing relative prices rather than the reverse. I have discussed the evidence of an economic motivation for conversion to Islam. The connection between long-distance traders and conversion to Islam is well established the world over. The fact that Islam has many institutions that facilitate trade, such as the *commenda*, which was used in interior trade with the Orma from the very first, adds strong circumstantial support for this thesis. Islam may have significantly reduced transaction costs for traders, and these benefits may have played a considerable role in motivating traders to convert others. The Orma may themselves have perceived these advantages.

Earlier in this volume we saw that the Orma responded quite readily to the economic incentives of the market. Their transition from subsistence cattle production to commercial ranching appears to have been in measured response to increases in their terms of trade for cattle, which followed in part from reductions in transaction costs. In spite of the fact that Orma ideology used to dictate that cattle not be sold, and that doing so was a sign of poor management, the attractiveness of increased terms of trade for livestock helped change such ideological resistance.

Even more dramatically, we saw that in the face of overwhelming costs in the form of environmental degradation and competition for territory, the Galole were able to overcome their ideological commitment to common grazing. Not all were in favor of this move, and some specifically noted the inconsistency between restricted access and prevailing ideology, but they lost the political struggle. In this case, not only economic imperatives but also the distribution of political power played a role in the outcome. The sedentarists had over the years become politically dominant, and the interests of the most powerful among them – the wealthiest and longest-term residents with fewest ties to the nomads – eventually carried the day.

Later we saw that, in a variety of ways, changes in relative prices worked their way through the entire social fabric. As young men gained economic independence through wage labor, many of the institutions of society previously controlled by the elders gave way: gerontocracy, clan, lineage, patron–client relations, and marriage. These changes ultimately resulted in a transfer of authority to the state, as the elders became incapable of using their institutional control to engineer consensus for the common good. They could no longer maintain social order without third-party enforcement.

Ideology and the inhibition of change

These examples are compelling evidence that changing relative prices have a significant effect on ideology. But we have also seen evidence that ideology may inhibit response to changing relative prices, or at least determine the path of such change. The transaction cost literature teaches us that the costs of negotiating, monitoring, and enforcing contracts are considerable and that these costs have important implications for the organization of economic activity. Furthermore, they may escalate beyond control if the ideological underpinnings of society are threatened, such that voluntary self-enforcement of contracts, on which most economic relations rest, is destroyed.[4] If this happens, it may not be cost effective to substitute third-party enforcement for the lost self-enforcement or informal compliance. Some institutional changes that in theory promise increased output may well have to be rejected because they are contrary to prevailing ideology. The consequence of not adjusting institutions to changing relative prices may well be the forfeiture of gains from trade and specialization.

We see evidence of this significant role for ideology in several elements of the account of economic change among the Orma. The dismantling of the commons ran contrary to Orma ideology, and especially so when efforts were made in 1987 to increase the restricted area sufficiently to accommodate cattle camps. Historically, Orma ideology would clearly have placed the needs of nomadic milking stock ahead of those of the cattle camps of the sedentarists. The effort to favor sedentary cattle camps undercut a significant ideological norm, and this may explain why it took more than twenty years for the sedentarists to get to the point of proposing this most dramatic escalation of the dismantling of the commons. While they were chipping away at prevailing norms as early as the 1960s, they could make a credible claim to be consistent with Orma ideology. They were restricting access to the territory around the permanent village in order to preserve sufficient grazing for the milking herds of the sedentarists. But by 1987 the sedentarists were prepared to assault the ideology head-on by arguing for a reserved territory for their cattle camps, which had no historical claim over nomadic milking stock. It is significant that they waited until the population of nomads had dwindled to a mere 37 percent of the total before they acted on this issue.[5] The specific timing of the initiative, immediately after the drought, when stocking rates were

---

4 Voluntary self-enforcement of contracts may be purely self-interested behavior and therefore cannot be taken as evidence of the legitimacy of institutions. For example, one may wish to protect one's reputation by behaving predictably, regardless of one's beliefs concerning the institutions within which one functions.
5 See Riker (1986) for numerous examples of how people frame issues to their benefit.

low and therefore direct harm to herds was least, was undoubtedly also significant in ensuring the success of their action. After all, they were by then acting in the interest of the majority of the population and chose a time that imposed the least cost (temporarily) on the losers.[6]

We have also seen the importance of ideology in labor relations. Given that sufficient supervision of hired herders in the cattle camps is hard to come by, herd owners resort to the creation of patron–client relations imbued with the ideological expectations of kin relations. While neo-classical economists expect it to be economically advantageous for herd owners to hire and fire herders at will as herd sizes warrant, and adjust wages to supply and demand, this is not yet the predominant pattern for expanding the labor pool. For the Orma, the best way to achieve the degree of trustworthiness associated primarily with kinship is to fabricate such bonds and capture the self-imposed monitoring that goes with them. In other words, the need for dependence on ideology, in the absence of third-party enforcement, has affected the choice of labor relations, at least for the time being. In this case we see that the exceptionally high agency costs associated with absentee herd ownership of cattle camps require the adoption of labor contracts imbued with ideological norms rather than those most responsive to market forces.

Thus far, we have seen cases where changing relative prices led to more or less direct changes in ideology, and cases where changes in relative prices did not lead to the changes we might have predicted, or at least not immediately so, perhaps because they would have undermined legitimacy to such a degree that transaction costs would have eaten up the expected economic savings.[7] While ideology may not have been the cause of economic change in these cases, it at least stalled or changed the direction or path of institutional change.

It seems logical that in any society one of the ideologies most resistant to change will be that governing the acceptable distribution of resources. Furthermore, legitimacy in this domain, more than most, may directly affect economic performance by affecting transaction costs. This is not

---

6 This timing probably also ensured less opposition from the nomads, who would have had greater difficulty overcoming their own collective action problems in order to mount resistance. Given that their stock were depleted in 1985, a loss of grazing would not be significantly felt for at least a few more years. Wade (1988) points to the size of loss or gain as a key element in overcoming the problems of collective action he observed in rural India.

7 While it is possible for systems with less "moral validity" to have greater legitimacy in the sense of "acceptance" because they serve one's other interests, it is nevertheless true that, all other things being equal, a decline in the "moral validity" of a system should increase transaction costs. It follows, therefore, that an increase in legitimacy does not necessarily mean an increase in the moral validity component of legitimacy. I am grateful to Jack Knight for clarifying my thinking on this subject.

to say that "equality" is necessary to ensure legitimacy (even its "moral validity" component), nor that it always yields lower transaction costs, for people may accept unequal outcomes based on fair play according to agreed-upon rules. The relationship between distribution and ideology is complex. In cases where the size of the pie remains the same but bargaining power is used to redistribute the shares, we may predict a threat to ideological legitimacy. If changes in relative prices are the cause of redistribution, it is harder to predict whether ideological legitimacy will be undermined. The situation is even more complicated in cases such as the Orma's, where the size of the pie is increasing, most shares are growing, and relative gaps are widening. To what degree does this situation threaten legitimacy, raise transaction costs, and impede economic performance, thus ultimately reducing the size of the pie once again?

One literature directly related to this subject concerns the "moral economy." As James Scott (1976) uses this term, it refers to the ideology of guaranteed subsistence to all members of peasant societies. It is worth looking in some detail at this issue with respect to the Orma, for if such a powerful ideology is found to be prevalent in many peasant societies and is threatened by market relations, as Scott argues, it might have serious implications for economic performance in the developing world.

Evidence for the moral economy

One could make the case that there has been deterioration in the "moral economy" of the Orma, that is, the guarantee that rich households will subsidize the subsistence of the poor. Indeed, poor, and even rich households often articulate this perspective.[8] One poor elder (who lives primarily from his sons' wages and aid from rich friends) described the situation in 1987 as follows:

There is a lot of change. In the old days no matter how poor a person was, even if he had only one cow, he milked his cow himself and divided the milk with his poor neighbor. That is how people helped in the past. This is one of the changes. It is not that people are now poorer because they lost their cattle. It is because people do not like to help each other. In the past this was one of the customs to follow. If [a man] were poor and his clan rich, it was a must that the clan give some of its animals to him. Everyone related could be forced to help. When someone is poor it is his clan and relatives who should pay the bridewealth.[9]

8 The Orma are not unanimous on this point, however; some poor and rich households maintain that a great deal of support is still being given to the poor.
9 Although poor, this old man has married seven different women over the years, several of whom he has divorced. He has had as many as three wives simultaneously. This is highly unusual for a poor man and may explain the fact that he is somewhat preoccupied with this issue.

This was one of our customs that was supposed to be respected. If someone was poor they had to be helped. In the old days the Orma really believed in the customs. Even if one came and asked for help, if you were in a position to help it was very hard to refuse. In the old days people would be surprised if they heard a rich man refused to help the poor and people would ask him why. He would be embarrassed if he didn't help. This is what explains the change. The young men think they have more authority than their parents over the cattle and each one cannot agree to give out the animals.[10] Even their own brother they don't want to help. Everyone thinks he is responsible for what he has. He won't agree to be forced to help. What he will say is that the other [the poor] should work harder.

There are many issues here. Have total transfers from rich to poor declined, and if so, is it a consequence of greediness on the part of the rich or decreased need on the part of the poor? Are these the appropriate measures of ideological commitment to a moral economy? It is necessary to address these issues before determining whether a moral economy ever existed and, if so, the extent to which it exists today and its effect on economic performance.

Historically, rich Orma households have loaned milking stock to neighboring poor households whose stock was insufficient to meet their subsistence needs. Milk was the dietary mainstay until the 1980s. For rich nomadic subsistence producers far from markets, the opportunity costs of these exchanges, that is, the forgone benefits from the next-best alternative use, were extremely low. Most rich households had more milk than they could either consume or convert to ghee for dry-season use.

All of this changed with commercial production and sedentarization. Permanent settlements rapidly succumbed to overgrazing, making it necessary for an increasing number of stock to be sent to remote cattle camps too far away to provide milk to village residents. Furthermore, while households attempted to keep as many milking stock at home as possible, they were constrained by fear of weakening the stock. For example, one wealthy herder in 1987 refused to keep *any* stock in the village for this reason. What is more, the milk yields of the stock that were kept there were greatly reduced owing to the unfavorable conditions. As a consequence, milk yields in settled villages fell considerably, and households increasingly relied on purchased food for subsistence. As the value of milk, as well as the cash costs of providing subsistence, increases, so obviously do the real costs of providing support for dependent house-

10 The elder is referring to the fact that while in the past only heads of households had authority to give, loan, and sell animals, young men are increasingly asserting such control even before their fathers die and while they are still living in their fathers' compounds. Several controversies arose in 1987 when young men protested what they considered to be overly generous gifts – in one case for bride-wealth, in another for *zakat* – given from the common herd by their elderly fathers.

holds. In Scott's (1976) terminology, the costs of continuing the "moral economy" have escalated.

How, then, has this translated into behavior? Have the costs of supporting dependents made the provision of subsistence so great that the ideology of the moral economy has been abandoned, or has the ideology stood up in the face of this assault? The answer is not straightforward. There has been a dramatic and oft-commented-on decline in the loaning of milking stock in settled villages.[11] In fact, the practice is now virtually nonexistent. In addition to the scarcity problem, rich households note that it is too risky to entrust stock to other households. Because of the poor conditions in the settled villages, the temptation to overmilk livestock is deemed too great to trust the care of one's livestock to other households. The provision of small quantities of milk, cash, and purchased food has not ceased, although in most people's estimation these transfers amount to far less support than was previously the case. The situation is further compounded by the fact that wage labor opportunities now exist for the poor that enable them in some cases to be self-sufficient. Some households with almost no stock are less in need of support than they were before.

In the Orma case we may conclude that total transfers from rich to poor have declined. Nevertheless, as we have seen, real income levels have risen, even for the poorest third of the population. To some extent this is explained by the increased self-sufficiency of some poor households now engaging in wage labor. It is also my impression that a small percentage of the poor, particularly the elderly, infirm, disabled, and newcomers to the area, who are not able to take advantage of the new employment prospects, are worse off than before. Even this is difficult to ascertain, since many elders argue that in the past everyone went hungry for longer periods of time than they do now. What we have documented is that the relative gap between rich and poor has increased. For the purpose of this discussion, let us also assume that some households are worse off in an absolute sense. Does this amount to the demise of a once "moral economy"?

In one sense we could argue that it does not. The real costs of aid were extremely low in the past (measured as the opportunity costs of surplus milk for which there was no market). I suggest that it is appropriate to measure the strength of an ideological commitment in terms of what people give up in its service. Time, resources, and risk may be reasonable measures. If, in fact, subsistence support cost the Orma very little in the past, we have weak evidence for the strength of commitment to this

---

11 See Wilson (1977: 185) for another African case of declining hospitality as a result of a decrease in the abundance of food.

principle. In other words, one could make the case that a "moral economy" never existed, or at least that we have no evidence of one.

From the point of view of the poor, the reality of social life was that subsistence needs were met with a great deal of predictability.[12] I am uncomfortable referring to this as a "moral economy," because to do so imputes an ideological motive to behavior that may have been the consequence of economic and ecological circumstances. The economics of the situation were that aid was "cheap," at least most of the time. And the ecological imperative was that wild environmental perturbations placed everyone at risk and made social insurance a sound investment. Faced now with a different set of economic parameters, which among other things have substituted market vulnerability for ecological vulnerability to some degree, people make different choices. The calculus of choice has not changed, but the context has, resulting in considerably different outcomes, which one could conclude are less "moral."

What we are left with, therefore, is a case of distributional change brought on by changes in relative prices, primarily the increased costs of subsistence support and decreased value of social insurance. This leaves unanswered the question of ideological legitimacy. Whether or not one chooses to refer to this case as the demise of a once "moral economy," I believe Scott has a point. Even when brought on by exogenous economic forces rather than political manipulation, the transition from a system that resulted in more equitable distribution to one that does not may have ideological consequences that weaken legitimacy.

A strong case can be made that the recent drought provided evidence of such a loss of legitimacy. While undoubtedly there has always been some stealing of animals from the cattle camps, during the 1985 drought such behavior got out of control. One celebrated case points directly to a legitimacy problem. This concerns an Arab (referred to by the pseudonym Mohammed Abdalla) whose family had long bought stock from the Orma and left large herds in the care of poor families until the time was right to bring the stock to market. This particular dispute involved

---

12 This does not mean that people never went without food. In fact, elders are in agreement that during droughts and harsh dry seasons earlier in the century, people suffered long periods of inadequate nutrition, often going for days with no food. It is very difficult to confirm whether this suffering was shared equally. I can attest to the fact that in 1980, when food shortages were chronic, people in the market town of Wayu were hiding food and sharing very little. Those who did have food often consumed it after dark so as to avoid sharing. At the same time, food appeared to be more openly consumed and shared in the partially nomadic villages farther from the market. This comparison is confounded by the fact that there were more people with serious needs competing for help in the market town, and food resources (milk and meat, not grain) were more abundant in the more distance villages.

an Orma who herded his stock in Galole. Mohammed Abdalla accused the man of having sold some of the stock in his care, then claiming that they had died. Most Orma to whom I spoke confirmed that the herder had indeed cheated Mohammed. In previous cases, the families of the men who stole repaid Mohammed in order to make good on the losses; those cases never went to court. In this case, however, the family refused to pay; Mohammed took the herder to court and was awarded eight cattle. Rather than pay, the herder served a six-month prison term. The problem was not that the family could not afford the payment. Here is how an Orma elder explains the change in Orma attitude, which as a result of this and other incidents led to the expulsion of all absentee Arab stock from the area:

People are more Muslim than before, but also more learned than before. Now people realize that they [Mohammed Abdalla's family] have been making a great deal of money from us. They [Mohammed Abdalla's family] have left stock with us for free.[13] Now people can swear on the Qur'an and go against their oath because the whole enterprise is bad.[14] Also, Mohammed Abdalla in the past could go to the father of a son if the son had cheated him and the father would make good [the loss]. This is no longer the case.

The numerous examples cited earlier of hired herders and even sons who stole cattle during the drought illustrate the degree to which ideology regarding fairness can undercut economic performance. Examples of the means by which workers undermine their employers abound in the peasant literature (see Scott 1985; Scott and Kerkvliet 1986). As "moral economies" give way to those based on market relations, workers' resistance may be effective in steering change away from some of the more draconian consequences of unbridled market forces.

Where does ideology come from?

As yet, we have not seen much evidence in the Orma case of a role for ideology that could be classified as proactive rather than reactive. This stems in part from the fact that this study has not focused on the types of organizations and institutions from which ideologies originate. Ideologies are formed in places where economists rarely do their research. Many values and beliefs about how the world works are forged in schools,

13 The usual arrangement was for the Arab family to pay 2/= a head per month for herding male stock and nothing for female stock. The family that herded the stock was able to use the milk of the female stock and often marketed ghee from the surplus.

14 It was widely reported that before leaving stock with the Orma, Mohammed Abdalla made Orma herders swear on the Qur'an that they would be trustworthy.

families, religious organizations, and social events with peers and through media and personal exposure to alternative customs.

Those who control centralized organs for ideological dissemination – schools, churches, and media – obviously have an "institutional" advantage in promoting ideologies that serve their own ends.[15] But such reasoning does not get us very far in the search for a proactive role for ideology. We are merely back to understanding where the power elite's ideological perspectives came from or, alternatively, assuming hegemonic or economic determinist incentives for their motives.

The current, young chief of the Galole Orma has very different values and models of how the world works than his grandfather did. Many of his peers share these differences, and in their behavior they are transforming Orma society. Some of these differences can be easily traced to campaigns by individuals and groups who had a vested interest in changing ideologies in order to speed changes in institutions that would better serve their economic interests. Here we can cite the campaign to legitimize the change in property rights. In the past those favoring more restrictive property rights tried to argue that schools were the reason for placing the needs of sedentarists above those of the nomads. Today they point to the Somali threat. Whatever the particular rationale, the motivation appears to be primarily economic self-interest. Similarly, the state has used its control of several organs of ideological dissemination to sway public opinion. The schools and the officers of the state, particularly civil servants and elected officials, are instrumental. These campaigns have undoubtedly contributed to the ideological shift toward institutions that favor the sedentary population. The state has considerable interest in this transition, for sedentary populations are far easier to govern than nomadic ones.

Religious leaders have also campaigned for changes that serve their ends. In 1987 there were numerous efforts during regular Friday prayers and special sermons accompanying large Muslim celebrations to praise the benefits of Qur'anic education over secular training. The Orma were instructed in particular by a visiting cleric from another tribe not to send their daughters to school. These efforts were met with hostile rebuttal by the chief, a staunch proponent of secular education for both girls and boys. As numerous villagers pointed out, however, no one was fooled by the Qur'anic teachers' preaching; they could see for themselves that those who had secondary schooling were getting good jobs, while higher education in Qur'anic schools was perceived to lead nowhere. This was

---

15 There is, of course, a large literature on the means by which rhetoric is used to promote these ends. For a fascinating account of the compatibility of interpretivist/ symbolic approaches with a strategic actor approach see Johnson (1991).

a straightforward case of a failed ideological campaign that could not overcome the reality of relative prices.

The relationship between ideological formation and changing relative prices is not at all clear. The complexity of this relationship is illustrated by Orma attitudes toward the sale of livestock. The current generation of young Orma do not have the same inhibitions about selling stock that some of their fathers and mothers do. Is this because the terms of trade are now more favorable and the elder generation just has not adjusted? Is it because fewer of the younger generation grew up in the cattle camps and therefore can more easily view cattle as a commodity? Is it because they have studied markets in school and internalized the concept of buying cheap and selling dear, which they apply to cattle with alacrity? Or is it because young people everywhere tend to be less concerned about security and more focused on consumption, and these views will change as they did for their parents in previous times?

Similar generational differences are evident in the attitude toward re-distribution of wealth. Young people are less inclined to favor giving generous gifts from the common herd. While this generational difference may be ancient, what is new is that young people have more authority now to act on that ideology. As young people earn independent incomes, they have an increasing say in the allocation of resources from the house-hold. The consequence appears to be fewer contributions to the bride-wealth and support of kin and clan and to Muslim alms (*zakat*). Again, we understand very little about the relationship between this change in the norms of social justice and its roots in the social experiences of young people.[16]

Most of the preceding examples have dealt with phenomena fairly directly tied to the economy. But many ideological beliefs appear super-ficially to have little relevance to the economy, and therefore are perhaps less likely to have been influenced by changing relative prices. One ex-ample is the deterioration of clan exogamy. In 1979, when clan exogamy was virtually the unbroken rule, one young man fell in love with a senior clansman's daughter. Their fathers had been close friends, and the daugh-ter had stayed for extended periods of time with the young man's family. Motivated by his love for the woman and desire to marry her, the young man set about campaigning to convince the population that clan ex-ogamy was an antiquated norm. He proceeded logically and methodi-cally. He went first to his senior relatives and clansmen, whom he deemed most likely to be sympathetic (not including his father), and then to the Qur'anic teachers in several prominent villages. His argument was simple; the Orma were now Muslim (having converted in the 1920s and 1930s),

16 See Kerkvliet (1990) for a case study of differential norms of social justice.

and according to Islam it was acceptable to marry even one's cousin; how, therefore, could there be any harm in marrying a woman to whom there was no known genealogical link? No one protested his logic. However, the young man eventually fell out of love with the woman and married the woman previously chosen for him by his mother and father. Perhaps not coincidentally, however, by 1987 many intraclan marriages had taken place, possibly facilitated by this young man's ideological groundwork. I argued earlier that this significant ideological change has some profound economic effects. Among other things, it undermines the strength of clans, which once served the interests of powerful lineages and the council of elders. This change also coincides with economic independence for young men who have wage incomes and as a consequence may not need their father's economic resources to marry. While the proximate impetus for this change may have been as simple as one young man's love, the timing and success of the ideological change are undoubtedly related to the overall changes witnessed in the political economy, including a change in the relative value of young men's labor and, consequently, their bargaining power with the elders.

Another example of an ideological change that would not on the surface appear to be driven by an economic imperative is the attitude toward the role of women in society. Young men claim that they learned in school that it was neither necessary nor desirable to beat their wives, and that they need not fear giving their wives more independence. Women concur that young wives are indeed treated differently than they were not many years ago.[17] The Orma believe that new ideas regarding gender relations come from school.[18] I suspect that the media – particularly radio and newspaper – and travel play a large role as well, due in part to the increasing exposure to other cultures' norms of behavior. It is also entirely possible, given the many shifts in balance of power (including that between elders and youth), that some young men's interests are now better served by a different treatment of women.

Several considerable changes in gender relations among the Orma have been discussed in this volume. One of the most notable was the change in norms regarding widow inheritance in levirate marriage. The rela-

---

17 Nevertheless, as recently as 1986 there was a brutal, nearly fatal wife beating of a young bride. Even in this case we see evidence of new norms reflected in the outcome. When the woman was released from the hospital after four months, her family insisted on a divorce; this might not have been her fate in earlier periods. Sadly, the young man's father, a generation earlier, had beaten the son's mother to death. It took the young man more than a year to find another wife, which was considered a long period. His behavior is widely judged to have been pathological.

18 See Keyes (1991) for other examples of case studies dealing with the effect of formal education on ideology.

tionship between this cultural practice and changing relative prices is particularly obvious, as noted by a senior elder:

In the old days, if someone died, his brother had to inherit everything. If that person failed to take care of the family properly, then the whole clan had to take responsibility for the family. In this way every person was well taken care of because even if the one failed, the clan helped. In the old days the brother who inherited the wife looked after the family exceptionally well. Nowadays, those who inherit don't take care of them very well at all. They sell the remaining animals and the relatives just watch. When this started, the government began to get involved. The change began with the people. So now a woman can refuse to be inherited. This is why the government is stepping in. A deceased brother may have ten brothers among whom a widow can choose. In the old days it was always the eldest brother who inherited. Now when there is such a case the government immediately comes in and people don't like that. In the old days if a woman refused to be inherited she was sent to her father, and the children and cattle stayed with the brother. Now she can have it all.

In many of the cases cited in this volume, ideological change had an effect on social institutions, which ultimately had an impact on economic performance. In some cases we can see clearly where economic or other factors motived those with power to attempt to change prevailing ideology so as to bring others' behavior more in line with their interests. More complicated, however, are the cases in which the connection between ideological change, power, and relative prices are less predictable, yet no less momentous in their ultimate effects on economic performance. Anthropologists have researched many of these issues in innumerable contexts. What we have not always done, however, is to trace the effects of changing relative prices on ideological change and the effects of ideological change on institutions and the economic behavior that results. If the case is to be made that ideological change can be proactive, the burden of proof is on those who make such claims to demonstrate where ideologies come from, and how they affect the economy in ways that we would not be likely to predict given assumptions of political hegemony or economic determinism.

CONCLUSIONS

Like many peoples in the developing world, the Orma are in a transitional period during which their institutional and ideological systems are adjusting to an international market economy. The speed and success of their economic transition are controlled not just by technological innovation, the adoption of new governmental institutions, and entrepreneurial ingenuity, but also by the process by which new institutions are legitimized. Economic growth invariably leads to a redistribution of wealth. The acceptance of such redistribution has an effect on the accumulation of more wealth. Of course, individuals realize this and use their privileged positions to campaign for changes in ideology to legitimize new distributions. They are not always successful, as some of the examples given in this volume illustrate. Economists have powerful theories about the relationships among technology, relative prices, and economic performance. As anthropologists know well, in the real world economists' predictions falter because of the unanticipated consequences of institutional, organizational, and ideological constraints, as well as the preexisting distribution of power. Because these issues are rarely considered together, we understand far less than we could about the actual processes of development. The new institutional economics offers great promise here.

References

GOVERNMENT DOCUMENTS

The following files from the Kenyan National Archives are cited:

Tana River District Annual Report
  Years: 1917/1918, 1923, 1925, 1929, 1933, 1934, 1935, 1936, 1937, 1938, 1941, 1942, 1949, 1950, 1952, 1953, 1954, 1955
Tana River District Handing Over Report
  Years: 1923, 1928, 1945

GENERAL REFERENCES

Abir, Mordechai. 1968. Caravan trade and history in the northern parts of East Africa. *Paideuma* 28:103–20.
Acheson, James M. 1975. The lobster fiefs: Economic and ecological effects of territoriality in the Maine lobster industry. *Human Ecology* 3:183–207.
  1982. Limitations on firm size in a Tarascan pueblo. *Human Organization* 41(4):323–9.
  1985. The Maine lobster market: Between market and hierarchy. *Journal of Law, Economics, and Organization* 1(2):385–98.
  1988. *The Lobster Gangs of Maine.* Hanover, NH: University Press of New England.
  1989a. Management of common property resources. In *Economic Anthropology,* pp. 351–78. Stuart Plattner, ed. Stanford, CA: Stanford University Press.
  1989b. The generation of firms in the developing world: A transactions cost analysis. Paper presented at the annual meeting of the American Anthropological Association, Washington, D.C., Nov. 15–19.
Adelman, Irma, and Cynthia Taft Morris. 1973. *Economic Growth and Social Equity in Developing Countries.* Stanford, CA: Stanford University Press.
  1978. Growth and impoverishment in the middle of the nineteenth century. *World Development* 6(Mar.):245–73.
Alston, Lee J. 1981. Tenure choice in southern agriculture, 1930–1960. *Explorations in Economic History* 18:211–32.
Alston, Lee J., and Joseph P. Ferrie. 1985. Labor costs, paternalism, and loyalty

in southern agriculture: A constraint on the growth of the welfare state. *Journal of Economic History* 45:95–118.

1989. Social control and labor relations in the American South before the mechanization of the cotton harvest in the 1950s. *Journal of Institutional and Theoretical Economics* 145:133–57.

Alston, Lee J., and Robert Higgs. 1982. Contractual mix in southern agriculture since the Civil War: Facts, hypotheses, and tests. *Journal of Economic History* 42(2):327–53.

Alston, Lee J., Samar Datta, and Jeffrey Nugent. 1984. Tenancy choice in a competitive framework with transactions costs. *Journal of Political Economy* 92(6):1121–33.

Amin, Samir. 1976. *Unequal Development.* New York: Monthly Review Press.

Amnesty International. 1987. *Kenya: Torture, Political Detention, and Unfair Trials.* New York: Amnesty International Publications.

Anderson, Jon. 1978. There are no Khans anymore: Economic development and social change in tribal Afghanistan. *Middle East Journal* 32:167–83.

Apter, David E., ed. 1964. *Ideology and Discontent.* New York: The Free Press.

Arc Angelo, Henry C. 1845. A rough sketch of the River Juba or Gochob (of Major Harris), native name Gowin, from a trip made up the river in January, 1844. *United Service Magazine* (Feb.):278–83.

Asad, Talal. 1972. Market model, class structure and consent: A reconsideration of Swat political organisation. *Man* 7(1):75–94.

1979. Anthropology and the analysis of ideology. *Man* 14:607–27.

Attwood, D. W. 1979. Why some of the poor get richer: Economic change and mobility in rural western India. *Current Anthropology* 20(3):495–516.

Axelrod, Robert. 1984. *The Evolution of Cooperation.* New York: Basic Books.

Bailey, F. G. 1965. Decisions by consensus in councils and committees with special reference to village and local government in India. In *Political Systems and the Distribution of Power,* pp. 1–20. M. Gluckman and F. Eggan, eds. New York: Praeger.

1968. Parapolitical systems. In *Local-Level Politics,* pp. 281–94. Marc Swartz, ed. Chicago: Aldine.

1969. *Stratagems and Spoils: A Social Anthropology of Politics.* Oxford: Basil Blackwell.

1977. *Morality and Expediency.* Oxford: Basil Blackwell.

1983. *The Tactical Uses of Passion: An Essay on Power, Reason, and Reality.* Ithaca, NY: Cornell University Press.

1988. *Humbuggery and Manipulation: The Art of Leadership.* Ithaca, NY: Cornell University Press.

1991. Why is information asymmetrical? Symbolic behavior in formal organizations. *Rationality and Society* 3(4):475–95.

Bardhan, Pranab, ed. 1989a. *The Economic Theory of Agrarian Institutions.* New York: Oxford University Press.

1989b. The new institutional economics and development theory: A brief critical assessment. *World Development* 17(9):1389–95.

Barkan, Joel D., and Michael Chege. 1989. Decentralising the state: District focus and the politics of reallocation in Kenya. *Journal of Modern African Studies* 27(3):431–53.

Barlett, Peggy F. 1982. *Agricultural Choice and Change: Decision Making in a Costa Rican Community.* New Brunswick, NJ: Rutgers University Press.

References

Barlett, Peggy F., ed. 1980. *Agricultural Decision Making: Anthropological Contributions to Rural Development*. New York: Academic Press.

Barth, Fredrik. 1965. *Political Leadership among Swat Pathans*. London: Athlone Press.

1966. *Models of Social Organization*. Occasional Papers No. 23. London: Royal Anthropological Institute.

1967. On the study of social change. *American Anthropologist* 69:661–9.

1981. *Process and Form in Social Life: Selected Essays of Fredrik Barth*, Vol. 1. London: Routledge & Kegan Paul.

Barth, Fredrik, ed. 1963. *The Role of the Entrepreneur in Social Change in Northern Norway*. Bergen: Norwegian Universities Press.

Barzel, Yoram. 1989. *The Economic Analysis of Property Rights*. Cambridge University Press.

Bates, Robert H. 1981. *Markets and States in Tropical Africa: The Political Basis of Agricultural Policies*. Berkeley and Los Angeles: University of California Press.

1983. *Essays on the Political Economy of Rural Africa*. Cambridge University Press.

1989. *Beyond the miracle of the market: The political economy of agrarian development in Kenya*. Cambridge University Press.

1990. Capital, kinship, and conflict: The structuring influence of capital in kinship societies. *Canadian Journal of African Studies* 24(2):151–64.

Bates, Robert H., ed. 1988. *Toward a Political Economy of Development: A Rational Choice Perspective*. Berkeley and Los Angeles: University of California Press.

Baxter, P. T. W. 1954. Social organization of the Galla of Northern Kenya. D. Phil., University of Oxford.

Baxter, P. T. W., and Richard Hogg, eds. 1990. *Property, Poverty and People: Changing Rights in Property and Problems of Pastoral Development*. Manchester: University of Manchester.

Beck, Lois. 1980. Herd owners and hired shepherds: The Qashqa'i of Iran. *Ethnology* 19(3):327–52.

1991. *Nomad: A Year in the Life of a Qashqa'i Tribesman in Iran*. Berkeley and Los Angeles: University of California Press.

Behnke, Roy. 1985. *Open-Range Management and Property Rights in Pastoral Africa: A Case of Spontaneous Range Enclosure in South Darfur, Sudan*. Pastoral Development Network Paper. London: Overseas Development Institute.

Belshaw, Cyril S. 1965. *Traditional Exchange and Modern Markets*. Englewood Cliffs, NJ: Prentice Hall.

1970. *The Conditions of Social Performance: An Exploratory Theory*. New York: Schocken Books.

Berman, Bruce J., and John Lonsdale. 1980. Crisis of accumulation, coercion and the colonial state: The development of the labor control system in Kenya, 1919–1929. *Canadian Journal of African Studies* 14(1):55–81.

Binger, Brian, and Elizabeth Hoffman. 1989. Institutional persistence and change: The question of efficiency. *Journal of Institutional and Theoretical Economics* 145:67–84.

Blau, Peter. 1964. *Exchange and Power in Social Life*. New York: Wiley.

Bloch, Maurice. 1977. The past and the present in the present. *Man* 12(2):278–92.

References

Blomquist, William, and Elinor Ostrom. 1985. Institutional capacity and the resolution of a commons dilemma. *Policy Studies Review* 5:383–93.

Boissevain, Jeremy. 1968. The place of non-groups in the social sciences. *Man* 3(4):542–56.

Boteler, Captain Thomas. 1835. *Narrative of a Voyage of Discovery to Africa and Arabia*, 2 vols. London: Richard Bentley.

Bradburd, Daniel. 1980. Never give a shepherd an even break: Class and labor among the Komachi. *American Ethnologist* 7(4):603–20.

1990. *Ambiguous Relations: Kin, Class, and Conflict Among Komachi Pastoralists*. Washington, DC: Smithsonian Institution Press.

Brenner, R. 1868. Richard Brenner's Forschungen in Ost-Africa. *Petermann's Mittheilungen*, 175–9, 361–7, 456–65.

Bromley, Daniel W. 1989. *Economic Interests and Institutions: The Conceptual Foundations of Public Policy*. Oxford: Basil Blackwell.

Bunger, Robert. 1979. *Islamization among the Upper Pokomo*, 2d ed. Syracuse, NY: Maxwell School of Citizenship and Public Affairs.

Burling, Robbins. 1968. Maximization theories and the study of economic anthropology. In *Economic Anthropology: Readings in Theory and Analysis*, pp. 168–86. E. E. J. LeClair and H. K. Schneider, eds. New York: Holt, Rinehart & Winston.

Campbell, B. K., and J. Loxley, eds. 1989. *Structural Adjustment in Africa*. New York: St. Martin's Press.

Cancian, Frank. 1968. Maximization as norm, strategy, and theory: A comment on programmatic statements in economic anthropology. In *Economic Anthropology: Readings in Theory and Analysis*, pp. 228–33. E. E. J. LeClair and H. K. Schneider, eds. New York: Holt, Rinehart & Winston.

1979. *The Innovator's Situation: Upper-Middle-Class Conservatism in Agricultural Communities*. Stanford, CA: Stanford University Press.

Forthcoming. *The Decline of Community in Zinacantan: Economy, Public Life, and Social Stratification, 1960 to 1987*. Stanford, CA: Stanford University Press.

Carneiro, R. L. 1970. A theory of the origin of the state. *Science* 169:733–8.

Cashdan, Elizabeth. 1990. Information costs and customary prices. In *Risk and Uncertainty in Tribal and Peasant Economies*, pp. 259–78. E. Cashdan, ed. Boulder, CO: Westview Press.

Cassanelli, Lee V. 1982. *The Shaping of Somali Society: Reconstructing the History of a Pastoral People, 1600–1900*. Philadelphia, PA: University of Pennsylvania Press.

Chong, Dennis. 1991. *Collective Action and the Civil Rights Movement*. Chicago: University of Chicago Press.

Coase, Ronald H. 1937. The nature of the firm. *Economica* 4(3):386–405.

Cohen, Abner. 1971. Cultural strategies in the organization of trading disporas. In *The Development of Indigenous Trade and Markets in West Africa*, pp. 266–84. C. Meillassoux, ed. London: Oxford University Press.

Cohen, Ronald. 1971. *Dominance and Defiance: A Study of Marital Instability in an Islamic African Society*. Washington DC: American Anthropological Association.

1975. Introduction. In *Origins of the State: The Anthropology of Political Evolution*, pp. 3–20. R. Cohen and E. Service, eds. Philadelphia: Institute for the Study of Human Issues.

References

1988. Introduction. In *State Formation and Political Legitimacy*, pp. 1–21. R. Cohen and J. D. Toland, eds. New Brunswick, NJ: Transaction Books.

Cohen, Ronald, and John Middleton, eds. 1970. *From Tribe to Nation in Africa: Studies in Incorporation Processes*. Scranton, PA: Chandler.

Coleman, James S. 1986. Social theory, social research, and a theory of action. *American Journal of Sociology* 91(6):1309–35.

Collier, Paul, and Deepak Lal. 1986. *Labour and Poverty in Kenya*. New York: Oxford University Press.

Colson, Elizabeth. 1974. *Tradition and Contract: The Problem of Order*. Chicago: Aldine.

Cook, Scott. 1968. The obsolete "anti-market" mentality: A critique of the substantive approach to economic anthropology. In *Economic Anthropology: Readings in Theory and Analysis*, pp. 208–27. E. E. J. LeClair and H. K. Schneider, eds. New York: Holt, Rinehart & Winston.

1977. Beyond the Formen: Towards a revised Marxist theory of precapitalist formations and the transition to capitalism. *Journal of Peasant Studies* 4(4):360–89.

1982. *Zapotec Stoneworkers: The Dynamics of Rural Simple Commodity Production in Modern Mexican Capitalism*. New York: University Press of America.

Cook, Karen Schweers, and Margaret Levi, eds. 1990. *The Limits of Rationality*. Chicago: University of Chicago Press.

Cowen, Michael P. 1982. The British state and agrarian accumulation in Kenya. In *Industry and Accumulation in Africa*, pp. 142–69. M. Fransman, ed. London: Heinemann.

Dahl, Gudrun. 1979. *Suffering Grass: Subsistence and Society of Waso Borana*. Stockholm: University of Stockholm Press.

Dahl, Gudrun, and Anders Hjort. 1976. *Having Herds: Pastoral Herd Growth and Household Economy*. Stockholm: University of Stockholm Press.

Dalleo, Peter. 1975. Trade and pastoralism: Economic factors in the history of the Somali of northeastern Kenya, 1890–1948. Ph.D. dissertation, Syracuse University.

Dalton, George. 1968. Economic theory and primitive society. In *Economic Anthropology: Readings in Theory and Analysis*, pp. 143–67. E. E. J. LeClair and H. K. Schneider, eds. New York: Holt, Rinehart & Winston.

David, Paul. 1985. Clio and the economics of QWERTY. *American Economic Review* 75:332–7.

Dawes, Robyn M., and Richard H. Thaler. 1988. Anomalies: Cooperation. *Journal of Economic Perspectives* 2(3):187–97.

Demsetz, H. 1967. Toward a theory of property rights. *American Economic Review* 57:347–59.

Dennen, R. Taylor. 1976. Cattlemen's associations and property rights in land in the American West. *Explorations in Economic History* 13:423–36.

De Soto, Hernando. 1989. *The Other Path: The Invisible Revolution in the Third World*. New York: Harper & Row.

Donham, Donald L. 1981. Beyond the domestic mode of production. *Man* 16(4):515–41.

1990. *History, Power, Ideology: Central Issues in Marxism and Anthropology*. Cambridge University Press.

Douglas, Mary. 1986. *How Institutions Think*. Syracuse, NY: Syracuse University Press.

References

Dubois, Felix. 1897. *Tombouctou la mysterieuse*. Paris.

Eggertsson, Thráinn. 1990. *Economic Behavior and Institutions: Principles of Neoinstitutional Economics*. Cambridge University Press.

Eisenstadt, S. N., and L. Roniger. 1984. *Patrons, Clients and Friends: Interpersonal Relations and the Structure of Trust in Society*. Cambridge University Press.

Ellickson, Robert C. 1991. *Order without Law: How Neighbors Settle Disputes*. Cambridge, MA: Harvard University Press.

Elster, Jon. 1985a. *Making Sense of Marx*. Cambridge University Press.

    1985b. *Sour Grapes: Studies in the Subversion of Rationality*. Cambridge University Press.

    1986. *Rational Choice*. New York University Press.

    1989a. *Nuts and Bolts*. Cambridge University Press.

    1989b. *The Cement of Society: A Study of Social Order*. Cambridge University Press.

    1990. *Ulysses and the Sirens: Studies in Rationality and Irrationality*. Cambridge University Press.

Emmanuel, Arrighi. 1972. *Unequal Exchange*. New York: Monthly Review Press.

Ensminger, Jean. 1984. Political economy among the pastoral Galole Orma: The effects of market integration. Ph.D. dissertation, Northwestern University.

    1987. Economic and political differentiation among Galole Orma women. *Ethnos* 52(1–2):28–49.

    1990. Co-opting the elders: The political economy of state incorporation in Africa. *American Anthropologist* 92(3):662–75.

    1991. Structural transformation and its consequences for Orma women pastoralists. In *Structural Adjustment and African Women Farmers*, pp. 281–300. C. H. Gladwin, ed. Gainesville: University of Florida Press.

Ensminger, Jean, and Andrew Rutten. 1991. The political economy of changing property rights: Dismantling a pastoral commons. *American Ethnologist* 18(4):683–99.

Epstein, T. S. 1962. *Economic Development and Social Change in South India*. Manchester: Manchester University Press.

Evans, Peter B., Dietrich Rueschemeyer, and Theda Skocpol. 1989. *Bringing the State Back In*. Cambridge University Press.

Evens, T. M. S. 1977. The predication of the individual in anthropological interactionism. *American Anthropologist* 79:579–97.

Fama, Eugene. 1980. Agency problems and the theory of the firm. *Journal of Political Economy* 88:288–307.

Fama, Eugene F., and Michael C. Jensen. 1983a. Agency problems and residual claims. *Journal of Law and Economics* 26:327–49.

    1983b. Separation of ownership and control. *Journal of Law and Economics* 26:301–26.

FAO. 1967. *FAO Production Yearbook*. Rome: Food and Agricultural Organization of the United Nations.

Feeny, David, Fikret Berkes, Bonnie J. McCay, and James M. Acheson. 1990. The tragedy of the commons: Twenty-two years later. *Human Ecology* 18(1):1–19.

Ferejohn, John. 1986. Logrolling in an institutional context: A case study of food stamp legislation. In *Congress and Policy Change*, pp. 223–56. Gerald Wright, Leroy Reiselbach, and Larence Dodd, eds. New York: Agathon Press.

References

Fernandes, Valentim. 1938. *Description de la Côte D'Afrique de Ceuta au Senegal*. P. Monod and T. de Cernival, eds. Paris: Larose.

Firth, Raymond. 1953. The study of values by social anthropologists. *Man* 231:146–53.

——— 1967. Themes in economic anthropology: A general comment. In *Themes in Economic Anthropology*, pp. 1–28. R. Firth, ed. London: Tavistock.

Fischer, G. A. 1877. Uber die Jetzigen Verhaltnisse Im Sudlichen Galla-Lande und Wito. *Mitteilungen der Geographischen in Hamburg*, 347–62.

Fjellman, Stephen M. 1976. Natural and unnatural decision-making. *Ethos* 4(1).

Foster, George M. 1963. The dyadic contract in Tzintzuntzan, II: Patron–client relationship. *American Anthropologist* 65(6):1280–94.

Foucault, Michel. 1980. *Power/Knowledge: Selected Interviews and Other Writings, 1972–1977*. C. Gordon, ed. New York: Pantheon Books.

Frank, Andre Gunder. 1967. *Capitalism and Underdevelopment in Latin America*. New York: Monthly Review Press.

Frank, Robert H. 1988. *Passions within Reason: The Strategic Role of the Emotions*. New York: Norton.

Frankel, Francine. 1971. *India's Green Revolution: Economic Gains and Political Costs*. Princeton, NJ: Princeton University Press.

Fratkin, Eliot. 1991. *Surviving Drought and Development: Ariaal Pastoralists of Northern Kenya*. Boulder, CO: Westview Press.

Fratkin, Eliot, and Eric A. Roth. Forthcoming. Drought and economic differentiation among Ariaal pastoralists of Kenya. *Human Ecology*.

Friedland, Roger, and A. F. Robertson. 1990. *Beyond the Marketplace: Rethinking Economy and Society*. New York: De Gruyter.

Galvin, Kathleen. 1985. Food procurement, diet, activities and nutrition of Ngisonyoka, Turkana pastoralists in an ecological and social context. Ph.D. dissertation, State University of New York at Binghamton.

Geertz, Clifford. 1968. *Islam Observed: Religious Development in Morocco and Indonesia*. Chicago: University of Chicago Press.

——— 1973. *The Interpretation of Cultures*. New York: Basic Books.

——— 1979. Suq: The bazaar economy in Sefrou. In *Meaning and Order in Moroccan Society: Three Essays in Cultural Analysis*, pp. 123–257. C. Geertz, H. Geertz, and L. Rosen. Cambridge University Press.

Gladwin, Christina. 1979. Production functions and decision models: Complementary models. *American Ethnologist* 6(4):653–74.

Gladwin, Christina H., ed. 1991. *Structural Adjustment and African Women Farmers*. Gainesville: University of Florida Press.

Gluckman, Max. 1956. *Custom and Conflict in Africa*. Oxford: Basil Blackwell.

Goldberg, Victor P. 1981. Bridges over contested terrain: Exploring the radical account of the employment relationship. In *Management under Differing Value Systems: Political, Social and Economic Perspectives in a Changing World*, pp. 375–403. Gunter Dlugos and Klaus Weiermair, eds. New York: De Gruyter.

Goldberg, Victor P., ed. 1989. *Readings in the Economics of Contract Law*. Cambridge University Press.

Gorham, A. B. 1977. *Developments in Primary Education in Kajiado District, 1963–1975*. Nairobi: University of Nairobi, Institute for Development Studies.

References

1978. *The Design and Management of Pastoral Development: The Provision of Education in Pastoral Areas*. Pastoral Network Paper 6b. London: Overseas Development Institute.

Government of Kenya. 1983. *District Focus for Rural Development*. Nairobi: Government Printing Office.

Granovetter, Mark. 1985. Economic action and social structure: The problem of embeddedness. *American Journal of Sociology* 91(3):481–510.

Gray, Richard, and David Birmingham, eds. 1970. *Pre-Colonial African Trade*. London: Oxford University Press.

Greif, Avner. 1989. Reputation and coalitions in medieval trade: Evidence on the Maghribi traders. *Journal of Economic History* 49(4):857–82.

Gulliver, P. H. 1972. *Family Herds*. London: Routledge & Kegan Paul.

Gunnarsson, Christer. 1991. What is new and what is institutional in the new institutional economics? An essay on old and new institutionalism and the role of the state in developing countries. *Scandinavian Economic History Review & Economy and History* 39(1):43–67.

Guyer, Jane I., with Olukemi Idowu. 1991. Women's agricultural work in a multimodal rural economy: Ibarapa District, Oyo State, Nigeria. In *Structural Adjustment and African Women Farmers*, pp. 257–80. Christina H. Gladwin, ed. Gainesville: University of Florida Press.

Halperin, Rhoda H. 1984. Polanyi, Marx, and the institutional paradigm in economic anthropology. *Research in Economic Anthropology* 6:245–72.

Hardin, Garrett. 1968. The tragedy of the commons. *Science* 162:1243–8.

Hardin, Garrett, and John Baden, eds. 1977. *Managing the Commons*. San Francisco: Freeman.

Harris, Marvin. 1979. *Cultural Materialism: The Struggle for a Science of Culture*. New York: Vintage Books.

Hart, Keith. 1982. *The Political Economy of West African Agriculture*. Cambridge University Press.

Hayek, F. A. 1978. Epilogue: The three sources of human values. In *Law, Legislation, and Liberty*, Vol. 3: *The Political Order of a Free People*. Chicago: University of Chicago Press.

Heath, Anthony. 1976. *Rational Choice and Social Exchange: A Critique of Exchange Theory*. Cambridge University Press.

Hechter, Michael. 1983. Karl Polanyi's social theory: A critique. In *Microfoundations of Macrosociology*, pp. 158–89. M. Hechter, ed. Philadelphia: Temple University Press.

1987. *Principles of Group Solidarity*. Berkeley and Los Angeles: University of California Press.

1990. Comment: On the inadequacy of game theory for the solution of real-world collective action problems. In *The Limits of Rationality*, pp. 240–9. K. S. Cook and M. Levi, eds. Chicago: University of Chicago Press.

Hechter, Michael, Karl-Dieter Opp, and Reinhard Wippler, eds. 1990. Introduction. In *Social Institutions: Their Emergence, Maintenance, and Effects*, pp. 1–12. New York: De Gruyter.

Hedican, Edward J. 1986. Some issues in the anthropology of transaction and exchange. *Canadian Review of Sociology and Anthropology* 23(1):97–117.

Helland, Johan. 1980. *Five Essays on the Study of Pastoralists and the Development of Pastoralism*. African Savannah Studies No. 20. University of Bergen.

References

Heyer, Judith. 1981. Agricultural development policy in Kenya from the colonial period to 1975. In *Rural Development in Tropical Africa*, pp. 90–120. J. Heyer, P. Roberts, and G. Williams, eds. New York: St. Martin's Press.

Higgs, Robert. 1971. *The Transformation of the American Economy, 1865–1914: An Essay in Interpretation*. New York: Wiley.

———. 1987. *Crisis and Leviathan: Critical Episodes in the Growth of American Government*. New York: Oxford University Press.

———. 1989. Organization, ideology and the free rider problem: Comment. *Journal of Institutional and Theoretical Economics* 145:232–7.

Hinich, Melvin, and Michael Munger. 1990. *Ideology and a General Theory of Politics*. Ann Arbor: University of Michigan Press.

Hitchcock, Robin. 1985. Water, land and livestock: The evolution of tenure and administration patterns in the grazing areas of Botswana. In *The Evolution of Modern Botswana*, pp. 84–121. L. Picard, ed. London: Rex Collins.

Hogg, Richard. 1980. Pastoralism and impoverishment: The case of the Isiolo Boran of northern Kenya. *Disasters* 4(3):299–310.

———. 1981. The social and economic organisation of the Boran of Isiolo District, Kenya. Ph.D. dissertation, Manchester University.

———. 1990. The politics of changing property rights among Isiolo Boran pastoralists in northern Kenya. In *Property, Poverty and People: Changing Rights in Property and Problems of Pastoral Development*, pp. 20–31. P. Baxter and R. Hogg, eds. Manchester: University of Manchester Press.

Homans, George C. 1961. *Social Behavior: Its Elementary Forms*. New York: Harcourt Brace Jovanovich.

Hornstein, Harvey A., Elisha Fisch, and Michael Holmes. 1968. Influence of a model's feeling about his behavior and his relevance as a comparison other on observers' helping behavior. *Journal of Personality and Social Psychology* 10(3):222–6.

Hornstein, Harvey A., Hugo N. Masor, Kenneth Sole, and Madeline Heilman. 1971. Effects of sentiment and completion of a helping act on observer helping: A case for socially mediated Zeigarnik effects. *Journal of Personality and Social Psychology* 17(1):107–12.

Howard, Alan, and Sutti Ortiz. 1971. Decision making and the study of social process. *Acta Sociologica* 14(4):213–26.

Hyden, Goran. 1980. *Beyond Ujamaa in Tanzania: Underdevelopment of an Uncaptured Peasantry*. Berkeley and Los Angeles: University of California Press.

Jensen, Michael C., and William H. Meckling. 1976. Theory of the firm: Managerial behavior, agency costs and ownership structure. *Journal of Financial Economics* 3:305–60.

Johnson, Allen W. 1972. Individuality and experimentation in traditional agriculture. *Human Ecology* 1(2):149–59.

Johnson, Allen W., and Timothy Earle. 1987. *The Evolution of Human Societies: From Foraging Group to Agrarian State*. Stanford, CA: Stanford University Press.

Johnson, James. 1991. Symbol and strategy: On the cultural analysis of politics. Ph.D. dissertation, University of Chicago.

Johnson, R. N., and G. D. Libecap. 1982. Contracting problems and regulation: The case of fishery. *American Economic Review* 72:1005–22.

Kahneman, Daniel, Jack L. Knetsch, and Richard Thaler. 1986a. Fairness and the assumptions of economics. *Journal of Business* 59:285–300.

References

1986b. Fairness as a constraint on profit seeking: Entitlements in the market. *American Economic Review* 76:728–41.

1986c. Perceptions of unfairness: Constraints on wealth seeking. *American Economic Review* 76:728–41.

Kalt, Joseph P., and Mark Zupan. 1984. Capture and ideology in the economic theory of politics. *American Economic Review* 74(3):279–300.

Kapferer, Bruce, ed. 1976. *Transaction and Meaning: Directions in the Anthropology of Exchange and Symbolic Behavior.* Philadelphia: Institute for the Study of Human Issues.

Kerkvliet, Benedict. 1990. *Everyday Politics in the Philippines: Class and Status Relations in a Central Luzon Village.* Berkeley and Los Angeles: University of California Press.

Keyes, Charles, ed. 1991. *Reshaping Local Worlds: Formal Education and Cultural Change in Rural Southeast Asia.* Monograph 36. New Haven, CT: Yale Southeast Asia Studies.

Kiser, Larry, and Elinor Ostrom. 1982. The three worlds of action: A metatheoretical synthesis of institutional approaches. In *Strategies of Political Inquiry,* pp. 179–222. E. Ostrom, ed. Newbury Park, CA: Sage.

Kitching, Gavin. 1980. *Class and Economic Change in Kenya: The Making of an African Petite Bourgeoisie, 1905–1970.* New Haven, CT: Yale University Press.

Knight, Jack. 1992. *Institutions and Social Conflict.* Cambridge University Press.

Krapf, Rev. J. Lewis. 1845. *A Forty Mile Journey to Takaongo North East of the Island of Mombasa.* London: Church Missionary Society archives.

1860. *Travels, Researches and Missionary Labours During an Eighteen Years' Residence in East Africa.* London: Trubner and Co.

Kuper, Adam. 1971. Council structure and decision-making. In *Councils in Action,* pp. 13–28. A. Richard and A. Kuper, eds. Cambridge University Press.

Langlois, Richard N. 1986. *Economics as a Process: Essays in the New Institutional Economics.* Cambridge University Press.

Last, Murray. 1979. Some economic aspects of conversion in Hausaland (Nigeria). In *Conversion to Islam,* pp. 236–46. Nehemia Levtzion, ed. New York: Holmes & Meier.

Leaf, Murray. 1984. *Song of Hope: The Green Revolution in a Punjab Village.* New Brunswick, NJ: Rutgers University Press.

LeClair, Edward E., Jr. 1968. Economic theory and economic anthropology. In *Economic Anthropology: Readings in Theory and Analysis,* pp. 187–207. E. E. J. LeClair and H. K. Schneider, eds. New York: Holt, Rinehart & Winston.

Leeds, Anthony. 1974. Housing settlement types, arrangements for living, proletarianization, and the social structure of the city. In *Anthropological Perspectives on Latin American Urbanization,* pp. 67–99. W. Cornelius and F. Trueblood, eds. Newbury Park, CA: Sage.

Legesse, Asmarom. 1973. *Gada: Three Approaches to the Study of African Society.* New York: The Free Press.

Lele, Uma. 1991. Women, structural adjustment, and transformation: Some lessons and questions from the African experience. In *Structural Adjustment and African Women Farmers,* pp. 46–80. C. H. Gladwin, ed. Gainesville: University of Florida Press.

Lenin, V. I. 1956. *The Development of Capitalism in Russia.* Moscow: Progress Publishers. (Originally published 1907.)

References

Leonard, David K. 1991. *African Successes: Four Public Managers of Kenyan Rural Development*. Berkeley and Los Angeles: University of California Press.

Levi, Margaret. 1988. *Of Rule and Revenue*. Berkeley and Los Angeles: University of California Press.

Lewis, David. 1968. *Convention: A Philosophical Study*. Cambridge, MA: Harvard University Press.

Lewis, Herbert J. 1966. The origins of the Galla and Somali. *Journal of African History* 7(1):27–46.

Lewis, I. M. 1960. The Somali conquest of the Horn of Africa. *Journal of African History* 1(2):213–29.

———. 1961. *A Pastoral Democracy*. London: Oxford University Press.

Leys, Colin. 1975. *Underdevelopment in Kenya: The Political Economy of Neo-Colonialism, 1964–1971*. London: Heinemann.

Libecap, Gary. 1989. *Contracting for Property Rights*. Cambridge University Press.

Li Causi, L. 1975. Anthropology and ideology. *Critique of Anthropology* 4:90–109.

Linton, Ralph. 1936. *The Study of Man: An Introduction*. New York: Appleton-Century.

Lipton, Michael. 1977. *Why Poor People Stay Poor: A Study of Urban Bias in World Development*. London: Maurice Temple Smith.

Little, Peter D. 1985a. Social differentiation and pastoralist sedentarization in northern Kenya. *Africa* 55(3):243–61.

———. 1985b. Absentee herd owners and part-time pastoralists: The political economy of resource use in northern Kenya. *Human Ecology* 13(2):136–51.

Lobo, Jeronimo. 1984. *The Itenerario of Jeronimo Lobo*. London: Hakluyt Society.

Lofchie, Michael F. 1990. Kenya: Still an economic miracle? *Current History* (May):209–12, 222–24.

Lovett, Margot. 1989. Gender relations, class formation, and the colonial state in Africa. In *Women and the State in Africa*, pp. 23–46. Jane L. Parpart and Kathleen A. Staudt, eds. Boulder, CO: Lynne Rienner.

Mair, Lucy. 1962. *Primitive Government*. Baltimore: Penguin Books.

Malinowski, Bronislaw. 1945. *The Dynamics of Culture Change: An Inquiry into Race Relations in Africa*. P. M. Kaberry, ed. New Haven, CT: Yale University Press.

Maliyamkono, T. L., and M. S. D. Bagachwa. 1990. *The Second Economy in Tanzania*. London: James Currey.

Mansbridge, Jane J. 1990a. The rise and fall of self-interest in the explanation of political life. In *Beyond Self-Interest*, pp. 3–24. J. J. Mansbridge, ed. Chicago: University of Chicago Press.

Mansbridge, Jane J., ed. 1990b. *Beyond Self-Interest*. Chicago: University of Chicago Press.

Marwell, Gerald, and Ruth E. Ames. 1981. Economists free ride, does anyone else? Experiments on the provision of public goods, IV. *Journal of Public Economics* 15:296–310.

Matthews, R. C. O. 1986. The economics of institutions and the sources of growth. *Economic Journal* 96:903–18.

Mauss, Marcel. 1967. *The Gift: Forms and Functions of Exchange in Archaic Societies*. New York: Norton.

References

McCabe, J. Terrence. 1990. Turkana pastoralism: A case against the tragedy of the commons. *Human Ecology* 18(1):81–103.

McCay, Bonnie, and James Acheson, eds. 1987. *The Question of the Commons: The Culture and Ecology of Communal Resources*. Tucson: University of Arizona Press.

Michie, Barry H. 1981. The transformation of agrarian patron–client relations: Illustrations from India. *American Ethnologist* 8(1):21–40.

Morgan, L. H. 1974. *Ancient Society*. Gloucester, MA: Peter Smith. (Originally published in 1877.)

Nabli, Mustapha K., and Jeffrey B. Nugent, eds. 1989. *The New Institutional Economics and Development: Theory and Applications to Tunisia*. New York: North Holland.

Nash, Manning. 1958. *Machine Age Maya: The Industrialization of a Guatemalan Community*. Chicago: University of Chicago Press.

——— 1968. The social context of economic choice in a small society. In *Economic Anthropology: Readings in Theory and Analysis*, pp. 311–22. H. K. Schneider and E. E. J. LeClair, eds. New York: Holt, Rinehart & Winston.

Netting, Robert M. 1968. *Hill Farmers of Nigeria: Cultural Ecology of the Kofyar of the Jos Plateau*. Seattle: University of Washington Press.

——— 1972. Of men and meadows: Strategies of alpine and land use. *Anthropological Quarterly* 45:132–44.

——— 1976. What alpine peasants have in common: Observations on communal tenure in a Swiss village. *Human Ecology* 4:135–46.

——— 1977. *Cultural Ecology*. Menlo Park, CA: Cummings.

——— 1982. Territory, property, and tenure. In *Behavioral and Social Science Research: A National Resource*, pp. 446–501. R. N. S. and D. J. Treiman Adams, eds. Washington, DC: National Academy Press.

Netting, Robert M., Priscilla M. Stone, and Glenn D. Stone. 1989. Kofyar cash-cropping: Choice and change in indigenous agricultural development. *Human Ecology* 17(3):299–320.

Netting, Robert M., Richard R. Wilk, and Eric J. Arnould, eds. 1984. *Households*. Berkeley and Los Angeles: University of California Press.

New, Charles. 1873. *Life, Wanderings, and Labours in Eastern Africa*. London: Hodder & Stoughton.

Nkinyangi, John A. 1981. Education for nomadic pastoralists: Development planning by trial and error. In *The Future of Pastoral Peoples*, pp. 183–96. J. G. Galaty, D. Aronson, P. C. Salzman, and A. Chouinard, eds. Ottawa: International Development Research Centre.

North, Douglass C. 1977. Markets and other allocation systems in history: The challenge of Karl Polanyi. *Journal of European Economic History* 6:703–16.

——— 1981. *Structure and Change in Economic History*. New York: Norton.

——— 1985. Transaction costs in history. *Journal of European Economic History* 14:557–76.

——— 1986. Is it worth making sense of Marx? *Inquiry* 29:57–63.

——— 1990. *Institutions, Institutional Change and Economic Performance*. Cambridge University Press.

North, Douglass C., and Robert Paul Thomas. 1973. *The Rise of the Western World: A New Economic History*. Cambridge University Press.

O'Brien, Stephen. 1991. Structural adjustment and structural transformation in sub-Saharan Africa. In *Structural Adjustment and African Women Farm-*

References

ers, pp. 25–45. Christina H. Gladwin, ed. Gainesville: University of Florida Press.

Olson, Mancur. 1965. *The Logic of Collective Action*. Cambridge, MA: Harvard University Press.

Ortiz, Sutti. 1967. The structure of decision-making among Indians of Colombia. In *Themes in Economic Anthropology*, pp. 191–228. R. Firth, ed. London: Tavistock.

Ostrom, Elinor. 1990. *Governing the Commons: The Evolution of Institutions for Collective Action*. Cambridge University Press.

Owen, Capt. W. F. W. 1833. *Narrative of Voyages to Explore the Shores of Africa, Arabia, and Madagascar*. London: Richard Bentley.

Oyugi, Walter Ouna. 1983. Local government in Kenya: A case of institutional decline. In *Local Government in the Third World: The Experience of Tropical Africa*, pp. 107–40. P. Mawhood, ed. New York: Wiley.

Paine, R. 1974. *Second Thoughts about Barth's Models*. Occasional Papers No. 32. London: Royal Anthropological Institute.

Perinbam, B. Marie. 1980. The Julas in western Sudanese history: Long-distance traders and developers of resources. In *West African Cultural Dynamics*, pp. 455–76. B. Schwarz and R. Dummett, eds. The Hague: Mouton.

Peters, Carl. 1891. From the mouth of the Tana to the source – Region of the Nile. *Scottish Geographical Magazine* 7:113–23.

Peters, Pauline E. 1984. Struggles over water, struggles over meaning: Cattle, water and the state in Botswana. *Africa* 54:29–49.

1987. Embedded systems and rooted models: The grazing lands of Botswana and the commons debate. In *The Question of the Commons: The Culture and Ecology of Communal Resources*, pp. 171–94. B. J. McCay and J. M. Acheson, eds. Tucson: University of Arizona Press.

1989. An anthropological critique of rational choice. Paper presented at the annual meetings of the African Studies Association, Atlanta, GA, November 2–5.

Plattner, Stuart. 1989. Economic behavior in markets. In *Economic Anthropology*, pp. 209–21. S. Plattner, ed. Stanford, CA: Stanford University Press.

Plattner, Stuart, ed. 1975. *Formal Methods in Economic Anthropology*. Washington, DC: American Anthropological Association.

Polanyi, Karl. 1944. *The Great Transformation: The Political and Economic Origins of Our Time*. Boston: Beacon Press.

1968. The economy as instituted process. In *Economic Anthropology: Readings in Theory and Analysis*, pp. 122–42. E. E. J. LeClair and H. K. Schneider, eds. New York: Holt, Rinehart & Winston.

Popkin, Samuel L. 1979. *The Rational Peasant: The Political Economy of Rural Society in Vietnam*. Berkeley and Los Angeles: University of California Press.

Prattis, J. Ian. 1970. *Dilemmas of Decision-Making: A Methodological Test Case in Economic Anthropology. Studies in Economic Anthropology*, Vol. 1. Vancouver: University of British Columbia Press.

1973. Strategizing man. *Man* 8(1):46–58.

1976. Situational logic, social structure, and highland Burma. *Current Anthropology* 17(1):97–100.

Przeworski, Adam. 1985. Marxism and rational choice. *Politics and Society* 14(4):379–409.

Quinn, Naomi. 1975. Decision models of social structure. *American Ethnologist* 2(1):19–46.

References

1978. Do Mfantse fish sellers estimate probabilities in their heads? *American Ethnologist* 5(2):206–26.

Riker, William. 1980. Implications from the disequilibrium of majority rule for the study of institutions. *American Political Science Review* 74:432–46.

1986. *The Art of Political Manipulation*. New Haven, CT: Yale University Press.

Roemer, John. 1982. *A General Theory of Exploitation and Class*. Cambridge, MA: Harvard University Press.

Rondinelli, Dennis A., John R. Nellis, and G. Shabbir Cheema. 1984. *Decentralization in Developing Countries: A Review of Recent Experience*. World Bank Staff Working Papers No. 581. Washington, DC: World Bank.

Roth, Eric A. 1991. Education, tradition, and household labor among Rendille pastoralists of N. Kenya. *Human Organization* 50(2):136–41.

Rowlands, J. S. S. 1955. An outline of Tana River history. Typescript in private collection, Lamu.

Rutten, Andrew. 1990. Review of *The Economic Thought of Karl Polanyi* [by J. R. Stanfield]. *Economics and Philosophy* 6(1):157–64.

Rutz, Henry J. 1977. Individual decisions and functional systems: Economic rationality and environmental adaptation. *American Ethnologist* 4(1):156–74.

Sahlins, Marshall. 1972. *Stone Age Economics*. New York: De Gruyter.

1976. *Culture and Practical Reason*. Chicago: University of Chicago Press.

Salisbury, Richard F. 1962. *From Stone to Steel: Economic Consequences of a Technological Change in New Guinea*. Cambridge University Press.

1969. Formal analysis in anthropological economics: The Rossel Island case. In *Game Theory in the Behavioral Sciences*, pp. 75–93. I. R. Buchler and H. G. Nutini, eds. Pittsburgh: University of Pittsburgh Press.

Schmidt, Lieutenant A. R. 1888. Deutsch-Witu-Land. *Globus Band* 54:129–34, 145–7, 173–5, 188–90.

Schneider, Harold K. 1974. *Economic Man: The Anthropology of Economics*. New York: The Free Press.

Schofield, Norman. 1986. Anarchy, altruism and cooperation. *Social Choice and Welfare* 2:207–19.

Scott, James C. 1976. *The Moral Economy of the Peasant: Rebellion and Subsistence in Southeast Asia*. New Haven, CT: Yale University Press.

1985. *Weapons of the Weak: Everyday Forms of Peasant Resistance*. New Haven, CT: Yale University Press.

Scott, James C., and Benedict Kerkvliet, eds. 1986. *Everyday Forms of Peasant Resistance in Southeast Asia*. London: Frank Cass.

Service, Elman. 1962. *Primitive Social Organization*. New York: Random House.

1975. *Origins of the State and Civilization: The Process of Cultural Evolution*. New York: Norton.

Siegenthaler, Hansjorg. 1989. Organization, ideology and the free rider problem. *Journal of Institutional and Theoretical Economics* 145:215–31.

Silverman, Sydel F. 1968. Agricultural organization, social structure, and values in Italy: Amoral familism reconsidered. *American Anthropologist* 70:1–20.

Simon, H. 1957. *Models of Man*. New York: Wiley.

Skocpol, Theda. 1985. Bringing the state back in: Strategies of analysis in current research. In *Bringing the State Back In*, pp. 3–37. Peter B. Evans, Dietrich Rueschemeyer, and Theda Skocpol, eds. Cambridge University Press.

Skvoretz, John V., Jr., and Richard H. Conviser. 1974. Interests and alliances:

References

A reformulation of Barth's models of social organization. *Man* 9(1): 53–67.

Smith, Adam. 1976. *The Wealth of Nations*. Chicago: University of Chicago Press. (Originally published in 1776.)

Spear, Thomas. 1981. *Kenya's Past*. London: Longman.

Sperling, Louise. 1984. *The Recruitment of Labor among Samburu Herders*. Working Paper No. 414. Nairobi, Kenya: University of Nairobi, Institute for Development Studies,

    1987. Wage employment among Samburu pastoralists of northcentral Kenya. *Research in Economic Anthropology* 9:167–90.

Swartz, Marc J., ed. 1968. *Local-Level Politics: Social and Cultural Perspectives*. Chicago: Aldine.

Tanner, J. M. 1978. *Foetus into Man: Physical Growth from Conception to Maturity*. Cambridge, MA: Harvard University Press.

Taylor, Michael. 1982. *Community, Anarchy and Liberty*. Cambridge University Press.

    1987. *The Possibility of Cooperation*. Cambridge University Press.

Torry, W. J. 1973. Subsistence economy among the Gabbra, nomads of the Kenya/Ethiopia frontier. Ph.D. dissertation, Columbia University.

Trimingham, J. Spencer. 1962. *A History of Islam in West Africa*. London: Oxford University Press.

Tullock, Gordon. 1976. *The Vote Motive*. London: Institute for Economic Affairs.

Turton, E. R. 1975. Bantu, Galla and Somali migrations in the Horn of Africa: A reassessment of the Juba/Tana area. *Journal of African History* 16(4):519–37.

Tversky, Amos, and Daniel Kahneman. 1987. Rational choice and the framing of decisions. In *Rational Choice: The Contrast Between Economics and Psychology*, pp. 67–94. R. M. and Melvin W. Reder Hogarth, eds. Chicago: University of Chicago Press.

Vayda, Andrew. 1969. *Environment and Cultural Behavior*. Garden City, NJ: Natural History Press.

Vayda, Andrew, and Bonnie McCay. 1975. New directions in ecology and ecological anthropology. In *Annual Review of Anthropology*, Vol. 4, pp. 477–97. B. J. Siegel, A. R. Beals, and S. A. Tyler, eds. Boston: Houghton Mifflin.

Vincent, Joan. 1978. Political anthropology: Manipulative strategies. *Annual Review of Anthropology* 7:175–94.

Wade, Robert. 1988. *Village Republics: Economic Conditions for Collective Action in South India*. Cambridge University Press.

Wallis, John Joseph, and Douglass C. North. 1986. Measuring the transaction sector in the American economy, 1870–1970. In *Long-Term Factors in American Economic Growth*, pp. 95–161. S. Engerman and R. Gallman, eds. Chicago: University of Chicago Press.

Weber, Max. 1947. *The Theory of Social and Economic Organization*. Glencoe, IL: The Free Press.

Werner, Alice. 1913a. The tribes of the Tana Valley. *Journal of East African and Ugandan Natural History Society* 4(7):37–46.

    1913b. Two Galla legends. *Man* 13(2):90–1.

    1913c. Some notes on the Wapokomo of Tana Valley. *Journal of the African Society* 12:359–84.

    1913d. A few notes on the Wasanye. *Man* 13(2):199–201.

References

1913e. A Pokomo funeral. *Man* 13(2):66–8.

1914. The Galla of the East African Protectorate. *Journal of the African Society* 13(11):121–42, 262–87.

1915. The Bantu coast tribes of the East Africa Protectorate. *Journal of the Royal Anthropological Institute* 45:326–54.

1919. The native tribes of British East Africa. *Journal of the African Society* 19:285–94.

White, Leslie. 1959. *The Evolution of Culture.* New York: McGraw-Hill.

Williamson, Oliver E. 1975. *Markets and Hierarchies: Analysis and Antitrust Implications.* New York: The Free Press.

1980. The organization of work. *Journal of Economic Behavior and Organization* 1:5–38.

1981. The economics of organization: The transaction cost approach. *American Journal of Sociology* 87(3):548–77.

1985. *The Economic Institutions of Capitalism: Firms, Markets, Relational Contracting.* New York: The Free Press.

Wilson, Monica. 1977. *For Men and Elders.* London: International African Institute.

World Bank. 1989. *World Development Report 1989.* New York: Oxford University Press.

Ylvisaker, Marguerite. 1979. *Lamu in the Nineteenth Century: Land, Trade, and Politics,* African Research Studies No. 13. Boston: Boston University African Studies Center.

Index

Index